# TWENTIETH CENTURY VIEWS

The aim of this series is to present the best
in contemporary critical opinion on major
authors, providing a twentieth century perspective on their changing status in an era
of profound revaluation.

Maynard Mack, *Series Editor*
Yale University

# BRECHT

## A COLLECTION OF CRITICAL ESSAYS

Edited by

*Peter Demetz*

A SPECTRUM BOOK

Prentice-Hall, Inc., *Englewood Cliffs, N.J.*

LIBRARY OF CONGRESS CATALOG CARD NO.: 62-13723

*Printed in the United States of America*

08177-C

# Table of Contents

# Introduction

### by Peter Demetz

Orthodox admirers of Brecht usually disregard his warnings and define his total achievement as "epic theater." When he was twenty-five years old, Brecht himself would have liked such a simplification, for the guitar-strumming young man preferred the commissar's leather jacket to the many-colored coat of diverse poetic talents which nature had given him. Only in his later years did Brecht try to discourage the monolithic beliefs of his students. "The whole débâcle started," he said, "when I wanted to have my plays staged properly and effectively and so—oh misery!—in order to define a non-Aristotelian dramaturgy I developed— oh calamity!—a theory of the epic theater." Brecht, late in life, more and more harked back to Hegel, the magician of change and creative development, and he never wearied of implying that he had continued to change his own ideas, to modify his attitudes, his concepts, and his plays. This is precisely the reason why Communist critics, the brilliant Georg Lukács as well as the more pedestrian Fritz Erpenbeck, were always suspicious of the cunning sage at the *Theater am Schiffbauerdamm*. Brecht, at least as far as his theatrical efforts were concerned, was not afraid to thrive on the clash of ideas, and to enjoy the tension; he achieved some of his most impressive results from the richness of contradictions in himself and in the world. Even his syntax is of the antithesis, the chiasmus, and the asyndeton. Brecht complained that people without a sense of humor would never be able to understand Hegel's dialectics. One might also say that these people will never be able to grasp some of the most vital implications of Brecht's art.

It is easy to forget the fact that Brecht also wrote a number of ingenious stories and witty prose parables; a dubious exercise in "socialist realism," *The Threepenny Novel*; and first-rate poetry. Many critics are tempted to agree with Martin Esslin who called Brecht "a poet, first and foremost." And Hannah Arendt, in 1950, said that Brecht was the greatest of all living German poets—in spite of the accomplishments of Brecht's contemporaries, Gottfried Benn and Wilhelm Lehmann, whose delicate art persuasively combines the traditions of the German *Naturgedicht* with the technical firmness of a late Parnassian.

In tone and structure, Brecht's poetry takes the shortest escape route

from the sphere of the lyric to reach the securer haven of a dramatic
and narrative mode. In the theater, we observe the playwright as poet;
in Brecht's verse, we encounter the poet as playwright. Brecht's poetry
is written, as Volker Klotz has pointed out, in characteristic, "objective"
forms: the legend, the ballad, the song, the epistle, and the dramatic
monologue of a masked speaker. Often Brecht prefers to report something he has read or heard; often an anecdotal first line will develop
into a short story in verse. It is surely justified to call him, as Hays does,
"the apostle of a reaction against individualism," for Brecht avoids the
introspection and the pitfalls of a sensibility which is too egotistical, and
does not indulge in poetry "in which individuals selfishly complain
about psychic anomalies." But the question is whether it is really a
sufficient explanation to say that the unique quality of Brecht's verse is
a result of his aversion to psychology and his turning away from the
pageant of the bleeding heart to the hard and dry universe of supra-
individual events. In his antiromantic attitude, Brecht gloriously, though
belatedly, conforms to the general development of modern European and
American poetry. Brecht's verse may have exclusive social inclinations,
but it is also certainly derived from the pathos of *le moi haïssable*
which characterizes the poems of Gautier, the Parnassians, the mature
Rilke, T. S. Eliot, Gottfried Benn, and Ezra Pound. Like these poets,
Brecht, as far as his language is concerned, was also a true conservative
revolutionary. He came to disdain the hectic idiom of the Expressionists,
the upper-class sublimity of Stefan George, and the bric-à-brac of Dada.
He looked for his models in those centuries which seemed to have lost
their fascination for the German writer. Ezra Pound, because he wanted
to pierce Victorian "obfuscation," longed for the sophistication of the
troubadours and the wit of Restoration poetry. Brecht, to revitalize the
German language, went back to Luther's translation of the Bible; to the
Church hymns of the sixteenth and seventeenth centuries; to the plain
words of the folk ballad. He used the old "to make things new."

It is perhaps most useful to read Brecht's poetry in conjunction with
his plays. Often, one form blends with another—a ballad is part of a
theatrical scene, a song is placed in a collection of verse. The development of his poetry, on the whole, reflects the transformations in his
dramatic art. The change is from the "rhetoric of decomposition"
(Lüthy), close to the language of *Baal* (1918), to the ascetic and partisan discipline of *Songs, Poems, Cantatas* (1934), which roughly corresponds to the didactic plays, and, finally, to the serene nostalgia of
the *Buckow Elegies* (1950), which is of the more tender hues of *The
Caucasian Chalk Circle* (1944-45). After he had studied the art of the
Far East, it was almost inevitable that Brecht would achieve in his work
a tight and ideogrammatic structure of strong visual appeal that could
be thoroughly enjoyed by even the most discriminating Anglo-Saxon
imagist. In his final impersonal serenity, as well as in his attempts to

write new poetry by reviving older linguistic norms, the Communist poet Brecht is much closer to the conservative masters of modern poetry than his partisan defenders, lost in the meditation of his politics, are willing to admit.

To consider Brecht primarily as the creator of the epic theater is to be aware of the temptation to rely too heavily on the traditional connotations of that term. For Brecht uses his central term in a very specific way: the word refers to the actor who "demonstrates" a figure on the stage while—as Diderot recommended—coolly preserving his own individuality. In performing *Galileo,* a play of Brecht's later years, the actor Charles Laughton "demonstrated" the figure of the scientist, but did not disappear into the character he was demonstrating. Brecht described the fundamental quality of the epic with the German verb *zeigen:* to point to, to refer to, as a teacher would point to an interesting drawing on his blackboard. Yet the epic method of acting, though perhaps the most important, is only one element in Brecht's over-all strategy of alienation, or estrangement (*Verfremdung*[1]). Epic acting, inscriptions projected upon the stage, a particular use of songs, music, choreography and scenic design, which counteracts the fable, commenting on rather than supporting it—all of these elements "alienate," as Brecht says, certain events of the play from the realm of the ordinary, natural, and expected, and makes them surprisingly new and strange, or *imprévu,* as nineteenth century critics would have said. Alienation techniques affect the total structure of the play: they weaken the "arc" of tight construction, they challenge the inevitability of events; the interruptions which divide the play into almost autonomous playlets contribute to the destruction of the lures of dramatic illusion. The knots of the texture, as Brecht remarks, become visible. Erwin Piscator, the greatest of the Expressionist stage producers, once interrupted one of his productions to play a record of Lenin's voice. Brecht must have remembered that archetypal alienation effect for a long, long time.

The "epic" quality of Brecht's theater is derived from the idea of pastness which, as a revolutionary writer's weapon, Brecht tries to turn against an audience hungry for illusion. Brecht, as Martin Esslin explains, "makes it apparent to the spectators that they are not witnessing

[1] I am less convinced than are John Willett and Hans Egon Holthusen that Brecht derived his famous term *Verfremdung* (as chic today as *Geworfenheit* once was) from the terminology of the Russian Formalists, of whose work he may have heard during his visit to Moscow in 1935. As early as in his *Notes to The Threepenny Opera* (1929) and *A Man's a Man* (1931), Brecht uses the terms *befremdlich* and *Fremdheit* (strange, strangeness) to denote the qualities of his new theatrical style. The Formalist term *ostrannenie,* if he really did encounter it at all four years later, may have confirmed rather than set in motion this terminological development. In 1740 the Swiss critic J. J. Breitinger demanded that the poet disguise truth in a totally strange but translucent mask (*verkleidet die Wahrheit in eine gantz fremde aber durchsichtige Maske*); in other words, Brecht's *Verfremdung* has definite German antecedents.

real events happening before their very eyes at this very moment, but that they are sitting in a theater, listening to an account . . . of things that have happened in the past at a certain time and a certain place." But Brecht's theory disregards the psychology of the audience and the pragmatic relationship of stage to spectator. Brecht cannot alter the fact that his epic theater creates the past event *here* and *now.* The artful immediacy of presentation endangers the entire technology of pastness. The stage, because it is of the present, triumphs over the past of the events narrated; the audience will again and again try to overcome the most violent shocks of alienation; ironically, the audience's desire for theatrical illusion may well be more richly gratified by Brecht's ingenious "counter-actions" than by the mechanical illusions of the "realistic" stage. Resistance does not necessarily make enjoyment impossible; it may even add to its charms.

Epic theater is the theater of destroyed illusions and the wide-awake audience. Brecht attacks the "conventional" theater, that of the Greeks and of Schiller, as well as the theater of his own time, that of Wagner and the "well-made" play. He sketches a rationalist's caricature of an audience victimized by emotional empathy and theatrical illusion: there they sit, almost motionless, with a slightly stupid expression on their faces, intoxicated, as if sleeping. Brecht prefers to ignore the fact that even in traditional theater the spectator only intermittently yields to theatrical illusion; to Brecht, the relative and intermittent phenomenon constitutes an absolute and central abomination of which the theater must be radically purified. Empathy and illusion are poisonous because they make man, a rational being, lose his critical abilities, and because they cloud his brain with wishful thinking and dreams of harmony founded on political ignorance. The epic theater, in which stage technique and Marxism finally correspond, strives to keep man sober, "cool," and critical. Alienation effects show relations and events in a new light; they demonstrate that the world is changeable and keep the audience , alert for practical political action—why it should be action along Communist lines, Brecht alone knows. Brecht's ideal spectator, one almost assumes, would follow the example of that Walloon audience which, one hot summer evening in 1830, was so inflamed by Auber's opera *La Muette de Portici* (a truly "culinary" work), that it ran out into the streets of Brussels and started one of the most successful revolutions in modern Europe. But the mature Brecht shifts his interest from the revolutionary *prodesse* to the artful *delectare;* in his *Little Organon for the Theater* (1948), he demonstratively uses the terms "enjoyment" and "pleasure" and makes light of any theatrical efforts, including the didactic, that fail to contribute to the pleasure of the senses. Shortly before his death in 1956, Brecht even seemed to be ready to discard the term "epic" altogether as insufficient and meaningless. He spoke instead of a *dialectical* theater—but, it is hard to say whether he did this to repudiate his early theories or merely to irritate his dogmatic friends and enemies. However, it is moving to see the man who had been both ascetic and picaro leave the world with words of praise on his lips for the "naïve."

In spite of the revolutionary gestures of his youth and his apodictic pronouncements later, Brecht's theatrical concepts were very much in the antirealistic tradition of the European theater. Brecht's concerns with breaking the dramatic continuity, with alienation and illusion, have their antecedents, as Oscar Büdel has pointed out, in the theater of Apollinaire, Marinetti, Pirandello, and Claudel, and may owe a considerable debt to the didacticism and the stage techniques of the German Expressionist producers—who in turn looked to Strindberg and to the Soviet "constructivist" concepts of Mayerhold. If Brecht's vitality and humor reflect the world of Karl Valentin and the folklore farce of the Munich beer halls, his technology and politics remind one of Erwin Piscator, the most outstanding among the German *Proletkult* (i.e. [Soviet] Cultural and Educational Organizations) disciples; of the expressionistic use of films, records, and slides to show the global context of the theatrical event; and of the staging of Alfons Paquet's *Flags* in 1924, which was announced as the first *epic* and *Marxist* play. Ernst Schumacher has compiled an impressive and indispensable volume of evidence concerning Brecht's involvement with the left-wing Expressionists, but because Schumacher is an orthodox Communist he also tries to disengage Brecht from Piscator and to minimize the Expressionist contamination—for, as it turns out, the left-wing Expressionists committed the unpardonable sin of "underestimating the political organization"—in other words, the Communist party—and did not accept its guidance. Fortunately for us, Brecht did continue to commit some of the sins of his Expressionist teachers. Though he was, at times, ready to exhort his unfortunate contemporaries "to embrace the butcher," and did stoop to producing political propaganda in the service of the Ulbricht regime, he did not yield as far as the essentials of his theater were concerned. The German Communist Party was not able to impose its will on a poet living in California, and the Ulbricht regime had its own reasons for wooing the returning exile who had so many friends in Western Germany. Thanks to his cunning and his great political luck, Brecht *lived* to be the only dramatist in the Communist sphere who did not submit to Zhdanov's demands and doctrines. He continued to attack the hegemony of Stanislavsky, patriarch of illusionist acting. By implication he supported Anna Seghers in her protest against Georg Lukács, who was determined to beat the exiled German left-wing writers into submission to the "realist" line. And, as if Moscow had never proclaimed "socialist realism" the binding discipline, Brecht went on speaking of his epic theater as the truly realistic and proletarian form of drama.

In a certain sense, Brecht succeeded in preserving the vitality of the "Twenties" through the dangerous "Forties" and the ossified "Fifties."

What we will admire as part of the future may well be, as Herbert Lüthy has suggested, but a reflex and an echo of the great flourishing of the theater and the arts during the Weimar Republic. Like Stendhal, in his own moment in history, Brecht belongs so much to the past that he is of the future.

Through the Expressionist left wing, Brecht's ideas and stage techniques relate to the bold Soviet experimenters of the Twenties, to their protest against Stanislavsky's methods of acting, to the revolutionary fervor of Kerzhentsev, and to the abstract stage of Mayerhold. Thus Brecht may be indebted to the Soviets—but Kerzhentsev and Mayerhold, from the point of view of contemporary orthodoxy, are the wrong kind of Soviet Russians, whose formalist skeletons orthodoxy prefers to keep in a well-locked closet rather than to have them walk the stages of Moscow and Leningrad. Brecht's famous *Berliner Ensemble*, the pride of Communist East Germany, went to Moscow only after Stalin was dead, when the air was alive with signs of a political and literary "thaw." In Fradkin's apology for Brecht one discovers something of the tortuous and heavy-handed subterfuge necessary to make the German poet palatable to Soviet audiences; Fradkin presents Brecht as an old enemy of formalism and as a good socialist realist, one who also happens to be in favor of moderate artistic innovation. One would rather have expected to hear that Brecht's theater revived the spirit of artistic independence and aesthetic experimentation crushed by the Soviet state in the early Thirties.

Historical considerations, like those of Schumacher and Büdel, tend to increase one's doubts whether Marxism and the epic theater are inevitable correlatives, as Brecht insists; or whether we owe these affinities to Brecht's brilliant stubbornness and to the ideas of some of his predecessors on the German Expressionist Left and in the Soviet *Proletkult*. Brecht's own explanations of the relationship are as meager as they are unconvincing. In his *Notes* to *The Threepenny Opera*, in 1929, for instance, he only states that epic elements follow in the wake of materialism, and contends that epic theater alone is capable of grasping and presenting the ever changing development of man as determined by the social environment. This is a difficult argument or, rather, a *non sequitur*. We certainly know "epic" theater unburdened by Marxism; and we are also aware of the fact that in most Communist countries the ideological message appears in the wholly traditional disguise of the bourgeois "well-made" play, derived from Scribe and Dumas. Brecht himself practiced "epic" theater long before he became a Marxist; and, more recently, Thornton Wilder, Max Frisch, and Friedrich Dürrenmatt, just to mention a few, continue to make productive use of techniques which are "epic" in the Brechtian sense. Conversely, some of the most impressive plays of world literature, though they are entirely unconcerned with alienation effects, offer deeply disturbing images of man tortured on the wheel of economics and history. Büchner's *Woyzeck* (1836-37) and Hauptmann's *The Weavers* (1892) are entirely within the conventions of realism or naturalism, they promote illusion and emotional empathy, are "hot" rather than "cool" theater, and yet Büchner's soldier Woyzeck or Hauptmann's old weaver Hilse are figures more alive than Brecht's epic Pelagea Vlassova acting against a background of statistics projected upon the stage. It seems that neither epic nor realist norms and conventions as such guarantee a deeper and a more inclusive grasp of man and his fate; in the final analysis it is dramatic genius that determines how far the playwright, using one or the other set of conventions, penetrates the human situation.

But it would amount to a failure of sensibility if these considerations were to blind us to the powerful liberating function of Brecht's theory of the epic theater. Brecht reinstitutes the antirealist tendencies of the stage, long languishing at the periphery of the modern drama (particularly in England, the United States, and Soviet Russia) at the vital center of the theater. And, as if taking a long-delayed revenge, he declares that the naturalist conventions, the stage of the missing fourth wall, of slavish *mimesis,* of the actors' entrances and exits carefully explained, is "reactionary" and obsolete. Brecht's theory rescues the theater from the heavy burden of having to copy nature—in practice, the upper middle-class drawing room—makes the stage translucent, aims at "art as Art" (Shklovsky) and at the "theatricality of the theater" (Büdel). The epic theater brings back to the stage the sister arts of music, scenic design, and choreography, long devaluated or excluded by naturalist dramaturgy because these elements were absent from that grey-flanneled daily life to be imitated. No longer does the stage suffer from the necessity of having to put real olives into real martinis or real butter on real bread (American Organization Men and Moscow Party officials occasionally agree on points of aesthetics). Epigrammatic, compressed gestures (*gestus*); sophisticated arrangements of movement; stylization; cool elegance; and a relaxed enjoyment of the technicalities of art replace a correct imitation which is true to "life." Man, facing history in difficult choices, no longer appears as a prisoner of the carefully duplicated confines of Greenwich (Connecticut) or Chelsea, but acts out his life in an expanding space: in exotic Georgia, imaginary Setzuan, hilarious India, or poetized Chicago —in the "never-never land of the philosophical parable" (Sokel).

But Brecht presents his doctrine of theatrical liberation in close alliance with an ideology of the individual's servitude. With one hand he destroys theatrical illusion, while recreating political illusions with the other. *The Little Organon for the Theater* (1948), for example, abounds with political ideas which are as obsolete as they are invalid. In paragraph 18 the famous Marxist "immiseration" theory emerges which, by now, belongs with the museum pieces of intellectual history, because our industrial civilization developed in ways not foreseen by Marx. To say, as Brecht does, "that an increase of production leads to an increase of misery" is to adhere to ideas which are demonstrably false. There we also read the pronouncement, in paragraphs 17-18, that the middle classes, even though they have scientifically analyzed nature, never dared to direct their scientific attention to society because they knew that a systematic social science would mean the end of their class domination. Of course, science (*Wissenschaft*) to Brecht means Marxism, and he prefers to ignore the entire development of sociology, which gave Marx a chance to spend the better part of his life in the British Museum excerpting the works of British and French middle-class economists. It is curious to see that Brecht's critical intelligence, brilliantly penetrating in its analysis of theatrical problems, suffers from the burden of ideas which, though valid in their analysis of nineteenth century phenomena, have totally failed to interpret the concrete problems of our time and have become an anachronism as obsolete as the conventions of the natural-ist stage. In his theoretical efforts, Brecht is like an eagle whose eyes triumphantly and sharply view the future of the arts—but the eagle's feet drag the rusty chains of Marxist iron and lead.

Brecht's theory does not necessarily add to our understanding or to our undisturbed evaluation of his plays. Although it would be misleading to say that the changing system of his ideas and the theatrical universe of his plays are far apart—for they converge in the Thirties—their re-lationship is, at best, a loose, intermittent and paradoxical one. As no other modern playwright, Brecht was constantly on the alert to prevent his audience from enjoying his plays incorrectly, but again and again the creations of the playwright defeated the efforts of the theorist; again and again the play itself assumed a radiant autonomy that calmly disdained any belated attempt to make it a servant to ideology or intent.

Brecht's early plays are exercises in assimilation, protest and provoca-tion. Brecht was never forced to discard his first attempts: hidden in the abrupt changes of manner and style, seminal motifs and stage techniques already appear which are later systematically defined. Marxism may have modified Brecht's use of the stage, but it did not disrupt Brecht's develop-ment as a playwright; his work "has an impressive unity; what is found in the later plays is found in the earlier ones, and vice versa" (Bentley). Communist interpreters of Brecht try hard to isolate *Baal* (1918), his first play, from contemporary Expressionism; they declare that the ma-terialist Brecht must certainly have disagreed with the idealism of the Expressionist poets. Yet from the core of the play emerges a burning *élan vital* untouched by the sterile dichotomy of matter and idea: Baal, the poet and the criminal, the lover of women and man, the brutal lumberjack and the tender admirer of pink clouds and blue plumtrees, incarnates pure stubbornness of being, the ecstasies of metaphoric idiom, and absolute moral irresponsibility. The hero of *Drums in the Night* (1919) seems much more a creation of the later, the political Brecht.

Andreas Kragler, a prisoner of war, returns to a contemporary, revolutionary Berlin. For the first time, Brecht raises the question of how a human being may survive in the vicissitudes of the world. But the answer which young Brecht offers is not yet Marxist: Andreas Kragler turns against the revolutionary obsessions of his proletarian friends, mocks their ideas as romantic illusions, and, refusing to fight, invites his fiancée to share his "great, white, broad bed." For the first time Brecht uses crude alienation effects—not to provoke political action in favor of the *Spartakus* but to destroy the belief that political action may have any meaning. Onstage, a paper moon falls into a river in which there is no water; the enduring, the *real* reality is a world too cold, too decayed, to be open to hope and improvement. In his third play, *In the Swamp* (1921-24), Brecht penetrates further into this darkened world, and revolution-torn Berlin changes into a strange Chicago which exudes the stark light of despair. Life has become a cruel fight to the finish; Brecht arranges the "inexorable wrestling match" between Shlink and George Garga to demonstrate that in a universe devoid of warmth and closeness even enmity may be something rewarding and unattainable. *In the Swamp*, "a series of pictures which, by their very surrealism, are intended to unmask reality" (U. Jarvis), constitutes Brecht's first and last contribution to the "absurd" theater of vanishing causality and inexplicable fates and events; perhaps it also indicates why Brecht, after exploring man's hopeless isolation, looked for a way to find hope and salvation in the Great and Imminent Togetherness.

*A Man's a Man* (1924-26) suddenly reveals Brecht's impeccable craftsmanship. Here, Eric Bentley insists, "emerges the Brecht the world knows." After the Chicago *spectacle noir*, Brecht creates a high comedy of clear outlines and—in spite of brainwashing and castration—a hilarious and elegant play that holds up the mirror to an age in which a man can be transformed and given a new function, like a car. Thus, innocent Galy Gay, going to market, may end up as a soldier at the Kipling frontier, not only not resisting his metamorphosis but joyfully accepting it and thriving on iron and blood (E. Bornemann). We have reached the first turning point. In the comic and epic strains of the play, pointing back to Baal's funny dialogue with his Bavarian landlady, and Kragler's paper moon, Brecht once again refines what he has sketched in his earliest plays; but in a character like sad, earthy, tenacious, and resolute Witwe Begbick, Brecht anticipates those vital and grand figures that dominate his late plays.

After the production of *A Man's a Man* (1926), Elisabeth Hauptmann noted that "Brecht acquired books on socialism and Marxism and asked for advice on which essential books he should read first." The initial result of these studies was Brecht's effort to create a new musical theater: both *The Threepenny Opera* (1928) and *The Rise and Fall of the*

*City of Mahagonny* (1928-29) are conceived as protests against the conventional, "culinary" opera which, as Brecht believed with Stravinsky, had lost its meaning. But Brecht, unlike Stravinsky, demands that the new opera, a first form of the epic theater, imply a critique of decaying bourgeois society, hiding the bitter didactic remedy in the sugar of attractive tunes. The culinary prevailed: in today's Greenwich Village as on the *Kurfürstendamm* of yore, middle-class audiences—in the puritan East both operas are ignored—continue to enjoy the "nostalgic melodies, the neat counterpoint and the harmonies disconcertingly prickly" (John Willett), and have little trouble in disregarding a social message which lacks direction, coherence, and a concrete target. In 1929 Brecht enters the ascetic and radically didactic period of his development (1929-1936/7). His *Schulstücke*, based upon the tradition of the medieval mystery plays and the *autos sacramentales,* are set on a liturgic stage on which immovable, abstract, allegorical figures and groups discuss the right (Communist) course of revolutionary action and the individual's mystical death and resurrection in the embrace of the collective. Issues, not techniques or characters, emerge as the center of theatrical interest. What Brecht demands of the individual amounts to a radically secularized *Entwerdung,* once defined in theological terms by the old German mystics. Not only does the individual have to give up extending a spontaneously charitable hand to his fellowman, as in *The Baden Cantata of Acquiescence* (1929) and *Saint Joan of the Stockyards* (1929-30), but, as Brecht insists in *The Measures Taken* (1930), he must submit to the Hegelian dictates of history, completely efface will and personality, and regress to the womb of the group, the whole, the (party) Organization. We are very close to Auden and Isherwood's *The Ascent of F6* (1936). Brecht's *The Measures Taken,* because of its admirable terseness and controlled craftsmanship, may well be the most accomplished and disturbing of the didactic pieces; yet it is doubtful whether one can really enjoy this "classic tragedy of communism" (as Esslin and Sokel seem to suggest). Unfortunately, it is based on the Hegelian disregard of individual dignity, a principle underlying both National Socialism and Communism; and possibly this "vile philosophy," to borrow T. S. Eliot's term, will interfere with aesthetic enjoyment unless one prefers to have artistic pleasures flavored with masochism.

Though Marxism may have helped Brecht to discipline his inner conflicts and to sharpen his innate dialectical powers, it did not necessarily make it easier for him to penetrate contemporary political events. "Truth is concrete," Brecht maintained throughout his life; but when, in the Thirties, he stepped beyond the parable stripped of all local color and tried to cope with present events, such as the rise of Hitler and the corruption of the German mind, the ideological dogma clouded his view. The "epic" version of Gorki's *Mother* (1930-32) provoked Sergey Tretiakov to utter some highly ironic remarks. *The Roundheads and the*

*Peakheads* (1932-34) tries to establish the point—not confirmed by the death camps of Treblinka, Dachau, and Osviedzyn—that Nazis and rich Jews are natural allies. *The Private Life of the Master Race* (1935-38) succeeds where it centers on idiom and character, but fails miserably whenever it touches on the concrete politics or economics of the *Third Reich*. And the *Resistible Rise of Arturo Ui* (1941), by ignoring the compulsive, if not the demonic aspect of National Socialism, reduces Hitler's way to catastrophe to an obsolete "Chicago gangster spectacle" (Willy Haas). Strangely enough, *Señora Carrar's Rifles* (1937), one of Brecht's more effective plays, written to support the worthy cause of the Spanish Republican government, clings no less to realist convention than does Hemingway's *The Fifth Column* (1938). Perhaps it was a sign that Brecht, after a period of unmitigated dogmatism, was ready to search for new tolerance and new dramatic interests.

The late Thirties are a decisive turning point in European intellectual history. After the Moscow trials, and the dubious interference of the Soviets in the Spanish War, the enthusiasm of the younger leftist writers and intellectuals began to cool: from Gide to Auden, from Silone to Spender, poets radically revised their commitments. It was the time when Franz Kafka was discovered by the Anglo-Saxon world, and Rilke's *Duino Elegies* were praised as valid explorations of man's ontological destiny— while, in the United States, the New Critics started to formulate their ideas in opposition to Edmund Wilson and *New Masses*. It is hard to believe that the general change of mood should not have affected a writer so responsive to his age as was Brecht. More important perhaps, as Eric Bentley suggests, the exile transformed Brecht's way of life as well as his poetic tasks: "Brecht was forced by Hitler into a withdrawal from political life in his own country. Living among foreigners who did not know him or his language, he ceased to be the writer he had recently decided to become—the political activist."

In attempting to describe the new quality of Brecht's late—the most important—plays, one cannot ignore the pervasive element of continuity. The late plays are of a more meditative cast and open to a number of conflicting interpretations; yet they ponder questions long present in the earlier plays. They are mellow, more disciplined, perhaps more traditional in their use of "epic" stage techniques, but they definitely rely on the alienation effects ruthlessly employed in the Twenties and Thirties. The later plays shift the central interest from technical experimentation and the discussion of ideological issues to an overwhelming creation of vital, "earthy," and impressive dramatic figures. These figures, however, are reincarnations of earlier characters whose substance, as in the reappearance of Witwe Begbick as Mother Courage, they preserve and refine.

As early as 1938-39, Brecht worked out his first version of *Galileo,* and he continued to revise the play almost until the time of his death. If Brecht earlier believed that the great change was imminent—and a mere matter of the sudden submission of the individual to the general will, ready to act—the world, though still changeable, now puts up a stiff resistance. "In the tension between the hero and reality, it is . . . the very unheroically depicted hero who gives in, adapts himself, and conforms" (H. Lüthy). Brecht's exploration of Galileo's life and failure has as much personal meaning as the early *Baal*. To a Communist poet who was commended by the Committee on Un-American Activities for his cooperation and who, not much later, went to East Berlin (his own Florence) where both lavish material support and a new Inquisition awaited him, the story of Galileo must have offered a fascinating chance to explore and to defend his own decisions. Brecht's Galileo may be a coward facing the Inquisition, but he demonstrates extraordinary courage when he continues his experiments during the days of the Black Death. Galileo does condemn himself in the presence of dear Andrea, but it is difficult to say whether his confession implies more sadness about his failure to stand up or hopeful pride that, now the *Discorsi* are completed and about to be smuggled out of the country, the personal failure may be weighed against the impersonal validity of his intellectual achievement. In the "West" we will always be tempted to measure Brecht's Galileo with the moral rod. In the "East" eager audiences will probably concentrate on other aspects of the play. There, private and public confessions, the necessity to continue daily cunning in order to preserve one's integrity, the art of dissimulation and the most intense self-hatred, because one does not dare to show one's real face, are basic, "existential" experiences. There, particularly after the East German workers' revolt, the Hungarian revolution and the Polish October, Galileo's passionate praise of the new age will fall upon understanding ears: "The Millenium of Faith is ended . . . this is the Millenium of Doubt." Whether Brecht wanted it or not, his *Galileo* has become a major document of what Soviet ideological language terms *revisionism,* and what we have come to recognize as a reawakened desire for independence and the destruction of an ossified system of oppressive ideas. In the intellectual constellation of Eastern Europe, Brecht's *Galileo* has its place very close to the philosophy of Ernst Bloch, and to the ideas of Harich and Kolakowski.

In his exile in Scandinavia and the United States, Brecht was again brooding over the question of how man, by nature good and charitable, may live in and resist a cruel universe of economic rapaciousness and exploding political evil. Andreas Kragler escaped into carnality, and Saint Joan of the Stockyards had her own rather simple answer: to be charitable is to betray the Revolution; it is better—to translate her message into plain political language—to be a Communist and aim at the great conflagration than to be a humble Social Democrat and be concerned with accident insurance and strike laws. The old question demanded a new answer: How was the *anima naturaliter christiana* to survive here and now? Thus we enter, as Esslin and Sokel have pointed out, the kingdom of Brecht's split characters. It is impossible to be good and to live. Either one creates an evil *Doppelgänger,* as does Shen Te (*The Good Woman of Setzuan*) or, like the Finnish Estate Owner, one may indulge in his innate goodness when drunk and sober up to the necessity of being inevitably evil. *Herr Puntila and His Man Matti* (1940) gloriously demonstrates Brecht's comic genius. It is not much of a play but it admirably develops individual situations, such as the parade of Puntila's brides, or his ascent of the Hatmal-Mountain built of "alienated" pieces of broken furniture, as well as the hilarious figure of Puntila himself. Indeed, Brecht so completely succeeds in making the picaresque capitalist live that he had difficulty explaining to his audience that the Communist chauffeur Matti should not be ignored—a singularly wooden-headed chap who plays up the proletarian class interest.

Unlike Puntila, the heroine in *The Good Woman of Setzuan* (1938-42) has no chance to escape the conflict of goodness versus survival. Even the three shabby little gods are helpless, and the iron law of "conditions" literally rends the golden-hearted prostitute apart.

> Shen Te would like to give all her possessions away to make everyone happy. . . . But her other self Shui Ta is compelled to be calculating, mean and profit-minded in order to save Shen Te's property and thereby make it possible for her to indulge in her generosity in the future. . . . As Shui Ta she safeguards her livelihood but cripples her life; as Shen Te she fulfills her life but forfeits her livelihood. (W. Sokel)

Unfortunately, the idea of the play counteracts its dramatic possibilities. Because Shen Te and Shui Ta may only consecutively appear on the stage and cannot clash head-on, *The Good Woman of Setzuan* suffers as drama. As in *Mother Courage* (1939), one is left "with a final despairing gesture," with the moving image of a suffering woman "helplessly caught in the web of circumstances" (Sokel). I do not understand why the American version of the play ignores the Epilogue with Brecht's final question about what should be done to make such suffering altogether impossible. The Epilogue will hardly persuade an audience to reply with the Marxist answer desired by Brecht. After one has observed the tragic fate of Shen Te, the question of the Epilogue rather points beyond the solution implied by the author. Brecht's merely rhetorical question turns into a legitimate one and, as Volker Klotz has pointed out, reveals the solution implied by Brecht as fragmentary and wholly insufficient.

The pathos of the final gesture and the tenacity of a hopeless existence relate Mother Courage to the Chinese girl, Shen Te. The vicissitudes of the German sutler woman and her children again demonstrate the difficulties of survival and the dangers of virtue: the sutler woman "cannot keep out of the war that is destroying her"; her son Eilif dies because he is too brave, her son Swiss Cheese because he is too honest, and her daughter Kattrin because she is too kind. True, *Mother Courage* does at times betray residues of an allegorical construction, but there is such a richness of local color, historical allusion, and concrete detail of idiom and costume that the message is far less obtrusive than in *The Good Woman of Setzuan.* For once Brecht's use of the South German (plebeian) language substantially adds to the "realistic" consistency of tone and character. If, in the case of Puntila, the Finnish capitalist, the Bavarian idiom is part of a highly effective comic alienation technique, in *Mother Courage* it rather furthers historical "authenticity" and considerably reduces the distance that usually separates Brecht from the great masters of German social drama, Georg Büchner and Gerhart Hauptmann. Far bigger than the play, Mother Courage herself has not failed to impress audiences in East and West. In vain, Brecht tried to point out her greed and her commercial participation in the murderous war in order to disengage the sutler woman from the emotional sympathies of the spectators. But Brecht was caught in his own snare: the more he put the stress on Mother Courage's greed and her moral deficiencies, the more clearly she emerged as a truly *mixed* character, who successfully invites the audience's empathy. Aristotle, Boileau and Lessing all knew that it is easier to feel with a human being than with a spotless hero. Precisely *because* the suffering sutler woman was eager to make her fast *Groschen* and was not without blemish, she turned into one of the unforgettable characters of the modern stage, completely defeated her author's intentions, and will go on pulling her wagon for as long as there is a theater and an audience longing to be moved by a symbol of supreme human tenacity.

But Brecht did not leave us without poetic consolation. In the last of his major plays, *The Caucasian Chalk Circle* (1944-45), charity and goodness are—as in fairy tales and old legends—rewarded by bliss and salvation. Brecht develops the story of the servant girl Grusha and the carnal judge Azdak with a serene and deceptive simplicity. As in a coda, or a final chord, many melodies and motifs of his earlier plays are here united in such pure and immaculate clarity that not even the Stalinist "frame" concerning the squabble of two agricultural collective farms can do any harm to it. In Grusha, the tender and simple peasant girl, all of Brecht's heroines, obsessed with kindness, reappear. In Azdak, Baal, Kragler, Puntila, and Galileo are reborn. Again, as in *Baal,* brittle nature, spring and winter, icicles and leaves of grass share the fate of men and women moving in wide, open, translucent spaces. Finally, Brecht admits to his most secret and most romantic dream about a "golden age almost of justice" out of which the poet, in the mask of a Homeric rhapsodist, steps forward to recite his tender tale.

The final question concerns our attitude toward Brecht's total achieve-

ment—so rich in grace and irritation, fruitful insight and terrible sim-
plifications, vitality and wit. To close our eyes for political reasons to the
charm of his theater would be as foolish as the blind admiration of his
orthodox devotees, who are willing to devour all of Brecht, lock, stock,
and trash. It is a pity that we are not in the happy position of T. S.
Eliot who, referring to Dante and Shelley, can calmly ponder the question of poetry and belief—which is the crux of our concern. With
Brecht, it is more difficult because the questions he asks and the answers
he offers do not yet belong to history. For having sent a telegram to
Ulbricht, Brecht has been boycotted by the Vienna theaters for years;
and after the East German Communists put up their Berlin wall on
August 13, 1961, many West German *Intendanten* immediately can-
celed their performances of *Mother Courage* and *The Caucasian Chalk
Circle*—as if Brecht were responsible for the brick and mortar. Strangely
enough, it may be quite fruitful to take Brecht's own advice seriously.
When he was young he always spoke of an *Epic "Smoking" Theater,* a
place where people could watch plays as if they were bicycle races or
boxing matches—spectators on their toes, critically aware of the technical
implications, *never permitting their cigars or cigarettes to go out.* This
sporting attitude may be the only one open to us who are involved in
political conflicts and are yet unwilling to make political categories the
last criterion of the arts. Deeply inhaling the recommended smoke, we
may discover that Brecht, in spite of his commitment, speaks to us as the
creator of vital characters like Begbick, Mother Courage, Shen Te,
Galileo, Azdak and Grusha, and in his comedies of Galy Gay and Puntila,
as the bitter Aristophanes of this age of little laughter.

# Bert Brecht

## by Sergey Tretiakov

The air is thick with cigar smoke. The only place where it gets any thicker is the smokers' car in the Berlin subway. People have drawn up their chairs and are sitting in a circle around a large ashtray. A telephone on a long cord is handed back and forth across the room as if it were a sugar bowl. The wires slide and tangle across the floor to the accompaniment of scraping chairs, scuffling feet and polite apologies.

The conversation proceeds in circular fashion (the way Georgians drink). Everyone speaks in an even tone, avoiding emphatic gestures or inflections. The craniums of the assembled intellectuals, economists, critics, men of politics, pamphleteers, and philosophers are like chemical retorts from which comments on the burning issues of the day dribble. No one interrupts; each waits his turn until the preceding speaker has squeezed out his last drop of utterance.

"Somewhere fascists, with knives, have attacked YCL'ers." (For this is Berlin in 1931.)

"Workers taken to jail in patrol wagons stick their fists through gratings and shout 'Rot Front!' "

"Another dozen factory chimneys have stopped smoking."

"Another thousand workers do not go out in the morning when the factory whistles blow."

"Another hundred women join the prostitutes on Berlin street corners."

Statements and aphorisms issue distilled, and perfectly bottled, from the human retorts. The most highly trained German minds discuss the situation. They hunt for formulas, formulas of cognition.

I am surprised. Formulas of cognition are all very well, but where are the formulas of action?

Climb out of your low armchair, Comrade Bert Brecht. Tell me why these people are here instead of in the Party units, or in the demonstrations of the unemployed? Why does the present welter of smoke and words remind me of the expression *"Stammtisch-Politik"*?

Every beerhall has its habitués. And these habitués have their table—

"Bert Brecht." Translator unknown. From *International Literature* (Moscow), May, 1937, pp. 60-70.

*"Stammtisch"*—where they swill beer and talk politics. They acquire distended livers from the beer and a complete aversion to political action from the talk.

"You're from the Soviet Union and a man of action," Brecht answers. "You do not appreciate to what extent the German intellectual requires a formula of cognition. People laugh at us Germans for our exaggerated sense of obedience and say we are prepared to regard every clause in the rules as a Kantian categorical imperative. This gives rise to the joke that Germans never will make revolutions, for in order to do so you must occupy the railway stations—and how can you do that without a pass? A logical formula has a hypnotic influence on the German mind.

"Today, the old saying that Germany is the country of thinkers and poets, *Denker und Dichter,* has been replaced by *Denker und Henker*—thinkers and hangmen."

And puffing on a poisonous black cigar of the kind Karl Marx used to smoke, Brecht adds with an upward flick of his fingers, "I suggest replacing the word *'Denker'* in the formula by the word *'Denkes.'* Germany is the land of 'Denkes'!" And he proceeds to explain. "Denke is the name of a criminal who killed people in order to use their corpses. He canned the meat and made soap from the fat, buttons from the bones, and purses from the skins. He placed his business on a scientific footing and was extremely surprised when, after his apprehension, he was sentenced to be executed. In the first place he couldn't see why the pointless sacrifice of thousands of people in wartime was considered legitimate! Why should the judges, prosecutors and lawyers make such a show of indignation? He had put his corpses to good practical uses; and he had utilized only second-grade people, human ballast, so to speak. He had never made a brief case out of a general's hide, or soap from the paunch of a factory owner or buttons from the skulls of journalists.

"I contend," Brecht continued, "that the best people of Germany, those who condemned Denke, failed to recognize the qualities of true German genius which the fellow displayed, namely: method, conscientiousness, cold-bloodedness, and the ability to base one's every act on a firm philosophical foundation. They should not have executed him; they should have made him a Ph.D. with *honoris causa."*

And resuming an interrupted argument, Brecht proceeds to weave a subtle web of refutations.

But Brecht himself is a living refutation. A full-fledged German from Swabia, he disconcerts all our notions of things German. Physically he resembles a note blown through a very slender clarinet. His hooked-nosed face recalls that of Voltaire or Ramses.

Berlin is the proverbial city of patent machinery and nickleplated automatons, but the elevator that takes you up to Brecht's sixth-floor garret lodgings is so shaky and dilapidated that you hesitate to enter it. It rises with jerks and spasms. And when you finally reach his landing you have to manipulate the lock for a long time before the door suddenly gives. It is the service elevator, used by delivery boys, housemaids, and writers who rent the garret rooms.

When a German is down and out the first thing he gives up is bread; next he sells his dishes; only after that does he part with his starched collar. I have seen unemployed Germans on the street give their ties to pushcart tailors to be pressed. Brecht, however, goes around in a rumpled shirt without a tie. He appears at brilliant first nights where everyone is in evening clothes, unshaven and wearing a black shirt!

His nose supports a pair of old-fashioned rimmed spectacles such as nobody else wears.

But do not imagine that he is an absent-minded sloven of the type of Kant, who once walked with one foot on the sidewalk and the other in the gutter and decided he was lame.

Brecht is a good chauffeur; he can assemble a machine or take it apart. The scar on his cheek he received in an automobile accident. Read Feuchtwanger's novel *Success*. His engineer Proeckl is patterned on Brecht.

In his native town of Augsburg Bert leads you past the huge cathedral. The drone of a lecture comes from the windows of the adjacent theological seminary. Brecht looks for the traces of bullets on the cornice and says: "I am a physician by education. As a boy I was mobilized in the war and placed in a hospital. I dressed wounds, applied iodine, gave enemas, performed blood transfusions. If the doctor ordered me: 'Amputate a leg, Brecht,' I would answer: 'Yes, your excellency,' and cut off the leg. If I was told: 'Make a trepanning,' I opened the man's skull and tinkered with his brains. I saw how they patched people up in order to ship them back to the front as soon as possible." In the evening, accompanying himself on the banjo, Brecht sings the *Ballad of the Dead Soldier*, the most famous of his ballads, describing how they dug up a soldier, patched him up and sent him back to the front.

Brecht did not write this ballad; he composed it orally and it traveled through the land by word of mouth. The "pure German gentlemen" answered this ballad with furious hatred.

"I was a member of the Augsburg Revolutionary Committee," Brecht continued. "Nearby, in Munich, Leviné raised the banner of Soviet power. Augsburg lived in the reflected glow of Munich. The hospital was the only military unit in the town. It elected me to the Revolutionary Committee. I still remember Georg Brem and the Polish Bolshevik Olshevsky. We did not boast a single Red Guardsman. We didn't have time to issue a single decree or nationalize a single bank or close a single church. In two days General Epp's troops came to town on their way to Munich. One of the members of the Revolutionary Committee hid at my house until he managed to escape."

In the days of the Hitlerite "beerhall" *Putsch*, Brecht's name was fifth on the fascist murder list, an honor earned by his *Ballad of the Dead Soldier*. He survived only because the Hitler *Putsch* failed.

Bavaria gave way to Berlin—ballads, plays, discussions, clashes. The solitary intellectual cynic took the field, one against many, puncturing hypocrisy with his pen, his only weapon.

He passed through a period of the cult of brawn and brute force. He wrote of huge hairy men with bulging muscles, who smelled of sweat, who took what they wanted, without asking.

"However," a neighbor recalls, "it was impossible to induce Brecht to do morning setting-up exercises. He would think up any excuse to get out of it."

Playwriting, Brecht's main literary expression, began in Munich.

He wrote *Drums in the Night*. This work contained echoes of the revolution. The drums of revolt persistently summon the man who has gone home. But the man prefers the quiet peace of his hearthside.

The work was a scathing satire on those who had deserted the revolution, and toasted themselves at their fireplaces. One should recall that Kapp launched his drive on Christmas Eve, calculating that many Red Guardsmen would have left their detachments for their family Christmas trees.

Brecht, the playwright, was at the same time Brecht the director. He himself staged all his own plays. His persistence, eagerness, and stubbornness trained a whole generation of actors. Carola Neher, who played in *The Threepenny Opera*; Helene Weigel who played in *A Man's a Man*, in *Mother* and in *The Measures Taken*; Ernst Busch—these are only a few of the actors trained by Brecht.

In his rehearsals Brecht strove not only for clarity of speech but for coordination of speech and gesture, that the speech might simply serve to complete and explain the gesture.

"The gesture precedes the word," says Brecht. And if the word is discordant with the gesture, he discards it for another.

Luther's language, in Brecht's opinion, is expressive because of its conformity to gesture. And one can learn much from Büchner and the early dramas of Goethe.

Brecht's plays usually bear several signatures. This is the result of his special way of working on them.

He does not write them but composes them, acting them out before a small group of collaborators.

The audience makes comments, objects to some expressions, and suggests others. When someone has a variant version to propose, he gets up and acts it. Arguments proceed over the form and meaning of the composition. Sometimes, at the opening of a scene, Brecht merely goes through the motions and instead of words intones a melody which only gradually evolves into words.

And when the play is produced, another phase begins. One must forget the bourgeois audience and critics and listen carefully to the comments of the proletarian audience.

Brecht received several hundred notes from workers after *The Measures Taken* was produced, and he inserted some twenty corrections in the play.

On one occasion the Vienna typesetters refused to set an episode which they considered incorrect, and someone had to be sent to convince them.

Thus, from antagonism to the audience the playwright went over to an alliance with that part of the audience whose friend, comrade-in-arms, teacher, and disciple he was.

I myself saw in 1931 how, after six performances, his play *A Man's a Man* was hastily taken off the stage of the *Schauspielhaus,* a theater which in importance compares with the Maly Theater in Moscow. In its respectable repertory Brecht's play fell under suspicion. The performance produced a tremendous impression on me, second only to Meyerhold's *Rogonosetz.*

Giant soldiers armed to the teeth and wearing jackets caked with lime, blood, and excrement stalk about the stage, holding onto wires to keep from falling off the stilts inside their trouser legs. According to the plot the soldiers belong to a British detachment in India, automatons for slaughter and pillage. And into the midst of these monsters wanders the softhearted civilian Galy Gay (the man who cannot say "no"). This is the plot:

While pillaging an invaded village a soldier disappears. Someone must be found to replace him—otherwise the whole company will be punished. The soldiers induce Galy Gay to stand on roll call with them, buying him beer and cigars; but they need him permanently and not just for this occasion. This means they must implicate him in a crime which will compel him to deny his own identity and remain with them. They persuade him to sell the regimental elephant. A fantastic deal ensues. Two soldiers, covered with an oilcloth table cover and the proboscis of a gas mask dangling in front of them, impersonate the elephant. As soon as the deal has been made, they arrest Galy Gay and tell him:

"A man by the name of Galy Gay has committed a triple crime. In the first place he sold an elephant that did not belong to him; in the second place he did not sell a real elephant; in the third place the elephant belongs to the regiment. It is a clear case of swindle and treason. You say you are not Galy Gay, but why then do you conceal your identity and what are you doing in camp? Are you a spy? The penalty for that is death."

The retreat back to the name of Galy Gay is thus cut off. What remains now is a man without a name. There are two alternatives. He is either a spy, and in that case he must be shot; or he is a soldier and he must hurry into line because the bugle has just blown. Galy Gay gives his answer. The soldiers cluster around him in a circle. When the circle opens, out of it rushes a man with a knife in his teeth, weighted down with hand grenades, in a uniform that stinks with trench filth. The shy, well-meaning civilian has been put through the mill, has been transformed into an efficient cog in that machine of extermination called a capitalist army. The intellectual of yesterday who could not say "no" is transformed into a fascist, for whom others say "no" and "yes," while all that is required of him is the unthinking yell "heil."

But the intelligent Berlin bourgeois does not go to the theater to be made to feel uncomfortable.

The spectator wants to be above the action of the play or at any rate on a level with it. He will not tolerate action that puzzles him and perhaps affronts his comforting sense of respectability. This is why women stamped their feet during Brecht's play. Indignant lawyers rushed out of the theater throwing crumpled program sheets at the actors on the way. In the cloakroom a sobbing woman snatched her coat from her husband and went to put it on in a far corner. She was guilty of having watched the performance without being roused to indignation.

Ossip Brik aptly remarked that Brecht's plays are usually in the form of court proceedings. This is true. Brecht the playwright is an able and resourceful casuist.

He is incomparable when he comes to litigation. He strips the time-honored concepts of "beauty," "truth," "justice," "honesty," "progress," forces them down on their bare knees and rubs their nose in the filth of the system which developed them.

I strolled with Brecht through a churchyard in a Bavarian village. The first-class dead were buried along the main path. The thick, short-armed marble crosses atop the family vaults were more substantial than bank entrances. Lists of names were chiseled in the stone, in which enameled portraits were imbedded. The words "druggist," "teacher," "miller," "*Ekonom*" preceded the names. "*Ekonom*" was the local title of the rich peasants, the kulaks, as we call them. These were all strictly respectable corpses.

The crosses in the second row were a bit thinner. "*Ekonoms*" who were more economical. This was the second-class area. It only cost sixty marks to lie here for a ten year period while in the first class it cost a hundred.

Third class was in a far corner.

There the crosses were so thin that from the side they were almost invisible. The inscriptions on the crosses were laconic, almost telegraphic in style. Beneath these frail monuments lay the inmates of the local "hospice." The hospice was a sort of alms house where couples who had "worked themselves out" were allowed to end their days. The majority of the war invalids, thrown out of the shops and shoved off the streets by the aggression of younger and stronger hands, ended up in the hospice.

A man climbed out of a grave and pulled a spade up after him. He invited us to the chapel to view the body of an old woman from the hospice, which was thinner, he said, than any corpse that had ever come to the cemetery before. He spoke of that corpse with genuine enthusiasm and was offended when we refused to inspect it, but he consoled himself by showing us his fourth-class tenants, the disreputable people, the suicides who occupied a strip along the churchyard wall. He was especially indignant over one grave. In it lay a motion picture operator from Munich and a girl, the daughter of a respectable local *"Ekonom."* The couple had shot themselves on a nearby mountain peak, visible over the top of the wall.

In its time doubtless each of these graves had stirred the imagination of the quiet hamlet, where generation after generation trod the well-worn path of changeless customs. The village felt the march of history and changes in the mould of life less through daily fluctuations of world economic and political indices than through the sudden shocks of local village tragedies.

The sexton passed over a fresh grave covered with wreaths. A cross stood over it. A peasant boy who had been apprenticed to a metal plant in the city had been buried here two days before. He had fallen in with company that wanted to live like gentlemen, to dress, eat, and amuse themselves like gentlemen. The boy ran short of money. He got into a mess and five days ago had been found with his skull perforated. The official certificate stated "killed at work by a falling rivet." The sexton explained: "By a bullet." And added: "The parents were very anxious that their son should not lie among the suicides. They got the curate to agree to this little white lie."

Brecht was beaming. He proceeded to compose the plot for a play about a youth who committed suicide, crashes the gates of heaven on false papers and places the celestial judge in an awkward position, as the latter must either discredit his agent, the curate, who forged the papers, or else keep quiet about the matter.

"I do not like plays to contain pathetic overtones," Brecht said, "they must be convincing, like court pleas. The main thing is to teach the spectator to reach a verdict. This trains the mind. Any fool knows how to feel sad and to share suffering. And not only fools. You should see the salty tears swindlers can shed when they are moved."

And he teaches people how to reach a verdict, transforming the spectator's chair into that of the judge.

His play *The Measures Taken,* the first of Brecht's plays on a Communist theme, is arranged like a court where the characters try to justify themselves for having killed a comrade and the judges (the chorus), who at the same time represent the audience, summarize the events and reach a verdict.

When he visited Moscow in 1932, Brecht told me his plan to organize a theater in Berlin which would re-enact the most interesting court trials in the history of mankind.

"The theater would function like a court room. Two trials an evening, each lasting an hour and a quarter. For example, the trial of Socrates, a witches' trial, the trial of Karl Marx's *Neue Rheinische Zeitung,* the trial of Georg Grosz on the charge of blasphemy for his cartoon *Christ in a Gasmask.*"

Brecht was carried away by his enthusiasm. He began to elaborate: "Let us suppose that the trial of Socrates is over. We organize a short witch's trial where the judges are armored knights who condemn the witch to the stake. Then the trial of Georg Grosz begins, but we forget to remove the knights from the stage. When the indignant prosecutor storms at the artist for having insulted our mild and compassionate God a terrific racket breaks loose, as though two dozen five-gallon samovars were applauding. The noise is caused by the knights who are moved to applause by the defender of the defenseless god.

"We shall stage an eviction trial against an unemployed worker in Germany," Brecht continued, "and alongside it a Soviet trial where a working woman wins a title to space in an apartment."

Brecht acquired a world reputation with his play *The Threepenny Opera.* The score is the work of the composer Weill. The plot is taken from an English melodrama. The peppery irony scattered through the play belongs to Brecht. The tremendous success of the *The Threepenny Opera* is not due to Brecht's text but to the veil of Weill's music, that conceals it.

The action proceeds on two planes—a false one and a real one. On the false plane a representative of the law catches a scoundrel and murderer concealed in a rat hole. On the real plane this same scoundrel and murderer stands revealed as the wielder of dictatorial power. The chief of police is his accomplice and is on his payroll. Is not this a parody of Chicago's Al Capone?

I know of nothing that Brecht despises more than *"Kitsch." "Kitsch"* is the German term for cheap sentimentalism and pseudo-heroics.

The applause received by the *The Threepenny Opera* is more than balanced by the catcalls and indignation which Brecht's other plays evoked. Everywhere the Philistine, who suddenly recognized his own image, took offense and forced play after play off the stage.

But Brecht's drama, the drama of paradox, began to develop more and more in the direction of the educational theater and epic drama, as the playwright came closer to the Communist movement.

Brecht conceived the idea of writing a play about the tariff tricks resorted to by the landowners in order to peg the price of grain. But this requires a knowledge of economics. The study of economics brought Brecht to Marx and Lenin, whose works became an indispensable part of his library.

Brecht studies and quotes Lenin as a great thinker and as a great master of prose.

Brecht bases the new departure in his drama on two propositions.

According to the first the theater must be epic in character. The epic theater must narrate events and compel the spectator to understand them, as opposed to the traditional theater, the Aristotelian theater, as Brecht calls it, which involves the spectator in a chain of emotional experience and acts upon his emotional responses. According to Brecht the theater should act upon the spectator's intellect. Brecht prefers the clash of judgment, the struggle of syllogisms, the conscious discovery of what is false and stupid in the world, to the emotional discovery of what is disgusting and bad.

| *1. The Aristotelian Theater* | *2. The Epic Theater* |
| --- | --- |
| *Action* | *Narrative* |
| Involves the spectator in the stage action and destroys his own will to action | Makes the spectator an observer and arouses his will to action |
| Touches | Calls for decisions and a world outlook |
| Emotional experience | |
| Suggestion | Argument |
| The spectator shares in emotional experience | The spectator is taught |
| Man is given as a known quantity | Man is a subject of investigation |
| Interest in the outcome of the action | Interest in the course of the action |
| Every scene preconditions the next | Every scene is independent |
| Organic development | Montage |
| Feeling | Intellect |

The traditional theater does not like argument on the stage. What usually convinces us in a play is not so much the correctness of the hero's arguments as his attractive personality or the emotional richness of his conduct.

The conflict of passions and not the conflict of judgments determines the character of the traditional theater.

In his efforts to establish a line of demarcation, Brecht published a chart showing where the center of gravity lies in each of these theaters.

The traditional drama portrays the struggle of class instincts. Brecht demands that the struggle of class instincts be replaced by the struggle of social consciousness, of social convictions. He maintains that the situation must not only be felt, but explained, crystallized into the idea which will overturn the world.

When I say "which will overturn the world," I am already intruding on the second proposition, which makes his drama not only epic, but didactic as well.

The creation of a rational theater along the lines we have outlined above, the transformation of the stage into the tribune, might easily lead to sophistry. The play of logic is just as liable to become the object of smug contemplation as the play of emotional outbursts.

Discussion for its own sake is just as socially retrograde and reactionary as emotional experience for its own sake. However, this does not occur in Brecht's drama. The full-blooded lyricism of the materialist artist breaks through his logical patterns.

The age taught the poet to be ashamed of sentiment and he conceals his emotion.

Brecht, the artist, has an extremely broad and varied range. He has composed many ballads, songs, and choruses on the subject of revolutionary ruthlessness. But these themes are dyed in many different hues. The play *The Measures Taken* still retains a considerable element of court proceedings, of paradox. Brecht's first truly epic drama is *Mother* (from Gorky's novel).

This production had a political significance, since it marked Gorky's jubilee in pre-Hitler Germany. Furthermore, it was not a simple adaptation of Gorky's novel to the stage. Gorky's *Mother* merely supplied the initial impulse for a new work which went beyond historical novels and which was addressed to all proletarian mothers of present-day Germany.

At first sight Brecht's *Mother* deals with the revolutionary development of the Tver working woman Pelagea Vlasova.

But this is misleading. It would be wrong to regard it as a historical play about a Russian working woman. Such an interpretation involves one absurdity after another.

Would a Russian teacher of the 1905 period spend his evenings over a beer mug, arguing with friends that science and technics are unable to better human life and that the only method is the moral transformation of the individual? Would such a teacher take footbaths at night and speak in a Spenglerean tone of the decline of civilization?

Would workers in Tver sit on a bench and discuss the nature of the lesser evil? Where in Russian history can you find agricultural workers, brought to the country from the city, who go on strike and throw stones at the strikebreakers?

Where could you find houseowners who evict their tenants and supply them with bibles for consolation?

Where, finally, in wartime Russia might you find women standing in queues before booths which accept patriotic offerings of copper utensils?

Of course none of this is Russia. It is Germany. Change the Russian names in the play to German ones and you will have the story of a contemporary German professional revolutionary woman doing her bit to enlighten millions of German Vlasovas who have not yet recognized reality.

This play is a whole seminar on methods of propaganda and tactics in revolutionary struggle. How should people be utilized in the struggle? How should one enlighten the ignorant, by frontal attacks or by incursions from the rear? How can one deceive the enemy? How can the experience of an alien culture be utilized? How to be disciplined? . . .

Regardless of whether Brecht likes it or not, I must mention the vividness of the teacher, the houseowner, the shopwoman, and the policeman in the play. The workers are hard to distinguish from each other; this is a general shortcoming of all Brecht's plays, which shows that he does not know the proletarian milieu intimately (this is a warning to him that he must get to know it so).

An exception is Vlasova. This professional working woman revolutionary has a face, a voice, and a stride that are peculiarly her own. She is unmistakable.

In this play the skeleton of Brecht's algebra is already clothed in the flesh of live circumstances and this immediately renders the play effective.

Brecht's play *Saint Joan of the Stockyards* is a parody of Schiller's *Maid of Orleans,* adapted to the present-day relations between the condors of finance and the quiet turtledoves of the Salvation Army. This play contains the phrase: "A sloven in the home nest," a term which stockbrokers use to describe a fellow broker who strips them by clever deals.

Brecht was just such a "sloven in the home nest" of the bourgeoisie until, by a decisive turn in the direction of Communism, he brought his drama face to face with a wholly new audience—the audience of the proletariat.

The nobles in Gogol's *Dead Souls* could vent their spleen on Nozdrev and even beat him, but for all that, he was a nobleman and therefore one of them.

So in Germany they jumped on Brecht for his earlier plays; but their indignation was coupled with the gloomy assertion: "There's always a ne'er-do-well in the family."

After *The Measures Taken* the newspapers became wary. When *Mother* appeared on the stage the howl of the press died down and the reviewers' voice was replaced by that of the police official. After thirty performances *Mother* was banned. It was only allowed to be read from the stage. The actors stood in a row and began to read.

"Halt!" the policeman shouted. "This is not a reading but a performance. Your actor turned toward another actor when delivering his reply."

The readers sat down and continued: "Halt!" the same voice rang out. "You made a gesture with your hand. This isn't a reading, it's a performance. I declare the reading discontinued."

*Saint Joan of the Stockyards* was produced in Darmstadt. Half an hour after the play began, the shouting and catcalling fascists provoked a brawl that put a stop to the performance.

Brecht's room is a living diagram of his literary biography. A dusty banjo hangs upon the wall. Brecht seldom sings his ballads to his own accompaniment now. Beside the gramophone lie records from the *The Threepenny Opera* sung by Brecht himself.

A sketch, intentionally rough and indecipherable, sprawls on a huge wooden panel. It is the work of the artist who designed the sets for *A Man's a Man,* where huge portraits of the characters took the place of stage scenery.

There is a plaster head of Brecht which looks for all the world as though it had been detached from the mummy of Ramses. A head of the same type protrudes from a Chinese robe on which the columns of Chinese characters compose a cartoon.

Brecht in the guise of Confucius. He is interested in Confucianism as a science of conduct. His bookshelf, however, contains books of science and action—Lenin.

The abstract logician finds the road to reality; he becomes Brecht the dialectician and activist. It is not enough to make cynical mock of reality—one must change it. Brecht regards the old forms of art as too static and passive. But he does not try to enliven art by concretizing the material from which the work is fashioned. He wants to concretize the action of the work of art upon men.

Brecht claims that art is a branch of pedagogy—that its purpose is to teach. Capitalism deforms education so that people consider themselves insulted by a didactic tone; its schools are a travesty on the human mind. Real education is something to be desired and the educated man is glad because he has become more intelligent and stronger. A good example of this is the attitude toward education in the Soviet Union.

Brecht favors an "intelligent theater." He wants conflicting opinions to be as absorbing as conflicting passions.

The point is not to leave the spectator purged by a cathartic but to leave him a changed man, or rather, to sow within him the seeds of changes which must be completed outside the theater.

The performance must not be a closed circle where the heroes and villains balance, where all accounts are settled. On the contrary it must be spiral in form, a circle which is sprung, which rises to new horizons; the spectator must be brought out of equilibrium.

In *Saint Joan* the dying heroine says:

> Make it not your goal
> That in the hour of death,
> You yourself be better.
> Let it be your goal
> That in the hour of death,
> You leave a bettered world.

What is the source of Brecht's strength? It is his implacable hatred of bigotry, hypocrisy, and all forms of conceit.

He hurls his trenchant aphorisms at the well-groomed and well-bred poetry of the symbolists. He constructs a sentence with biblical sedateness and then shatters it with a sudden whack. He makes stockbrokers talk in Shakespearean pentameters but he makes his pentameters stagger like drunkards.

On the wavering heights of intellectual tightrope walking Brecht came, by guidance of Lenin's articles, to Communism, and reached the place where men fight for their living cause. He applied his training in argument and logic to specific work. In collaboration with Hanns Eisler he wrote songs for the proletarian stage, for demonstrations, and mass choruses. He wrote the *Ballad of Paragraph 218, Lullabies for Proletarian Mothers,* the *Solidarity Song.*

The man who sat in a smoke-filled room where synthetic opinions dribbled from human chemical retorts has walked over to the window. He has flung the window wide open and heard the police whistles, and the thud of police clubs, the "Heil" of brown-shirted shopkeepers, the hum of the underground Communist press.

He goes out on the street. He no longer confines himself to scathing epigrams which only a refined intellectual audience can fathom. He speaks the truth in simple words. He talks to the proletariat of Wedding, Neukölln, Essen, and Hamburg. And they answer with thunderous laughter and applause.

Brecht writes about a worker who goes from a breadline into a storm-troop detachment. Put to music by Hanns Eisler, Brecht's song breathes over the shoulder of the worker who does not know that his shirt is brown because it is caked with the blood of his class brothers.

Brecht's old archenemy back in Munich, Adolf Hitler, takes power. Brecht emigrates abroad. He answers with the play *The Roundheads and the Peakheads,* which tells us how a certain dictator averted the approaching social revolution by dividing the population into two racial types and pitting them against each other. The scene of action is presumably Peru. But it is clear to everybody that the Peru in question does not border on Chile, but on France and Poland.

Abroad Brecht collaborates even more closely with Eisler. His poetry has a firmer and truer ring. The poet's pen attacks the enemy with un-relenting fury.

The positive strain also grows. It was already audible in the chorus of *The Measures Taken.* But abstract formulas were posited then. As time goes on, however, the arithmetic of a warm, living reality intrudes more and more insistently upon Brecht's algebra. This living reality was lacking in the earlier Brecht, who developed his concepts in terms of imaginary Perus, Chinas, Englands, and Russias, removed from specific historic epochs.

Brecht came to the Soviet Union twice and while here searched eagerly for episodes from our construction which contained crystallized thoughts and which at the same time would provide concrete samples of socialist reality.

The mathematician Leverier who calculated the location of the planet Neptune on paper was not even interested in seeing his discovery through the telescope.

Brecht likewise enumerates in the formulas of the epic theater, the laws of growth of the new man. He, however, is not satisfied with that. He wants to touch the new man and feel the threads that lead to him from the geniuses who foretold and who organized the October Revolution.

If not for this trend of Brecht's, away from dead schematism to throbbing life, he could not have conceived the proletarian mothers with their lullabies and the rugmakers of Kuyan-Bulak who honor the immortal name of Lenin.

"The things you create are so unique in human history," Brecht says, "that they should be recorded in the rock, just as the ancients recorded victories or the founding of cities.

"Your subway is lined with marble slabs but they contain not a single word as to what a miracle in the history of humanity this undertaking was."

# From the Testimony of
# Berthold Brecht

*(Accompanied by Counsel, Mr. Kenny, and Mr. Crum)*

HEARINGS OF THE HOUSE COMMITTEE

ON UN-AMERICAN ACTIVITIES,

OCTOBER 30, 1947

MR. STRIPLING. Mr. Brecht, will you please state your full name and present address for the record, please? Speak into the microphone.

MR. BRECHT. My name is Berthold Brecht. I am living at 34 West Seventy-third Street, New York. I was born in Augsburg, Germany, February 10, 1898.

MR. STRIPLING. Mr. Brecht, the committee has a——

The CHAIRMAN. What was that date again?

MR. STRIPLING. Would you give the date again?

The CHAIRMAN. Tenth of February 1898.

MR. McDOWELL. 1898?

MR. BRECHT. 1898.

MR. STRIPLING. Mr. Chairman, the committee has here an interpreter, if you desire the use of an interpreter.

MR. CRUM. Would you like an interpreter?

The CHAIRMAN. Do you desire an interpreter?

MR. BRECHT. Yes.

The CHAIRMAN. Mr. Interpreter, will you stand and raise your right hand, please?

Mr. Interpreter, do you solemnly swear you will diligently and correctly translate from English into German all questions which may be propounded to this witness and as diligently and correctly translate from German into English all answers made by him, so help you God?

MR. BAUMGARDT. I do.

The CHAIRMAN. Sit down.

(Mr. David Baumgardt was seated beside the witness as interpreter.)

. . .

MR. STRIPLING. Now, Mr. Brecht, will you state to the committee whether or not you are a citizen of the United States?

MR. BRECHT. I am not a citizen of the United States; I have only my first papers.

MR. STRIPLING. When did you acquire your first papers?

MR. BRECHT. In 1941 when I came to the country.

MR. STRIPLING. When did you arrive in the United States?

MR. BRECHT. May I find out exactly? I arrived July 21 at San Pedro.

MR. STRIPLING. July 21, 1941?

MR. BRECHT. That is right.

MR. STRIPLING. At San Pedro, California?

MR. BRECHT. Yes.

MR. STRIPLING. You were born in Augsburg, Bavaria, Germany, on February 10, 1888; is that correct?

MR. BRECHT. Yes.

MR. STRIPLING. I am reading from the immigration records——

MR. CRUM. I think, Mr. Stripling, it was 1898.

MR. BRECHT. 1898.

MR. STRIPLING. I beg your pardon.

MR. CRUM. I think the witness tried to say 1898.

MR. STRIPLING. I want to know whether the immigration records are correct on that. Is it '88 or '98?

MR. BRECHT. '98.

MR. STRIPLING. Were you issued a quota immigration visa by the American vice consul on May 3, 1941, at Helsinki, Finland?

MR. BRECHT. That is correct.

MR. STRIPLING. And you entered this country on that visa?

MR. BRECHT. Yes.

MR. STRIPLING. Where had you resided prior to going to Helsinki, Finland?

MR. BRECHT. May I read my statement? In that statement——

The CHAIRMAN. First, Mr. Brecht, we are trying to identify you. The identification won't be very long.

MR. BRECHT. I had to leave Germany in 1933, in February, when Hitler took power. Then I went to Denmark but when war seemed imminent in '39 I had to leave for Sweden, Stockholm. I remained there for one year and then Hitler invaded Norway and Denmark and I had to leave Sweden and I went to Finland, there to wait for my visa for the United States.

MR. STRIPLING. Now, Mr. Brecht, what is your occupation?

MR. BRECHT. I am a playwright and a poet.

MR. STRIPLING. A playwright and a poet?

MR. BRECHT. Yes.

MR. STRIPLING. Where are you presently employed?

MR. BRECHT. I am not employed.

MR. STRIPLING. Were you ever employed in the motion-picture industry?

MR. BRECHT. Yes; I—yes. I sold a story to a Hollywood firm, "Hangmen Also Die," but I did not write the screenplay myself. I am not a professional screenplay writer. I wrote another story for a Hollywood firm but that story was not produced.

MR. STRIPLING. "Hangmen Also Die"—whom did you sell to, what studio?

MR. BRECHT. That was to, I think, an independent firm, Pressburger at United Artists.

MR. STRIPLING. United Artists?

MR. BRECHT. Yes.

MR. STRIPLING. When did you sell the play to United Artists?

MR. BRECHT. The story—I don't remember exactly, maybe around '43 or '44; I don't remember, quite.

MR. STRIPLING. And what other studios have you sold material to?

MR. BRECHT. No other studio. Besides the last story I spoke of I wrote for Enterprise Studios.

MR. STRIPLING. Are you familiar with Hanns Eisler? Do you know Johannes Eisler?

MR. BRECHT. Yes.

MR. STRIPLING. How long have you known Johannes Eisler?

MR. BRECHT. I think since the middle of the Twenties, twenty years or so.

MR. STRIPLING. Have you collaborated with him on a number of works?

MR. BRECHT. Yes.

MR. STRIPLING. Mr. Brecht, are you a member of the Communist Party or have you ever been a member of the Communist Party?

MR. BRECHT. May I read my statement? I will answer this question but may I read my statement?

MR. STRIPLING. Would you submit your statement to the chairman?

MR. BRECHT. Yes.

The CHAIRMAN. All right, let's see the statement.

(Mr. Brecht hands the statement to the chairman.)

The CHAIRMAN. Mr. Brecht, the committee has carefully gone over the statement. It is a very interesting story of German life but it is not at all pertinent to this inquiry. Therefore, we do not care to have you read the statement.

Mr. Stripling.

MR. STRIPLING. Mr. Brecht, before we go on with the questions, I would like to put into the record the subpoena which was served upon you on September 19, calling for your appearance before the committee. You are here in response to a subpoena, are you not?

MR. BRECHT. Yes.

MR. STRIPLING. Now, I will repeat the original question. Are you now or have you ever been a member of the Communist Party of any country?

MR. BRECHT. Mr. Chairman, I have heard my colleagues when they considered this question not as proper, but I am a guest in this country and do not want to enter into any legal arguments, so I will answer your question fully as well I can.

I was not a member or am not a member of any Communist Party.

The CHAIRMAN. Your answer is, then, that you have never been a member of the Communist Party?

MR. BRECHT. That is correct.

MR. STRIPLING. You were not a member of the Communist Party in Germany?

MR. BRECHT. No; I was not.

MR. STRIPLING. Mr. Brecht, is it true that you have written a number of very revolutionary poems, plays, and other writings?

MR. BRECHT. I have written a number of poems and songs and plays in the fight against Hitler and, of course, they can be considered, therefore, as revolutionary because I, of course, was for the overthrow of that government.

The CHAIRMAN. Mr. Stripling, we are not interested in any works that he might have written advocating the overthrow of Germany or the government there.

MR. STRIPLING. Yes; I understand.

Well, from an examination of the works which Mr. Brecht has written, particularly in collaboration with Mr. Hanns Eisler, he seems to be a person of international importance to the Communist revolutionary movement.

Now, Mr. Brecht, is it true or do you know whether or not you have written articles which have appeared in publications in the Soviet zone of Germany within the past few months?

MR. BRECHT. No; I do not remember to have written such articles. I have not seen any of them printed. I have not written any such articles just now. I write very few articles, if any.

MR. STRIPLING. I have here, Mr. Chairman, a document which I will hand to the translator and ask him to identify it for the committee and to refer to an article which refers on page 72.

MR. BRECHT. May I speak to that publication?

MR. STRIPLING. I beg your pardon?

MR. BRECHT. May I explain this publication?

MR. STRIPLING. Yes. Will you identify the publication?

MR. BRECHT. Oh, yes. That is not an article, that is a scene out of a play I wrote in, I think, 1937 or 1938 in Denmark. The play is called *The Private Life of the Master Race*, and this scene is one of the scenes out of this play about a Jewish woman in Berlin in the year of '36 or '37. It was, I see, printed in this magazine *Ost und West*, July 1946.

MR. STRIPLING. Mr. Translator, would you translate the frontispiece of the magazine, please?

MR. BAUMGARDT. "East and West, Contributions to Cultural and Political Questions of the Time, edited by Alfred Kantorowicz, Berlin, July 1947, first year of publication enterprise."

MR. STRIPLING. Mr. Brecht, do you know the gentleman who is the editor of the publication whose name was just read?

MR. BRECHT. Yes; I know him from Berlin and I met him in New York again.

MR. STRIPLING. Do you know him to be a member of the Communist Party of Germany?

MR. BRECHT. When I met him in Germany I think he was a journalist on the Ullstein Press. That is not a Communist—was not a Communist—there were no Communist Party papers so I do not know exactly whether he was a member of the Communist Party of Germany.

MR. STRIPLING. You don't know whether he was a member of the Communist Party or not?

MR. BRECHT. I don't know, no; I don't know.

MR. STRIPLING. In 1930 did you, with Hanns Eisler, write a play entitled, *Die Massnahme [The Measures Taken]*?

MR. BRECHT. *Die Massnahme.*

MR. STRIPLING. Did you write such a play?

MR. BRECHT. Yes; yes.

MR. STRIPLING. Would you explain to the committee the theme of that play—what it dealt with?

MR. BRECHT. Yes; I will try to.

MR. STRIPLING. First, explain what the title means.

MR. BRECHT. "Die Massnahme" means [speaking in German].

MR. BAUMGARDT. Measures to be taken, or steps to be taken—measures.

MR. STRIPLING. Could it mean disciplinary measures?

MR. BAUMGARDT. No; not disciplinary measures; no. It means measures to be taken.

MR. McDOWELL. Speak into the microphone.

MR. BAUMGARDT. It means only measures or steps to be taken.

MR. STRIPLING. All right.

You tell the committee now, Mr. Brecht——

MR. BRECHT. Yes.

MR. STRIPLING (continuing). What this play dealt with.

MR. BRECHT. Yes. This play is the adaptation of an old religious Japanese play and is called No Play, and follows quite closely this old story which shows the devotion for an ideal until death.

MR. STRIPLING. What was that ideal, Mr. Brecht?

MR. BRECHT. The idea in the old play was a religious idea. This young people——

MR. STRIPLING. Didn't it have to do with the Communist Party?

MR. BRECHT. Yes.

MR. STRIPLING. And discipline within the Communist Party?

MR. BRECHT. Yes, yes; it is a new play, an adaptation. It had as a background the Russia-China of the years 1918 or 1919, or so. There some Communist agitators went to a sort of no man's land between the Russia which then was not a state and had no real——

MR. STRIPLING. Mr. Brecht, may I interrupt you? Would you consider the play to be pro-Communist or anti-Communist, or would it take a neutral position regarding Communists?

MR. BRECHT. No; I would say—you see, literature has the right and the duty to give to the public the ideas of the time. Now, in this play— of course, I wrote about twenty plays, but in this play I tried to express the feelings and the ideas of the German workers who then fought against Hitler. I also formulated in an artistic——

MR. STRIPLING. Fighting against Hitler, did you say?

MR. BRECHT. Yes.

MR. STRIPLING. Written in 1930?

MR. BRECHT. Yes, yes; oh, yes. That fight started in 1923.

MR. STRIPLING. You say it is about China, though; it has nothing to do with Germany?

MR. BRECHT. No, it had nothing to do about it.

MR. STRIPLING. Let me read this to you.

MR. BRECHT. Yes.

MR. STRIPLING. Throughout the play reference is made to the theories and teachings of Lenin, the A, B, C of communism and other Communist classics, and the activities of the Chinese Communist Party in general. The following are excerpts from the play:

> The Four Agitators: We came from Moscow as agitators; we were to travel to the city of Mukden to start propaganda and to create, in the factories, the Chinese Party. We were to report to party headquarters closest to the border and to requisition a guide. There, in the anteroom, a young comrade came toward us and spoke of the nature of our mission. We are repeating the conversation.
>
> The Young Comrade: I am the secretary of the party headquarters which is the last toward the border. My heart is beating for the revolution. The witnessing of wrongdoing drove me into the lines of the fighters. Man must help man. I am for freedom. I believe in mankind. And I am for the rules of the Communist Party which fights for the classless society against exploitation and ignorance.
>
> The Three Agitators: We come from Moscow.
>
> The Young Comrade: The two of us have to defend a revolution here. Surely you have a letter to us from the central committee which tells us what to do?
>
> The Three Agitators: So it is. We bring you nothing. But across the border, to Mukden, we bring to the Chinese workers the teachings of the classics and of the propagandists: The ABC of communism; to the ignorant,

the truth about their situation; to the oppressed, class consciousness; and to the class conscious, the experience of the revolution. From you we shall requisition an automobile and a guide.

The Four Agitators: We went as Chinese to Mukden—four men and a woman—to spread propaganda and to create the Chinese Party through the teachings of the classics and of the propagandists—the ABC of communism; to bring truth to the ignorant about their situation; the oppressed class conscious, and class conscious, the experience of the revolution.

The Young Comrade: The individual has two, the party has a thousand eyes. The party sees seven states. The party has many hours. The party cannot be destroyed, for it fights with the methods of the classics which are drawn from the knowledge of reality and are destined to be changed in that the teachings spread through the masses. Who, however, is the party? Is it sitting in a house with telephones? Are its thoughts secret, its revolutions unknown? Who is it? It is all of us. We are the party. You and I and all of you—all of us. In your suit it is, Comrade, and in your head it thinks; wherever I live there is its home and where you are attacked there it fights.

Now, Mr. Brecht, will you tell the committee whether or not one of the characters in this play was murdered by his comrade because it was in the best interest of the party, of the Communist Party; is that true?

MR. BRECHT. No, it is not quite according to the story.

MR. STRIPLING. Because he would not bow to discipline he was murdered by his comrades, isn't that true?

MR. BRECHT. No; it is not really in it. You will find when you read it carefully, like in the old Japanese play where other ideas were at stake, this young man who died was convinced that he had done damage to the mission he believed in and he agreed to that and he was about ready to die in order not to make greater such damage. So, he asks his comrades to help him, and all of them together help him to die. He jumps into an abyss and they lead him tenderly to that abyss, and that is the story.

The CHAIRMAN. I gather from your remarks, from your answer, that he was just killed, he was not murdered?

MR. BRECHT. He wanted to die.

The CHAIRMAN. So they killed him?

MR. BRECHT. No; they did not kill him—not in this story. He killed himself. They supported him, but of course they had told him it were better when he disappeared, for him and them and the cause he also believed in.

MR. STRIPLING. Mr. Brecht, could you tell the committee how many times you have been to Moscow?

MR. BRECHT. Yes. I was invited to Moscow two times.

MR. STRIPLING. Who invited you?

MR. BRECHT. The first time I was invited by the Volks Organization for Cultural Exchange. I was invited to show a picture, a documentary picture I had helped to make in Berlin.

MR. STRIPLING. What was the name of that picture?

MR. BRECHT. The name—it is the name of a suburb of Berlin, Kuhle Wampe.

MR. STRIPLING. While you were in Moscow, did you meet Sergi Tretyakov—S-e-r-g-i T-r-e-t-y-a-k-o-v; Tretyakov?

MR. BRECHT. Tretyakov; yes. That is a Russian playwright.

MR. STRIPLING. A writer?

MR. BRECHT. Yes. He translated some of my poems and, I think one play.

MR. STRIPLING. Mr. Chairman, *International Literature,* No. 5, 1937, published by the State Literary Art Publishing House in Moscow had an article by Sergi Tretyakov, leading Soviet writer, on an interview he had with Mr. Brecht. On page 60, it states—he is quoting Mr. Brecht—

"I was a member of the Augsburg Revolutionary Committee," Brecht continued. "Nearby, in Munich, Leviné raised the banner of Soviet power. Augsburg lived in the reflected glow of Munich. The hospital was the only military unit in the town. It elected me to the revolutionary committee. I still remember Georg Brem and the Polish Bolshevik Olshevsky. We did not boast a single Red guardsman. We didn't have time to issue a single decree or nationalize a single bank or close a church. In two days General Epp's troops came to town on their way to Munich. One of the members of the revolutionary committee hid at my house until he managed to escape."

He wrote *Drums in the Night.* This work contained echoes of the revolution. The drums of revolt persistently summon the man who has gone home. But the man prefers [the] quiet peace of his hearthside.

The work was a scathing satire on those who had deserted the revolution and toasted themselves at their fireplaces. One should recall that Kapp launched his drive on Christmas Eve, calculating that many Red guardsmen would have left their detachments for the family Christmas trees.

His play *Die Massnahme,* the first of Brecht's plays on a Communist theme, is arranged like a court where the characters try to justify themselves for having killed a comrade, and judges, who at the same time represent the audience, summarize the events, and reach a verdict.

When he visited in Moscow in 1932, Brecht told me his plan to organize a theater in Berlin which would re-enact the most interesting court trials in the history of mankind.

Brecht conceived the idea of writing a play about the terrorist tricks resorted to by the landowners in order to peg the price of grain. But this requires a knowledge of economics. The study of economics brought Brecht to Marx and Lenin, whose works became an invaluable part of his library.

Brecht studies and quotes Lenin as a great thinker and as a great master of prose.

The traditional drama portrays the struggle of class instincts. Brecht demands that the struggle of class instincts be replaced by the struggle of social consciousness, of social convictions. He maintains that the situation must not only be felt, but explained—crystallized into the idea which will overturn the world.

Do you recall that interview, Mr. Brecht?

MR. BRECHT. No. [Laughter.] It must have been written twenty years ago or so.

MR. STRIPLING. I will show you the magazine, Mr. Brecht.

MR. BRECHT. Yes. I do not recall there was an interview. [Book handed to the witness.] I do not recall—Mr. Stripling, I do not recall the interview in exact. I think it is a more or less journalistic summary of talks or discussions about many things.

MR. STRIPLING. Yes. Have many of your writings been based upon the philosophy of Lenin and Marx?

MR. BRECHT. No; I don't think that is quite correct but, of course, I studied, had to study as a playwright who wrote historical plays. I, of course, had to study Marx's ideas about history. I do not think intelligent plays today can be written without such study. Also, history now written now is vitally influenced by the studies of Marx about history.


·   ·   ·


MR. STRIPLING. Are you familiar with the magazine *New Masses*?

MR. BRECHT. No.

MR. STRIPLING. You never heard of it?

MR. BRECHT. Yes; of course.

MR. STRIPLING. Did you ever contribute anything to it?

MR. BRECHT. No.

MR. STRIPLING. Did they ever publish any of your work?

MR. BRECHT. That I do not know. They might have published some translation of a poem, but I had no direct connection with it, nor did I send them anything.

MR. STRIPLING. Did you collaborate with Hanns Eisler on the song "In Praise of Learning"?

MR. BRECHT. Yes; I collaborated. I wrote that song and he only wrote the music.

MR. STRIPLING. You wrote the song?

MR. BRECHT. I wrote the song.

MR. STRIPLING. Would you recite to the committee the words of that song?

MR. BRECHT. Yes; I would. May I point out that song comes from another adaptation I made of Gorky's play, *Mother*. In this song a Russian worker woman addresses all the poor people.

MR. STRIPLING. It was produced in this country, wasn't it?

MR. BRECHT. Yes. '35, New York.

MR. STRIPLING. Now, I will read the words and ask you if this is the one.

MR. BRECHT. Please.

MR. STRIPLING. (reading):

> Learn now the simple truth, you for whom the time has come at last; it is not too late.
> Learn now the ABC. It is not enough but learn it still.
> Fear not, be not downhearted. Again you must learn the lesson, you must be ready to take over—

MR. BRECHT. No, excuse me, that is the wrong translation. That is not right. [Laughter.] Just one second, and I will give you the correct text.

MR. STRIPLING. That is not a correct translation?

MR. BRECHT. That is not correct, no; that is not the meaning. It is not very beautiful, but I am not speaking about that.

MR. STRIPLING. What does it mean? I have here a portion of *The People*, which was issued by the Communist Party of the United States, published by the Workers' Library Publishers. Page 24 says:

> In praise of learning, by Bert Brecht; music by Hanns Èisler.

It says here:

> You must be ready to take over; learn it.
> Men on the dole, learn it; men in the prisons, learn it; women in the kitchen, learn it; men of sixty-five, learn it. You must be ready to take over—

and goes right on through. That is the core of it—

> You must be ready to take over.

MR. BRECHT. Mr. Stripling, maybe his translation——

MR. BAUMGARDT. The correct translation would be, "You must take the lead."

The CHAIRMAN. "You must take the lead"?

MR. BAUMGARDT. "The lead." It definitely says, "The lead." It is not "You must take over." The translation is not a literal translation of the German.

MR. STRIPLING. Well, Mr. Brecht, as it has been published in these publications of the Communist Party, then, if that is incorrect, what did you mean?

MR. BRECHT. I don't remember never—I never got that book myself.

I must not have been in the country when it was published. I think it was published as a song, one of the songs Eisler had written the music to. I did not give any permission to publish it. I don't see—I think I never saw the translation.

Mr. Stripling. Do you have the words there before you?

Mr. Brecht. In German, yes.

Mr. Stripling. Of the song?

Mr. Brecht. Oh, yes; in the book.

Mr. Stripling. Not in the original.

Mr. Brecht. In the German book.

Mr. Stripling. It goes on:

You must be ready to take over; you must be ready to take over. Don't hesitate to ask questions, stay in there. Don't hesitate to ask questions, comrade——

Mr. Brecht. Why not let him translate from the German, word for word?

Mr. Baumgardt. I think you are mainly interested in this translation which comes from——

The Chairman. I cannot understand the interpreter any more than I can the witness.

Mr. Baumgardt. Mr. Chairman, I apologize. I shall make use of this.

The Chairman. Just speak in that microphone and maybe we can make out.

Mr. Baumgardt. The last line of all three verses is correctly to be translated: "You must take over the lead," and not "You must take over." "You must take the lead," would be the best, most correct, most accurate translation.

Mr. Stripling. Mr. Brecht, did you ever make application to join the Communist Party?

Mr. Brecht. I do not understand the question. Did I make——

Mr. Stripling. Have you ever made application to join the Communist Party?

Mr. Brecht. No, no, no, no, no, never.

Mr. Stripling. Mr. Chairman, we have here——

Mr. Brecht. I was an independent writer and wanted to be an independent writer and I point that out and also theoretically, I think, it was the best for me not to join any party whatever. And all these things you read here were not only written for the German communists, but they were also written for workers of any other kind; Social Democrat workers were in these performances; so were Catholic workers from Catholic unions; so were workers which never had been in a party or didn't want to go into a party.

The CHAIRMAN. Mr. Brecht, did Gerhart Eisler ever ask you to join the Communist Party?

MR. BRECHT. No, no.

The CHAIRMAN. Did Hanns Eisler ever ask you to join the Communist Party?

MR. BRECHT. No; he did not. I think they considered me just as a writer who wanted to write and do as he saw it, but not as a political figure.

The CHAIRMAN. Do you recall anyone ever having asked you to join the Communist Party?

MR. BRECHT. Some people might have suggested it to me, but then I found out that it was not my business.

The CHAIRMAN. Who were those people who asked you to join the Communist Party?

MR. BRECHT. Oh, readers.

The CHAIRMAN. Who?

MR. BRECHT. Readers of my poems or people from the audiences. You mean—there was never an official approach to me to publish——

The CHAIRMAN. Some people did ask you to join the Communist Party.

MR. KENNY. In Germany. [Aside to witness.]

MR. BRECHT. In Germany, you mean in Germany?

The CHAIRMAN. No; I mean in the United States.

MR. BRECHT. No, no, no.

The CHAIRMAN. He is doing all right. He is doing much better than many other witnesses you have brought here.

Do you recall whether anyone in the United States ever asked you to join the Communist Party?

MR. BRECHT. No; I don't.

The CHAIRMAN. Mr. McDowell, do you have any questions?

MR. McDOWELL. No; no questions.

The CHAIRMAN. Mr. Vail?

MR. VAIL. No questions.

The CHAIRMAN. Mr. Stripling, do you have any more questions?

MR. STRIPLING. I would like to ask Mr. Brecht whether or not he wrote a poem, a song, rather, entitled, "Forward, We've Not Forgotten."

MR. McDOWELL. "Forward," what?

MR. STRIPLING. "Forward, We've Not Forgotten."

MR. BRECHT. I can't think of that. The English title may be the reason.

MR. STRIPLING. Would you translate it for him into German?

(Mr. Baumgardt translates into German.)

MR. BRECHT. Oh, now I know; yes.

MR. STRIPLING. You are familiar with the words to that?

MR. BRECHT. Yes.

MR. STRIPLING. Would the committee like me to read that?

The CHAIRMAN. Yes; without objection, go ahead.

MR. STRIPLING (reading):

Forward, we've not forgotten our strength in the fights we've won;
No matter what may threaten, forward, not forgotten how strong we are as one;
Only these our hands now acting, build the road, the walls, the towers.
All the world is of our making.
What of it can we call ours?

The refrain:

Forward. March on to the tower, through the city, by land the world;
Forward. Advance it on. Just whose city is the city? Just whose world is the world?
Forward, we've not forgotten our union in hunger and pain, no matter what may threaten, forward, we've not forgotten.
We have a world to gain. We shall free the world of shadow; every shop and every room, every road and every meadow.
All the world will be our own.

Did you write that, Mr. Brecht?

MR. BRECHT. No. I wrote a German poem, but that is very different from this. [Laughter.]

MR. STRIPLING. That is all the questions I have, Mr. Chairman.

The CHAIRMAN. Thank you very much, Mr. Brecht. You are a good example to the witnesses of Mr. Kenny and Mr. Crum.

We will recess until two o'clock this afternoon.

(Whereupon, at 12:15 P.M., a recess was taken until 2 P.M. of the same day.)

# The Poet Bertolt Brecht

## by Hannah Arendt

It is difficult to know what attitude to maintain toward poets, and the case of Brecht does not make it any easier for us. A committee of American poets, whose members have the most varied political convictions, unanimously awarded the prize for the best poetry of 1949 to the same Ezra Pound who vigorously pursued his fascist and anti-Semitic convictions on the Italian radio as a propagandist during the war, and who was spared a trial for high treason in the United States only by a judgment of mental incompetence. I do not know what the committee of poets had in mind with this award. They obviously did not take seriously Pound's medically certified mental derangement. Since the prize was awarded by poets, a certain measure of self-knowledge may have played its part, so that they may have wanted to stress the unsuitability of regarding the political convictions of poets and artists with excessive seriousness.

"Poets do not sin so grievously." Any given editor, however, who by appealing to their desire for fame induces them to write otherwise than they actually wish, can more easily corrupt them than the much calumniated annual pension that the French government used to pay Heine. The artist is only corrupted (to remain with our example, which is admittedly somewhat obsolete) if he takes the subsidizing government seriously and responds to his duties with the same joy in responsibility as any government official. But then the matter is settled anyway; he does not paint any more, he daubs some kind of vulgar trash; he does not write poetry any more, he rhymes together some battle hymns. These creations, moreover, usually turn out to be even worse than the propaganda current at that moment. Money or even political conviction—the things commonly believed to be the source of corruption—have nothing to do with this. What is actually fatal is that the poet has taken political advice seriously.

Consequently in Brecht's case it is not so serious that he wrote *The Measures Taken* in order to glorify a totalitarian party, but rather that,

"The Poet Bertolt Brecht." Translated by J. F. Sammons. From *Die Neue Rundschau*, LXI (1950), 53-67. Reprinted by permission of the author and S. Fischer Verlag.

for a while, he experimented in all earnestness with the "socialist realism" which has brought the Soviet Russian intelligentsia—insofar as it physically survived the party purges—to its demise. In *The Private Life of the Master Race* he presented hunger and unemployment in the manner of "socialist realism" just when both had disappeared from the social reality of Nazi Germany. He succeeded in a poem, "The Jew, a Misfortune for the People," in producing an argument which, far from carrying anti-Semitism *ad absurdum,* is very common among anti-Semites: "Everyone knows/ That the regime is a misfortune for the people; if therefore / All misfortune comes from the Jews, then / The regime must come from the Jews. / This is clearly evident." Indeed it is so evident that neither Hitler nor Roosevelt are safe from logical speculation about their Jewish origin. This naïve ignorance of reality, which is otherwise completely uncharacteristic of Brecht, typifies almost all his poems in this period of "socialist realism." Typical is "The Burial of the Agitator in a Zinc Coffin." It is about an agitator whose purpose was "eating his fill / And living in clover / And feeding the kids / And watching his nickels"—clearly a mad agitator, because those who were not mad were driven to despair by the discovery of how few people know that they are oppressed when they have enough to eat, live securely, and can feed their children. Thus Brecht shared with them, the fellow travelers (and not with the revolutionaries), the complete incomprehension that the only interesting thing about the agitator was the zinc coffin, and that the old materialistic categories of oppression had as much to do with totalitarian reality as with the state of affairs on the moon.

However, one cannot claim that Brecht never really understood the conditions of totalitarianism—although it seems evident to me that his best poems grew out of his genuinely revolutionary mood in the Twenties and his report on that *status quo* to which Hitler put such a thorough end. *The Measures Taken,* written at the end of the Twenties, was to the point and told the truth about the basic rules of a totalitarian party. But there is something strange about this truth which Brecht quite simply praised: the absolute subjugation of the individual, the *sacrificium intellectus,* the human sacrifice made to the Moloch of the mass movement —it revealed exactly that side of the matter which the party wanted to keep secret at any price. In the fervor of creating, Brecht did what all poets do when they are left alone; he told tales out of school. He found what he told wonderful, and others found it abominable. The issue may be argued back and forth; one thing is certain: within a totalitarian dictatorship it is relatively indifferent where the sympathies of the men of letters lie; as long as they create they will tell the truth and thus tell tales out of school. It is well-known that in many countries this truthfulness incurs the death penalty.

Something similar, only not quite so dangerous, had already happened to Brecht once before. Just as *The Measures Taken* did not help those whom he wanted to help, so *The Threepenny Opera* did not hurt those whom it attacked. This, perhaps the most successful play of the pre-Hitler theater, was supposed to expose the attitudes of the bourgeoisie and make the duly authorized guardians of civil order appear as criminals —the characters of the underworld, on the other hand, as businessmen. For a year after the first performance all of Germany was whistling "First comes the grub, then come the morals." The *épater le bourgeois* this time did not shock anyone any more and least of all the bourgeoisie, which, tired of its burdensome hypocrisy and mendacity, agreed in serious enthusiasm with the ironically meant banalities—according to which they were used to ordering their lives anyway. In other words, the bourgeoisie discovered the deep wisdom of its attitudes. The underworld, on the other hand, which in those years was growing so alarmingly and from which the bourgeoisie after all recruited its best accomplices in times of crisis, naïvely thought that it was a simple defense of gangsterism, which it naturally applauded. The intellectual, revolutionary elite was the only group that understood what it was about, but they did not understand that such attacks on bourgeois morality and its mendacity were trying to break down doors already open.

Every time Brecht wanted to create a direct political effect he fumbled. He could never break through the boundaries within which a poet is constrained, despite all his political-aesthetic argumentation. Always he only bore witness: he testified to the power machinery of totalitarian parties which every truly totalitarian politician sought to hide, and to the mendacity of postwar and even more of prewar Germany. But this testimony remains poetically valid, even if it reveals itself as politically obsolete, because the whole world was just then trying to throw off the mask of hypocrisy and regarded the "compliment to virtue" as super-fluous. (Such testimony would probably have confused him, and rightly so, since it would obviously be valid for all totalitarian governments; the precision of poetry moves too much in the general sphere to operate with purely political, temporal, and tactical distinctions.) When he did *not* bear witness, as in the above-mentioned creations of the Thirties, he wrote plays and poems which, of no consequence whatever, helped no one and hurt no one.

Just how dangerous the precise generality of the literary art is can best be shown in one of his most recent plays, *Galileo*. Here a scientist is described who has discovered something—the earth revolves around the sun—which contradicts the doctrines of an authoritarian ruling apparatus (the Catholic Church and the Inquisition). There is no question that this drama fits both the Bolshevik and the Nazi dictatorship with equal precision. When it was produced in New York, people were tempted to believe that Brecht had become an anti-Stalinist.

I have no doubt that Bertolt Brecht is the greatest living German poet. Perhaps he is also the greatest living European playwright. Born in

1898, he belongs to the first of those "lost generations" whose productive
talents again and again fall victim to private bitterness and sentimental
self-pity. If Hebbel is right that "the highest thing still is quiet, pure
development," then these "lost ones" are right, too, and in any case are
not lost to creativity. The battlefields of the First World War introduced
the first generation of the twentieth century to life; inflation and unemployment decisively conditioned the second; and the members of the
third had their choice whether they wanted to thank the shock of Nazism
(in Germany) or the Spanish Civil War (in other countries of Europe)
or the Moscow Trials (in the whole world) for the decisive experience
of their youth, the beginning of the "pure, quiet development." It is
characteristic of the wild tempo of this century that these three generations, which, seen historically, belong to three physiognomically different
epochs, are so close in age that they could still go into the Second World
War together—as soldiers or as civilians under a rain of bombs, as
refugees and exiles, as members of resistance and underground movements, or as inmates of concentration camps. Thus it happened that not
only the situation of the "lost generation" repeated itself formally over
and over again, but also that poets and writers today in the various
European countries, whether old or young, exhibit the same spiritual
and biographical pattern. If they try to come to terms with themselves
in the awareness of a personal development constantly interrupted by
events of world politics, even the youngest among them are still tempted
to measure their productive possibilities of a personal and practical kind
with the yardsticks of the nineteenth century. Over and over again, with
an amazing and depressing monotony, they produce variations of the
same literature, in which individuals selfishly complain about psychic
anomalies and the intolerability of social norms—as if the world had intentionally cheated them of something and history had taken place only
to rob them of their illusions.

This individualistic stand, at bottom filled with resentment, which
does not become less individualistic when dealing with the *decay* of the
individual, and no less resentful when dealing with the *decay* of society,
never played any part in Brecht's poems and dramas. He must have decided at a very young age to care more about the misfortune of his
times than about his own, and, whether his personal problems were
solved or not, to keep them at a distance with a gesture of superior
equanimity. . . .

Brecht's stoicism in "gloomy times" is the truly antibourgeois element
in him. His line "If my luck expires, I am lost" betrays such an enor-
mously calm and imperturbable certainty of self-reliance; he can stand to
face the fact that what has been spared thus far survives only by accident
and it is not to be reckoned as a gain; he can bear possible disaster
without self-doubt.

Brecht knows no envy for the past and would rather remain with his view of what will have been left behind in the future. He never let himself be seduced by purely psychological considerations and always saw the comedy of a sentimentality which would like to measure the maelstrom of events with the yardstick of individual aspirations. It is not only psychological suicide, it is also comic, when the jobless man feels the international catastrophe of unemployment as a personal failure, or when people in the face of the catastrophe of war complain that they are no longer able to become well-rounded personalities, or when exiled writers grieve for their lost fame.

Brecht's literary forms—the ballad in contrast to the lyric poem, and "epic theater" in contrast to tragedy—can be derived from this anti-psychological insistence upon the events themselves. Epic theater differs from traditional dramaturgy in that it is not concerned with characters, their development in the world, and their conflicts with it, but with certain series of events under particular circumstances, which the public is to understand as its own in typified form, and in which types act, whose modes of behavior are measured against the events themselves. The types are not necessarily abstract, although Brecht in his early "didactic plays" often abstracted to the point of mannerism. To be sure, Galileo (in the play of the same name) and the heroes of *The Good Woman of Setzuan* are almost individualized; still they are not characters. Only they have lost the young Brecht's mistrust of the good gifts of the earth; Galileo loves "old wine and new thoughts" and does not only moralize about the "invigorating effect of money." He is nevertheless a type—the human being interested essentially in truth, a truth in fact which becomes an active component of the whole basic structure of life and the world. The good woman of Setzuan, who in order to remain good—i.e., to be neither annihilated by the misery of the world nor taken in by its evil—must split herself into two roles, is lovable and unforgettable as a female figure also. But the pure problem of character, that the same person can and must be good and bad, is totally resolved into something functional by the double role. Behind this double role a primitive, instinctive good nature becomes visible which in itself is without conflict and consequently undramatic.

Just as Brecht avoids characters on the stage, so in his poems he avoids those individual moods which in their lyrical formation can become enchanting melodies of all existence. The ballads treat an important part of an event, and their heroes (in contrast to stage heroes who are men of action and seek to create an impact on the world) find their greatness in suffering a catastrophe created by man or nature. The ballads celebrate the virtues of men; their half-cynical, half-puerile fearlessness, their unruly pride, and their untameable curiosity in the midst of the unchaining of destructive and horrifying forces. With Brecht the ballad once again became a street song and could express the essential experience of the First World War, the total helplessness, because the telling of sad events with an anticipated unhappy ending was intensively practiced in this form by the cabaret, as well as by the *Dienstbotenpoesie* (servants' poetry). The "virtuous" heroes, too, are very similar to those who at least in song have "led the servant girls astray" from time immemorial: adventurers, pirates, mercenaries, in whose company infanticides and youthful parricides are found. Brecht's sympathies with these, the damned and rejected, still had no social note of any kind in the *Domestic Breviary (Hauspostille)*, the first collection of poems. One required no philosophical persuasion and no dialectic to side with the "murderers whom great misery has befallen."

Murder, death, destruction, and dissolution were popular themes of the Twenties, and it is easy to misinterpret Brecht. Gottfried Benn in Germany and Céline in France, for example, who both felt themselves irresistibly attracted by National Socialism, have, with their gifted and half-pathological glorification of physical collapse, their half-neurotic fascination with everything that arouses disgust, hardly anything in common with the exciting, wild, and triumphant beauty of the early Brecht poems. . . .

Brecht's pirates and adventurers and drowned girls have the devilish pride of absolutely carefree creatures, of people who, with stoic equanimity, submit only to catastrophes, and never to considerations of propriety or to higher ones of eternal salvation. Brecht saw in "God's death" only the intoxicating possibility of a release from all fear on earth, and he was obviously of the opinion that anything is better than hoping for paradise or fearing hell in the midst of life. "Praise the cold, the darkness and corruption! / Behold it: / It's not your concern / And you can die uncaring."

It has often been remarked that this "vitalism" rooted in the elements arose directly out of the mass warfare of the First World War. What it is actually about has been explicated recently by Sartre in an essay "Qu'est-ce que la littérature?" Sartre says: "When all instruments are smashed and useless, when all plans have come to nought and every conscious effort is senseless, then suddenly the world appears in a new childlike and frightening freshness, hovering freely and without marked paths." The inhuman innocence of Brecht's ballad heroes, who are all, like Jakob Apfelböck who murdered his parents, "lilies of the field," corresponded exactly to this inhuman freshness of the world, out of which mass warfare had extinguished all humane traces, all instruments and plans, all efforts and well-trod paths, so that nothing seemed to be left of the world but the pure elements, and no one seemed to be at home in it but those pirates who knew how to conspire with them. "Oh, heavens, gleaming azure! / Enormous wind, inflate the sails! / Let wind and heavens pass away! Only / Leave us the sea round Saint Marie."

Compared with this rejoicing cynicism, all the other poetry of the Twenties which follows traditional ways seems consciously or unconsciously to be taking part in a "clearance sale of values." The tradition was torn, its instruments were smashed; the more classicistically or traditionally poetry behaved, the closer it came to being mere literature— which no one has proved in a more gifted manner than Rudolf Borchardt. The true danger threatening the tradition did not come from those who did not believe it capable, sight unseen, of carrying new content but rather from those who bombastically or sentimentally wrote in it as though nothing had happened.

Brecht's attitude toward the tradition expresses itself most unambiguously in his parodies of classical poems. Technically mastered and poetically unimpeachable are the choruses in *St. Joan of the Stockyards* or the "Liturgy of Breath," a parody of Goethe's "Over All the Peaks Lies Peace." Goethe's poem is used here to show that peace means, among other things, peacefully looking on while an old woman starves; that "the little birds in the forest" are silent also because silence is supposed to envelop the murder of a man who was not peaceful and who was not silent. In these parodies an extraordinary respect for tradition becomes apparent in the amazing beauty of his purely technical precision; at the same time there is also the conviction that whoever cannot maintain this mastery of traditional forms does not understand the trade of a German poet. The parodistic element, on the other hand, is turned less against the tradition itself than against those who with its help wish to lull us about our own problems, against the *classicists* and not against the *classical poets*. Brecht's parody solves in the most concrete manner the problem of leading away from tradition and at the same time conserving it. Brecht's rebellion in this, his most intimately personal area, is never destructive and never modernistic. He is not interested in experiments which are a means to help a new sensibility find its expression. He claims only that beauty is, among other things, misused to hide the really existing ugliness, but he leaves beauty itself actually inviolable. And since the passion for truth is probably the central passion of the "Brecht hungering for knowledge"—so central indeed that despite all his technical mastery he writes with incredible incompetence as soon as he is prevented from telling the truth—his way of coming to terms with tradition by breaking through it is a more effective means of genuine continuity and a better school even for the purely formal comprehension of the past than all the patchwork of quotations with which the Germans have attempted to come upon an idiom of their own after the horror of Hitler's barbarism.

Brecht's mistrust of the tradition, his predilection for popular forms not recognized as art have still another and probably more decisive motivation. Behind his socialist speeches and the philosophy of dialectical materialism which he so loves to display there lies hidden a genuinely revolutionary temperament—something which does not appear often in Germany. His fundamental bitterness is directed against the world of

victors and vanquished—a world in whose history the cause of the defeated was always excluded from human memory because the victors
wrote history. What rouses him to anger is not so much poverty, oppression, and exploitation, but rather the fact that the poor, the oppressed,
and the exploited have never been able to make their voices heard, that
their voices have been irrevocably stifled, that the insult of oblivion is
always added to the injury of defeat and misfortune. "For the ones they
are in darkness / And the others are in light; / And you see the ones
in brightness / Those in darkness drop from sight."

This "history of philosophy" has nothing to do either with socialist
realism or with proletarian poetry. It deals with something much more
general, and at the same time much more precise, namely the construction of a world in which all men are equally visible, and with the
planning of a history which does not remember few and forget many,
which does not lead to forgetting under the pretext of remembering,
which does not have some take part and the others be the instrument
of events. . . .

This, then, is the real reason why Brecht loves the ballad form so
much and why we owe his finest poems to this form. Popular tradition
chose the ballad to secure in it its own unwritten tradition, which alongside of and independent of the great artistic tradition bore witness to
a forgotten and neglected history. It is a form in which the people endeavored to create its own poetic immortality in street song, *Dienstbotenpoesie*, folk song, and *chanson*. Brecht the poet did not join the party
of the oppressed when he began to occupy himself with Marxism, but
rather when he began to use the ballad form and give it distinction.
And no one will be able to take this distinction away from him, "no
god, no emperor, or tribune," not even his own delusion.

# On Brecht's *In the Swamp,*
# *A Man's a Man,* and
# *Saint Joan of the Stockyards*

## *by Eric Bentley*

### *In the Swamp*

*Emotional Dynamics.* Brecht's later plays were so unconventionally constructed that the drama critics, being the men they are, were bound to think them badly constructed. *In the Swamp* is well-constructed and, for all the absence of act divisions, is constructed in a fairly conventional way. Brecht's originality shows less in the overarching main structure than in the details of his rendering of the emotions and their dynamics.

The word *dynamics* may at first seem inapplicable because the subject is passivity. But human passivity has its own negative dynamics—as has a donkey that refuses to budge, a possum that pretends to be dead, or a poodle that begs to be whipped. It would be arbitrary to assume that there is less drama in cessation than in initiation, in refusal than acceptance, in surrender than resistance. Nor is the passive man consistently passive. He is passive so much that occasionally he has to be the opposite. He overcompensates for inaction by action that is rash, sudden, and extreme. No lack of dynamics here! Combining the negative dynamics of refusal with the insane lunges of passivity interrupted, the young Brecht makes a drama out of apparently undramatic materials. Very modern materials. Critics have not been slow to see the connection between the Brecht of 1920 and the plays of Beckett in the Fifties. If only Beckett had a quarter of Brecht's constructive power! It seems to me that the later author, for all his true theatricality, could not find the emotional dynamics to animate a full-length play. . . .

Speaking of the aggressions of the passive type of person, the works of Brecht embody aggressions of colossal proportions, and make a special

appeal to persons who harbor such aggressions of their own. I have
known many Brechtians intimately: one and all persons positively possessed by aggression. This is something to think about when you read
some of the current French and British Brechtians, who can give their
writing a coolness of tone that accords with the theories of the Meister.
Those theories came into being to create such a rational coolness of tone
—and conceal the heat and irrationality of the aggressive impulse.

*The Menagerie of Bertolt Brecht.* Between the art of Bertolt Brecht and
the discussion of that art, a great gulf has been fixed. Maybe it was Brecht
who fixed it by becoming a Marxist and letting us know about his art,
even his early art, only in Marxist terms. Hence, for example, if you
read about Mackie the Knife in Brecht's Notes, you would expect anything but the Mackie the Knife of Brecht's own play. The Notes are
about capitalism and the world around us. The play shows . . . well,
what? If this type of figure must be characterized in one word, that word
will have to be *grotesque.* Yes, a grotesque figure may *represent* capitalism
and the world around us, but here we are changing the subject to the
author's intentions. What has he *done?* He has created a group of gro-
tesques. This creation in no way results from Marxism; it antedates
Brecht's reading of Marx. What one should rather observe is the way in
which Brecht, when he joins the Left, brings his menagerie with him.
All he has to do is rename his jackals capitalists.

By this time (1961), there are many people who approve of Brecht on
the ground that he was a Communist. But is that why they are attracted
to his work? Rather, he is approved for one reason and enjoyed for
another. Some of the enjoyment may indeed be rather improper, almost
illicit. An unbeatable combination!

*Amerika.* The menagerie is all complete in *In the Swamp.* In Garga and
Shlink we already hear the sentiments and accents of Peachum. Worm
and Baboon are our first Brechtian henchmen. The nickelodeon plays
*Ave Maria*; a Salvation Army officer shoots himself after uttering the last
words of Frederick the Great; and a lynch gang goes into action at the
bidding of the police! It is the Amerika that was discovered not by C. C.
but by B. B. It is the Amerika of *Mahagonny* and *The Seven Deadly
Sins.*

*Homosexuality.* The modern subject *par excellence?* Yet still an unusual
subject for a play when Brecht wrote *In the Swamp*; and it seems that
people can read this play and miss it. They miss a lot. If homosexuality
is not talked about, it is as fully implicit as in Genet's *Deathwatch.*

There is candor and candor. If homosexuality is now a standard subject
of sentimental commercial literature, that literature can be trusted to
impose its own limitations on the subject as it did on previous "daring"

subjects. For example, Broadway plays on the theme only permit us to *discover* that the hero is homosexual just as older plays let us discover that the unmarried heroine was pregnant.

Homosexuality can appear in commercial culture only by way of pathetic romance. A homosexual disposition is accepted as arbitrarily *there*. Society is "arraigned" for its failure to see this. Here, as it were, is a group of people who prefer strawberries to raspberries, and society has made the eating of strawberries illegal: pathos! Brecht on the other hand, while he does not tag characters with clinical labels, reaches what clinicians will recognize as the big facts.

One reason the treatment of homosexuality seems not very explicit in *In the Swamp* is that the author clearly puts sex in its place—the place for this kind of sex being entitled masochism. As in Genet, eros is subordinated to the struggle for power; in which struggle Brecht's characters tend to wish to lose.

*Nihilism: a Query.* Discussions of Brecht's philosophy—of this period *or later*—would gain from an understanding of his emotions and attitudes. His philosophy as of this period is always described as nihilism. But is nihilism a philosophy? Is it not rather an emotional attitude in a philosophically minded person? The philosophy is pessimistic, but pessimism becomes nihilist only when espoused with resentment and rage. Nihilists are destroyers, though to study particular nihilists is often to find that they were very passive men. Are they men who become active only in destruction? And when they are converted to causes which make high moral claims, can their nihilism be discarded as a mere opinion?

## A Man's a Man

*A New Brecht.* The protagonists of the earlier plays—Baal, Kragler, and Garga—were mouthpieces for Brecht's own yearnings and agonies. We are still not as far as he liked to think from the agonized-ecstatic dramas of the Expressionists. With *A Man's a Man* emerges the Brecht the world knows. The transition is rather an abrupt one, and I wonder that more has not been made of it. Formally speaking, it could be taken as a switch from tragedy to comedy. Brecht's final attitude would be vehemently antitragic. The newfangled notion of Epic Theater can be construed as a synonym for traditional comedy.

*Influences.* None, luckily, are as marked as those of Rimbaud and Büchner on *Baal* and *In the Swamp*. Yet surely Charlie Chaplin runs these pretty close. It would be hard to prove this, of course, though Brecht's admiration of Chaplin is a matter of record, and the latter's influence is obvious enough in such later plays as *Puntila* and *Schweyk in World War II*. As far as *A Man's a Man* is concerned, one need not stress

Chaplin individually: I would judge the influence to be that of American silent movie comedy in general. It was this influence (among others) that enabled Brecht to write, as he already wished to, much more impersonally. He was able to dispel the Expressionistic penumbra, and draw his own creatures on white paper, as it were, in hard black lines. Georg Grosz may have been as valuable to him as Chaplin.

*Later Revisions.* He succeeded so well that later he was able to believe that *A Man's a Man* was Marxist before the fact: all it needed was a few extra touches, and it would be the model anticapitalist and antiwar play. The extra touches involved the omission of the superb final scenes (10, 11), and hence the blurring of the crucial Bloody Five-Galy Gay relationship. It was perhaps the puritanism of his Communist friends that made Brecht omit the castration episode (as it certainly made him tone down or omit the racier jokes). Brecht's famous revisions were usually doctrinaire and were seldom improvements.

*Structure.* The first version of *A Man's a Man* has a very clear structure. The accident to Jip provides only the point of departure. At the center of the action is Uriah. It is Uriah who decides that, since men are all interchangeable, Jip can be replaced: it is just a matter of picking out Galy Gay, making sure that Jesse and Polly go along, and then keeping at it. While Uriah conducts his experiment on Galy Gay, Bloody Five conducts one on himself. What's in a name?—the phrase would make a good title for the play. Bloody Five changes into a civilian at the bidding of Widow Begbick. His humiliations in the role persuade him to change back again and cling to the name Bloody Five at any cost. "It is not important that I eat; it is important that I am Bloody Five." Well, Bloody is successful by his own standard, but Galy Gay is even more successful by drawing the opposite conclusion: one should not make a "fuss about a name" and "it is very important that I eat." Final Curtain.

*Pirandello.* Within this clear structure, there are some less clear, but no less fascinating, things, such as the one piece of spoken verse in the play (Scene 9, Sixth Number), in which Brecht goes far beyond a sociological statement and enters the depths of personal confusion. Indeed, the whole of the Fourth and Sixth Numbers bears witness to a very intimate kind of distress concerning lack of identity, and the vehicle that Brecht finds to carry the sense is singularly Pirandellian:

> URIAH: Fire!
> GALY GAY *falls in a faint.*
> POLLY: Stop! He fell all by himself!
> URIAH: Shoot! So he'll hear he's dead!
> *They shoot.*

*Is* A Man's a Man *Topical?* In some ways, not. As of 1960, our Galy Gays would not be so easily persuaded that war is pleasant. In some ways, too, this play was old-fashioned even in 1925. The imperialism envisaged seems to be that of the Nineties ("We're soldiers of the Queen, my lads"), of jingoism, and the days when swords still had glamor, and Orientals seemed to some a lesser breed without the law.

The play belongs to the era of Georg Kaiser's critique of the Machine Age—man dwarfed by his machinery and caught in it—whereas in 1960 Professor Galbraith tells us that the machine is on the decline and that in the Affluent Society persons will be important. This last argument, however, is not really damaging to *A Man's a Man,* for *in what way* are our new managers and executives important? As organization men—as interchangeable ciphers. In their world, Bertolt Brecht's message is still pertinent: a man is most definitely a man.

Martin Esslin has remarked that the play is a prophecy of brain-washing. A good point, but the fable of brainwashing is combined, at least in the first and best version, with one that contradicts it: a fable of a sorcerer's apprentice or Frankenstein's monster. Uriah's brainwashing of Galy Gay can hardly be deemed successful if then Galy Gay eats Uriah's rations! Perhaps the right conclusion is that Brecht's fable happily transcends the topical applications that will crop up from time to time. Of the latter, here is one from *The Nation,* June 11, 1960:

> Rockefeller, the most intellectual advocate of strong Civil Defense, detailed his argument in the April, 1960, issue of *Foreign Affairs.* . . . Rockefeller's words harmonize with the ponderous theorizing of other *Foreign Affairs* contributors who talk in terms of numbers and percentages instead of horror and anguish, as if war were a chess game. . . . When we concentrate on numbers, survival, and victory, as Rockefeller does, and drive from our minds visions of writhing bodies and screaming flesh, then war becomes thinkable. . . .

*Cruelty.* It would be hasty to imagine that, in finding his own genre, Brecht could change his emotional system. The emotional patterns of *In the Swamp* are found in the later plays in this or that disguise.

*The Brechtian world revolves about an axis which has sadism and masochism as its north and south poles.* In one play after another, Brecht saw the humaneness in human nature swamped out by inhumanity, by the cruelty of what he at first thought of as the universe and later as capitalist society. The standard ending of Brecht plays is the total victory of this cruelty. If, near the end of *Days of the Commune,* he indicates in a song that the workers may do better later on, the fact remains that he chose as his subject a classic defeat. *In Brecht's world, badness is active, while goodness is usually passive.* That antithesis is well rendered in *A Man's a Man* in Uriah and Galy Gay. It will be the making of the split good-and-bad ladies of *The Seven Deadly Sins* and *The Good Woman of*

*Setzuan.* And, as Ernest Borneman has added, the passivity is not simply good, it has its perverse aspect—Galy Gay relishes his humiliations.

At the end of *King Lear,* Kent sees the world as a rack on which human beings are stretched. That's Brechtian. People talk of the lack of emotion in his plays. Perhaps they mean in his theory of his plays, or perhaps they mean the lack of pleasant emotions. Being tortured in a violent emotional experience, and Brecht's characters, from the earliest plays on, live (it is his own metaphor, taken from Rimbaud) in an inferno. Shlink is lynched, Bloody Five castrates himself, Galy Gay is brainwashed. . . . What of the later plays written (we are told) in the spirit of rationalistic positivism and permitting the audience to keep cool? Self-castration occurs again in *The Private Tutor. The Good Woman* is the story of the rending asunder, all but literally, of a young woman. In *Courage,* we watch a mother lose all three children by the deliberate brutality of men. In *Galileo* (as not in actual history), everything hinges on the threat of physical torture. Though torture cannot very well (*pace* Shakespeare) be shown on stage, Brecht devised scenes which suggest great physical violence without showing it and push mental torment to the limits of the bearable.

Are we to take plays like *A Man's a Man* and *Mahagonny* as forecasts of the Nazi regime or even as comments on the already active Nazi movement? If so, we shall have to characterize as "Nazis" certain characters in the very earliest Brecht plays. The fact is that if the Nazis had never existed, Brecht would have invented them.

The scene in which Mother Courage is asked to identify the corpse of her son is thought by some to derive straight from such incidents in recent history—one of which is shown directly by Brecht in "The Zinc Box" (*The Private Life of the Master Race*). But is not the essence of the matter already present in that scene in *A Man's a Man* where the corpse of Galy Gay is supposed to be in a crate and the actual (or former) Galy Gay makes a tormented speech about it?

Brecht the stage director was always insisting that the perpetrators of cruelty not be presented demonstratively. Instead of gesticulating and declaiming, they were to be businesslike, *sachlich.* The actors usually found the reason for this in "the Brecht style," "the alienation-effect and all that," but what Brecht chiefly wanted was to make the cruelty real instead of stagey. And he had in mind a different sort of cruelty from that which the average actor would tend to think of—the cruelty of men who live by cruelty and by little else, men who can order tortures as matter-of-factly as an actor orders a cocktail. Here Brecht pierces through into the pathological—the pathology of a Himmler or an Eichmann.

Whatever else is said of cruelty in Brecht's plays, the nature and quantity of it defeat any attempt on the spectator's part to remain detached in the manner recommended in Brecht's theoretical writings. Brecht's theater is a theater of *more than usually violent* emotion. It is a theater for sadists, masochists, sado-masochists, and all others with any slight tendency in these directions—certainly, then, a theater for everybody.

## Saint Joan of the Stockyards

Here Bernard Shaw's Joan enters the menagerie of Bertolt Brecht, Chicago being its location in no less than three Brecht plays—*In the Swamp* and *Arturo Ui* are the others.

*Parody.* Parody is more important to modern than to any previous school of comedy. Already in Shaw, parody had become very serious—a way of calling attention to dangerous fallacies.

It has been said that good parody parodies good authors and does not decrease your respect for them. The authors parodied in this play are Shakespeare, Goethe, and Schiller, and certainly they are not the target. One could begin to explain what the target is by mentioning that many supporters of Hitler could and did quote all three of these authors a great deal.

To Shaw, Bertolt Brecht's attitude was ambivalent. Already in a tribute he paid the older author in 1926, Brecht had said in passing that the most treasured possessions of Shaw characters were opinions. What Brecht thought of the right to your own opinions had already been indicated in certain speeches of Shlink and Uriah. Hence, he is at pains to ensure that *his* Joan is entangled in circumstances, not besieged by epigrams.

Whether Brecht had understood Shaw is another matter. It is by circumstances—those of the capitalist system, as interpreted by a Marx or a Brecht—that Shaw's Major Barbara is trapped. Nor are the opinions of Brecht's Joan Dark held to be immaterial. It is to an opinion (atheism) that she is finally won over, and Brecht tips the audience the wink that, had she lived any longer, she would have accepted that last word in opinions: Communism.

Now as to Brecht's use of works by Goethe and Schiller, Shakespeare and Shaw in this play, the first two had better be ignored by readers of an English translation, for even the reader who spots the allusions to *Faust II* and *The Maid of Orleans* is still in the dark. The "light" is the reverent acceptance by the German Philistine public of their classics, a reverence that precludes any positive critical interpretation. To the English-speaking audience, the Shakespearean blank verse should, on the other hand, have something to say. For we know the emptiness of our Anglo-Saxon acceptance of Shakespeare, and we can see how serious Brecht's verse has to be to express the utter falsity of the mode of life depicted. In the Brechtian parody, this falsity is quite the reverse of self-proclaimed. The speeches of Mauler and Cridle and the rest are a good

deal more dignified, intelligent, plausible than many speeches in the
Congressional Record.

*Shavianism.* As for Shaw, as I said, ambivalence reigns. He is parodied
and he is plagiarized. The borrowings are less from *Saint Joan* than from
*Major Barbara*. The essence of Brecht's tale, like Shaw's, is that a girl of
superior caliber joins the Salvation Army but is later disenchanted by
discovering that the Army is involved in "the contradictions of the capitalist system." (Shaw and Brecht were the only good "Marxist playwrights"—partly, no doubt, because they regarded the dialectic as dramatic and not just as valid.) More interesting still is the adoption by both
playwrights, in their maturer vein, of fine young women with shining
eyes, and a limited or nonexistent interest in men, as the bearers of the
banner of the ideal.

*Communism.* On the Communist question this play is discreet but clear.
The Communists are very seldom mentioned by name—but every
mention is also a genuflection.

Yet the Communist critic Schumacher observes that Brecht's treatment
of the masses is "abstract"—for him a very dirty word. The Communist
critic Kurella observed that such bourgeois converts to leftism as Brecht
were obsessed with the conversion of bourgeois to leftism. It was a Communist critic who shows no knowledge of Brecht's work, Christopher
Caudwell, who wrote the classic denunciation of such converts in the
last chapter of his *Illusion and Reality* (1937). Though today the fellow
travelers are shocked to hear Brecht accused of "unconscious dishonesty,"
that formula was applied by Caudwell to the whole class that Brecht
belonged to—bourgeois writers with Communist leanings.

Official, or semiofficial, Party writers never had much of a liking for
Brecht's attempts to deal with working-class life. It is true that he got it
all out of books, out of brief slumming expeditions, out of his imagination. *The menagerie would do very well as capitalists, but how to
render the proletariat?* Generally, we get those incarnations of sterling
simplicity that many believe in and few have met with—I paraphrase
one of the few great proletarian artists, D. H. Lawrence. The mother in
Brecht's adaptation of Gorky's novel is an example. Another tack is that
of Agit-Prop: treat the workers as a group and present them on stage as
a singing or verse-speaking choir. *Saint Joan of the Stockyards* belongs to
Brecht's Agit-Prop phase.

# Contemporary Theater
# and Aesthetic Distance

### by Oscar Büdel

Giue me That Man,
Who when the Plague of an Impostumd Braynes
(Breaking out) infects a Theater, and hotly raignes,
Killing the Hearers Hearts.

(Th. Dekker)

Il teatro, voi vedete, signori, è la bocca
spalancata d'un grande macchinario che ha fame.

(L. Pirandello)

Car le théâtre ne doit pas être
un art en trompe-l'œil.

(G. Apollinaire)

## I

In confuting Schlegel's ideas on the role of the chorus in Greek
tragedy, Nietzsche said that he believed in an aesthetic audience and
thought the single spectator to be the more capable, the more he was
able to take the work of art as art, namely aesthetically.[1] Some forty years
thereafter modern drama felt called upon to awaken the spectator from
his "illusionist period"—as if there had been any danger that, again in
Nietzsche's words, the ideal spectator might rush onto the stage to free
the God from his torment. Yet to prevent this once and for all seems to

"Contemporary Theater and Aesthetic Distance." From *PMLA*, LXXVI (1961), 277-
291. Reprinted by permission of the Modern Language Association of America.
[1] F. Nietzsche, *Die Geburt der Tragödie aus dem Geiste der Musik*, Musarion Ausgabe
(München, 1920), III, 52-53.
My essay was written in the summer of 1958 before the appearance of P. A.
Michelis, "Aesthetic Distance and the Charm of Contemporary Art," *Journal of
Aesthetics and Art Criticism*, XVIII (1959), of which it therefore does not take ac-
count. Discussion of affinitive questions will have to be reserved for a further study.

have been one of the foremost axioms of the Expressionist and kindred revolts of the first decade of this century.

Ibsen's theater had already destroyed the illusion of "the" human personality, and this procedure was to become with Strindberg and Pirandello the central theme and preoccupation. But then a further step was taken in order to accomplish the same destruction of "illusion" in terms of the play itself, both from within its own structure (i.e., on the level of the play) and with respect to the form of the stage; for Ibsen's destruction of the "illusion" of the human personality had for the most part still happened in a play and on a stage which were on the whole in no way different from the ones of the "illusionist" period.

Whereas the Expressionist revolution may have been a salutary reaction against an era of "illusionism" (and as such stressed again the theatricality of theater), its implications seem to have created tendencies which perhaps have gone beyond original intentions. These tendencies may destroy more than mere theatrical "illusionism"; they indeed seem to reach to the very roots of theater. One of these trends appears to point toward a destruction of aesthetic distance with reference to the spectators, thereby reducing or eliminating the tension between actor and spectator, between stage and audience, which seems to be a *conditio sine qua non* for the theater.

Edward Bullough in a searching article some time ago pointed out at length: "All art requires a Distance-limit beyond which, and a Distance within which only, aesthetic appreciation becomes possible." [2] This, in other terms, says nothing more than that a loss of distance actually entails and means loss of aesthetic appreciation. That, however, appears to be what the spectator demands of the theater, since by dint of his being a spectator of a *spectacle,* which he knows is put on not for its "reality" but for its art, he expects to take it as such; for in spite of the worries of modern playwrights we may take Fielding's Partridges as being relatively scarce.

At about the same time Julien Benda took issue with what he called the "religion de l'émotion" [3] in modern literary trends. In a polemical tone quite different from Bullough's impartial inquiry he pointed out some of the foremost characteristics of these new tendencies singularly incapable of rendering an aesthetic emotion:

> L'art doit saisir les choses *dans leur principe de vie.* . . . L'art doit *s'unir* à ce principe; il ne doit pas le regarder, le décrire, ce qui implique *en rester distinct,* il doit *s'y unir,* plus précisément *s'y fondre, s'y confondre.*

[2] Edward Bullough, "Psychical Distance as a Factor in Art and an Aesthetic Principle," *British Journal of Psychology,* V (1912-13), p. 98.

[3] Julien Benda, *Belphégor. Essai sur l'esthetique de la présente société française* (Paris, 1918), p. xi. Although published after the First World War, this book was written for the most part before 1914.

. . . L'art doit être une *perception immédiate* des choses, supprimer tout intermédiaire, tout "voile interposé" entre le monde et nous (ce "voile," c'est les formes de la représentation). . . . Le plus remarquable, c'est la supériorité qu'ils [the modern artists] confèrent à qui se montre capable d'une telle perception, comme si la marque principale de la hauteur d'un être dans l'échelle des vivants n'était pas précisément la faculté qu'il a de remplacer la perception directe par l'indirecte.[4]

It is not difficult to see how Benda's ideas are diametrically opposed to those of Bergson, one of the main disseminators of concepts with which modern literature experimented. Consequently, Benda took issue especially with Bergson's "thèse" *Essai sur les données immédiates de la conscience.*

It seems ironic that Expressionist practices as they were applied to theater should have brought about a loss of distance, for the first steps of the movement went in the right direction of no longer tricking the spectator with the deception that it is "reality" which he sees; on another plane, however, it moved beyond its original emphasis of the play-character of theater and engulfed a much larger realm than it perhaps set out to do. Thus, contemporary dramatic practice has striven more and more to decrease aesthetic distance to the point of almost eliminating it; and the propagators of phrases such as "activating the audience," "restoring the unity of audience and stage," even those among them who pretend to arrive at their conclusions by means of historical considerations, misconceive the nature of the theater. On the other hand, we observe to a lesser degree, a tendency to overdistance, as in Brecht's theater; but this in the end achieves the same results as does its counterpart: loss, destruction of aesthetic distance.[5]

In the following pages the effect of this loss of aesthetic distance on contemporary dramatic practice will be investigated on the structural level as well as from within the play, and also in terms of mere spatial distance. It should be stated in advance that this study is concerned exclusively with the formal elements and the formal aspect of modern drama, leaving the more complex feature of its content for another essay.

## II

On the structural level one of the first things to give way in the wake of the Expressionist and related revolts was the outer form of the piece (this in itself, of course, not necessarily producing a loss of distance). That is, the piece built upon acts changed into the tableau-type drama, the

---

[4] Benda, pp. 6, 7, 15, 16.
[5] For further pertinent and more detailed discussion of this aspect see Bullough, pp. 92 ff.

*Stationendrama,* of which Strindberg's *Till Damaskus* was not so much
the prototype, as is sometimes held,[6] but rather the immediate example
at hand. Essentially the same technique had been used in Goethe's *Götz
von Berlichingen* (and there were, furthermore, Büchner's *Woyzek,*
Ibsen's *Peer Gynt,* and Strindberg's own *Fröken Julie*). It is interesting
that this "epic" *Stationendrama* actually grew out of a misunderstanding
of Shakespeare on the part of his German admirers, foremost among
them young Goethe. Wilhelm Dilthey pointed this out almost a hundred
years ago.[7]

Werfel's word "Den Marmor deiner Form zerbrich" may be taken as
expressing symbolically the feeling of the time also toward artistic form
in general, and may stand as the motto of the new drama, for which any
preconceived order or logical concatenation of causes was held to violate
life. Thus, Guillaume Apollinaire in the prologue to *Les Mamelles de
Tirésias* set forth his aesthetic of the new theater speaking of:

> Le grand déploiement de notre art moderne
> Mariant souvent sans lien apparent comme dans la vie
> Les sons les gestes les couleurs les cris les bruits
> La musique la danse l'acrobatie la poésie la peinture
> Les chœurs les actions et les décors multiples[8]

The bilingual Ivan Goll, equally at home in the pre-World War I
Expressionist circles of Berlin as he was later in the Cubist and Surrealist
entourage of Apollinaire, demanded *post festum* in the preface to his two
*Überdramen:* "Zunächst wird alle äußere Form zu zerschlagen sein." [9] A
tangible example of these tendencies was stated by Jean Cocteau in his
farce *Les Mariés de la Tour Eiffel,* performed in 1921, which is indeed
not very much unlike Apollinaire's play, although Cocteau took great
pains to explain that this was the first work of his in which he owed
nothing to anyone. But one might ask what claims can really be made by
the writer of a piece whose characters do not speak, and which relies

---

[6] Cf. Paolo Chiarini, "Espressionismo," in *Enciclopedia dello Spettacolo* (Roma,
1957), IV, 1633.

[7] W. Dilthey, "Die Technik des Dramas," in *Die große Phantasiedichtung* (Göttingen,
1954), p. 138. Originally published 1863 in the *Berliner Allgemeine Zeitung.* Recently
Siegfried Melchinger pointed out the same fact in discussing the original concept of
"epic theater." (*Theater der Gegenwart,* Frankfurt/M-Hamburg, 1956, p. 143.)

[8] *Les Mamelles de Tirésias* (Paris, 1946), p. 31. The prologue was added in 1916 to
the play which was itself written in 1903, and first produced 24 June 1917. A few
years later, in 1919, Virginia Woolf, proclaiming her *Life-is-a-luminous-halo* theory,
will demand the same for the novel. Cf. "Modern Fiction," in *The Common Reader.
First and Second Series* (New York: Harcourt, 1948).

[9] *Die Unsterblichen* (Berlin, 1920). Goll's is a typical case for how closely the different movements of Expressionism, Futurism, Surrealism, and Cubism were related to
one another. For this see Francis J. Carmody, "L'œuvre d'Yvan Goll," in *Yvan Goll.
Quatre Études* (Paris, 1956).

heavily on the pantomime, music, and other artistic forms, wanting thus to achieve "the plastic expression of poetry" the success of which is no longer dependent on the word.[10]

The basic ideas, however, which were expressed by Apollinaire in his prologue (and in his wake by Goll, Cocteau, and others) had already been vented in F. T. Marinetti's several Futurist manifestoes, where the concepts of Time and Space were left behind for the *Absolute*. In the *Manifesto del teatro futurista sintetico* (1915), Marinetti had already used the terms "sinfonizzare la sensibilità del pubblico" and "compenetrazione di ambienti e di tempi diversi." [11] He had even given an early example of this kind of theater with his satire *Le Roi Bombance,* which was performed on 3 April 1909 at the *Théâtre de l'Œuvre* in Paris. Although Marinetti and writers of his group, like Francesco Cangiullo, hardly scored a lasting success, their importance as innovators, as well as the fact that they prepared the ground for the *Teatro grottesco* and especially for Pirandello in Italy, should not be underestimated. How much Marinetti (who ended up as an academician of Mussolini's Italian Academy) thought of himself as the sole originator of ideas which brought more success to other playwrights than to him, is shown by Silvio d'Amico's remembering him interrupting performances of *Our Town,* and shouting: "Ma questo è un plagio, questo sintetismo l'ho inventato io." [12]

An example of how closely related all these revolutionary and antinaturalistic movements were is the fact that in 1914 Apollinaire himself wrote one of the many Futurist manifestoes which appeared in Papini's *Lacerba,* then temporarily the official organ of Futurism. But Papini, Soffici, and most of the *Vociani* thought differently about these ideas after World War I, and Papini himself cautioned against a "creazione che si rifà semplice azione." Autodidact though he was, he clearly perceived the end results of such attempts: "Arte che torna natura greggia." [13] Benda, who, with tongue in cheek, had given his *Essai* the Bossuet motto "Le charme de sentir est-il donc si fort?" stated his doubts more bluntly: "L'artiste ne doit pas devenir l'âme des choses *pour ensuite la mieux dire,* il doit la devenir *et s'en tenir là.*" [14]

---

[10] Cf. the foreword to *Les Mariés de la Tour Eiffel* (written in 1922). Also the opinion André Gide gives in his *Journal* on *Parade,* a previous *ballet réaliste* by Cocteau. For a more detailed and very sensitive analysis of Cocteau's debut see Neal Oxenhandler, *Scandal and Parade. The Theater of Jean Cocteau* (New Brunswick: Rutgers University Press, 1957).

[11] Marinetti, Settimelli, Corra, "Manifesto del teatro futurista sintetico," in *Il teatro futurista sintetico,* Biblioteca Teatrale dell'Istituto [n.d. but 1915]. Similar ideas Marinetti had already expressed in "Il teatro di varietà," in *Lacerba,* I, No. 19 (1 Oct. 1913); published also in *Daily Mail,* 21 Nov. 1913.

[12] *Il Futurismo. Il Novecentismo,* a cura di Enrico Falqui (Torino, 1953), p. 59.

[13] *Il Futurismo. Il Novecentismo,* p. 43.

[14] Benda, p. 11 (Italics in the text).

So much for the matter of form, which in the field of theater manifested itself as an abandoning of the old structure of the piece in acts. As mentioned previously, the *Stationendrama* in itself does not necessarily cause a loss of distance, even though it has often been used with such an intent. Pirandello, for example, in his *teatro sul teatro* trilogy adheres essentially to the idea and form of the *Stationendrama* and achieves his acts and subdivisions by means of some event or foreign element which breaks off the action at the "right" place. Thus in *Sei personaggi* the operator drops the curtain "by mistake" when he hears the director shout "Benissimo: sì, benissimo! E allora, sipario, sipario!" [15]—meaning only to indicate the act should end in the way just "improvised" by the characters. The frame of *Ciascuno a suo modo* is built on the same principle, and it is not very difficult to see an analogical situation also in Thornton Wilder's *The Skin of Our Teeth,* where Act III is interrupted by Mr. Antrobus' statement about the actors who cannot take part in the play.

Connected with the idea of the *Stationendrama* and its tempting loose structure are furthermore the plays which are built on an inversion of the time concept and its aspect of cause and effect. Thus, Act II may chronologically follow Act III as in Priestley's *Time and the Conways,* or it may precede acts I and III as in Gherardo Gherardi's little-known *Lettere d'amore.* It is doubtful, however, whether Gherardi may be called the first to make use of a blending back in time on the stage,[16] for Priestley's three time plays had then already appeared. It is true that Gherardi is in no way interested in theorizing, yet it seems hardly plausible to explain his ridding himself of the time concept entirely in terms of the tradition of the *Commedia dell'arte.* To establish a precedence here seems to be a difficult and, moreover, an idle task. Theater may have taken its cue from the film, as Hauser suggests,[17] yet preoccupation with the time element and the idea of breaking away from the concept of a time meaningful only in a successive cause and effect relationship was as common in the other arts. Granted that the establishment of one common denominator for Space and Time, and of their equality, was one of the conventions of the film, it was an Expressionist maxim as well.[18] Thus it would seem that the situation had deeper implications than those of a simple borrowing of other media from other arts: it seems to have been one of necessity, and one that had long been prepared by psychological as well as philosophical insights and per-

[15] Luigi Pirandello, *Maschere nude* (Milano, 1958), I, 99.

[16] Cf. Joseph Gregor, *Der Schauspielführer* (Stuttgart, 1955), III, 2, 8.

[17] Arnold Hauser, *Sozialgeschichte der Kunst und Literatur* (München, 1953), II, 498. Hauser uses in this connection the term *Verräumlichung der Zeit.*

[18] See Paul Kornfeld's "Betrachtungen über den 'beseelten und den psychologischen Menschen'" in A. Soergel, *Dichtung und Dichter der Zeit. Im Banne des Expressionismus* (Leipzig, 1925), p. 643: "Die Situation möge kopfstehen."

ceptions. Bergson in his *Thèse* had already implied a utilization by aesthetics of William James's ideas, and stated there himself: "Il est a présumer que le temps, entendu au sens d'un milieu où l'on distingue et où l'on compte, n'est que de l'espace."[19] Such ideas as well as the later expounded "simultanéité des états d'âme" were not without repercussions in literature. Although the question of direct influence, especially in Proust's case, is still denied and affirmed with the same vigor,[20] there should be no doubt that works like Proust's *A la recherche du temps perdu* or Thomas Mann's *Zauberberg* can hardly be thought of outside the realm of contemporary philosophy. As for the theater, Priestley, for instance, acknowledges indebtedness to Ouspensky's work *A New Model of the Universe*,[21] and the impact of Bergson's ideas may be found without any specific and dogmatic, or even conscious, reference here and there in the many considerations of playwrights who also expressed themselves theoretically.

Bert Brecht thus rejects any intentional finality in his theater:

> Die epische Dramatik, materialistisch eingestellt, an Gefühlsinvestierungen ihres Zuschauers wenig interessiert, kennt eigentlich kein Ziel [sic!], sondern nur ein Ende, und kennt eine andere Zwangsläufigkeit—in der der Lauf nicht nur in gerader Linie, sondern auch in Kurven, ja sogar in Sprüngen erfolgen kann.[22]

Yet this intent to change the basic dramatic characteristic involves some difficulties which Schiller already had remarked upon discussing with Goethe the dramatic and epic qualities: "Der Dramatiker steht unter der Kategorie der Kausalität, der Epiker unter der der Substantialität, dort kann und darf etwas als Ursache von was anderm da sein, hier muß alles sich selbst um seiner selbst willen geltend machen" (Letter of 25 April 1797).

Brecht sought to compensate for this loss of tension in stating that the new dramatics must be allowed to make use of connections to all sides, and that a tension would exist between its single components which "charged" them mutually. The epic form, therefore, would be anything but a revuelike assemblage. Brecht takes issue with what he calls the German *Pseudoklassik*, which mistakes, according to him, the dynamics of representation (*Dynamik der Darstellung*) for the dynamics of the

---

[19] *Essai sur les données immédiates de la conscience* (Paris, 1946), p. 68.

[20] Cf. Vittorio Mathieu, "Tempo, memoria, eternità: Bergson e Proust," in *Il Tempo*, ed. E. Castelli (Padova, 1958), p. 164; also Hans Mayer, "Welt und Wirkung Henri Bergsons," in *Deutsche Literatur und Weltliteratur* (Berlin, 1957), p. 528.

[21] *Three Time Plays* (London, 1952), p. xi. Cf. also Erwin Stürzl, "Die Zeit in den Dramen J. B. Priestleys," *GRM*, XXXVIII (1957), 37-52.

[22] "Literarisierung des Theaters," in *Schriften zum Theater* (Berlin-Frankfurt/M, 1957), p. 33.

matter to be represented (*Dynamik des Darzustellenden*). Yet he does
not seem to have made much progress in this direction himself when, in
the same essay, he describes the epic form so dear to him as the only
one which can encompass all those processes which serve the theater to
express an all-embracing *Weltbild* today. For if the German *Pseudoklassik*
had its individual "organized" systematically, Brecht has his disinte-
grated [23] according to modern creed, and he shows this as well on the
representational level, perhaps no less revolting to a Schiller, if he were
still alive, than Schiller's ideas are to Brecht.

It is, however, questionable—even in modern drama—whether (to
follow Brecht's terminology) the dynamics of representation must be
mistaken for the dynamics of the matter to be represented. In this connection Siegfried Melchinger recently undertook to demonstrate (using
contemporary French theater, and there especially Anouilh as the exception to prove the "rule") that the destruction of form in modern
theater is not necessarily a consequence of anti-illusionism.[24]

## III

Among the elements or devices used which affect aesthetic distance
from within the play, we may discern both a tendency to underdistance
as well as one to the opposite, to overdistance. Both of these effects are
achieved by breaking up the one-level performance of the play, and by
activating the audience;[25] although applying different means, both in
the end achieve the same effect: loss or removal of aesthetic distance.

The theater within the theater technique is one of the preferred means
of achieving an underdistancing. This technique in itself is, of course,
a hoary and venerable device, but the modern playwright using it is
not content to show the audience how a play is put together, as it were,
and thereby to advance whatever cause he has in mind; he will go one
step further and insinuate the internal play upon the audience by means
of making the audience one with the performers in the external play. In
other words, we first look at the internal play by watching the actors (in
the external play) carry on the mechanics of rehearsal while bickering
among themselves, etc. But suddenly the "stage manager" rushes down
the aisle of the theater, perhaps brushing our arm as he charges by, to

[23] Cf. "Literarisierung des Theaters," p. 34: "als ob nicht das Individuum schon lang
einfach auseinandergefallen wäre."

[24] *Theater der Gegenwart* (Frankfurt/M-Hamburg, 1956), p. 163 f. Interesting are the
testimonies supplied in the cases of Anouilh and Sartre. Gustaf Gründgens reports that
Sartre, when questioned by Germans as to whether the production of *Les Mouches* in
Paris had been classical or romantic, replied that it definitely had been classical, fully
corresponding with his intentions.

[25] Apollinaire: "les grossissements qui s'imposent si l'on veut frapper le spectateur"
(Foreword to *Les Mamelles de Tirésias*, p. 14). Cf. also Marinetti's and Cangiullo's concept of a "Teatro a sorpresa."

object to something within the play. In doing this, he is, in effect, putting himself completely on the level of the audience, that of a genuine spectator; and at the same time he is elevating the audience to his level as actors in the external play. All this, of course, makes active participants of us, and we are no longer watching so much as we are emotionally participating. In the process we lose our objectivity toward the external play (which is actually the piece of art that must convey the experience) and become emotionally involved to the point where our critical sense is eclipsed.[26]

We go to the theater not to see re-enacted a scene from life, not to see re-enacted an experience we may have had in our own lives, but rather to see this experience re-enacted in such a way that we may become aware of its *essence,* of what it represents on the scale of human values. If we are participants in this experience, then and there, our emotions become such that the *essences* are lost on us, and we become concerned only with saying bitter things and perhaps swinging our fists. In other words, art should "illuminate" life, not reflect it. Does this not mean that the artist has an obligation to maintain a perspective, allowing the spectator to derive an experience from the artistic product rather than to clutter it up with what all too often are but phony gimmicks[27] which rob the spectator of his honest critical-emotional response? After all, a play which relies for its effect upon a "stage manager" running up and down the aisles of the theater is not too far removed from the motion picture which relies upon three-dimensional representation and stereophonic sound to get its point across. When the actor swings his lethal fists in a 3-D movie, the whole audience involuntarily ducks. All right, the producer has been able to fool its reflex mechanism. What has that to do with art?

Looking at the end products of the Expressionist revolt today, it is interesting to see to what an extent the movement has drifted away from its original demands. Paul Kornfeld, one of the promoters of the "new drama," asked exactly for such an awareness of the essence of theater: "So befreie sich also der Schauspieler von der Wirklichkeit und abstrahiere [sic!] von den Attributen der Realität und sei nichts als der Vertreter des Gedankens, Gefühls oder Schicksals." [28]

As we have already seen, one device used in the theater within the theater technique to reduce aesthetic distance is that of the "stage

---

[26] Cf. Lipps's and Volkelt's concept of *Einfühlung,* not too different from Bergson's ideas on theatrical audiences as set forth in *Le Rire.*

[27] Such features, moreover, do not make for dramatic qualities. Cf. Hugo von Hofmannsthal: "Je stärker ein dramatischer Dialog ist, desto mehr von diesen Spannungen der Atmosphäre wird er mit sich tragen und desto weniger wird er den Bühnenanweisungen anvertrauen." (*Gesammelte Werke* (Frankfurt/M., 1955), Prosa IV, 197.)

[28] Soergel, p. 640.

director" who directs the play within the play from the audience, thereby establishing an emotional link between audience and actors, and serving as a rather suggestive agent for the activating of the audience. Another expedient which goes a step further is the placing of the spectator-actors of the play within the play among the real spectators, thereby also insinuating the play atmosphere upon the audience. The classic example for, this combined with the use of a "stage manager" going back and forth between audience and stage, is Pirandello's *Questa sera si recita a soggetto*. An idea of how much the distinction between the real audience (the audience of the external play) and the "play-audience" (the audience of the internal play) has been effaced in this piece, is already given us in the stage directions at the beginning: "Il pubblico, nell'improvvisa penombra, si fa dapprima attento; non udendo il gong che di solito annunzia l'aprirsi del sipario, comincia ad agitarsi un po'." [29]

The odd situation here is that this actually was not written for the "play-audience" alone, but also for the real one, which, of course, is not subject to stage directions at all and must not act accordingly. Stylistically, such a situation would require the future of probability ("si farà," "comincerà") instead of the declarative present indicative. When the "spectator-actors," distributed throughout the real audience, begin their play in discussing the goings-on behind the curtain, they simulate and insinuate to the real audience that they are indeed part of it. Then Dr. Hinkfuss, who has just entered the theater, rushes down the aisle to address the "audience" (the simulated and the real one). In bickering with the simulated audience (seated among the real one), he insinuates again the whole atmosphere upon the real audience. This is heightened to full irony in the scene where Dr. Hinkfuss tries to quiet the simulated audience by saying that he could not possibly answer all the questions asked of him while the play was going on, and then asserts to one of the "spectator-actors" who objects that the play really has not begun yet that it indeed has. This might seem to be the *non plus ultra* in reaching a state of almost complete identification of audience and actors, thereby reducing aesthetic distance to a level where any critical sense is eclipsed.

But this effect is intensified further by not only having single "spectator-actors" argue with the stage director, but also by stressing the collective side of these bickerings. Thus many stage directions read: "Qualcuno ride," "Molti, nelle poltrone, nei palchi e in platea, ridono," "Si ride"; and even direct lines are prescribed for: "Alcuni nella sala," "Altri," "Voci nella sala." [30] But this is still not enough: Dr. Hinkfuss tells the audience that also among it there will be a performance by the actors on a stage prepared for them there, indicating, moreover, a direct participation by the audience (which in the end is always the simulated

[29] *Maschere nude,* I, 255.
[30] *Ibid.,* pp. 255-260.

one): "e allora anche voi tutti parteciperete all'azione." [31] Furthermore, he directs attention to the *Intermezzo* during which the play will be carried into real life: the actors of the play within the play will perform simultaneously in separate groups "with the greatest ease," intermingled with the real audience in the foyer, "da spettatori tra gli spettatori." [32] This is theatricalization to a point where no further step is possible.[33] The actor's space has been made to coincide with, is the same as, the actual space of the audience. The play element has been carried into the reality of life to the point where both seem inextricably intermingled, thus suggesting, making, proclaiming theatricality as a form of life.[34]

We find an analogous situation in Schnitzler's one-act play *Der grüne Kakadu* (1899), some thirty years before Pirandello wrote *Questa sera si recita a soggetto*.[35] There Prosper, a former theater manager, has set up a cellar tavern in Paris at the time of the French Revolution and former members of his troupe, playing rascals, criminals, and whores, entertain his guests, consisting mostly of the nobility of the Ancien Régime. Under the cloak of this play-atmosphere the actors allow themselves jokes with the nobility which would be impossible in reality, thus creating a bewildering atmosphere between essence and appearance, the real and the unreal.[36] This atmosphere is crowned by the real murder of a noble rival by the main actor who just before had been reciting the scene of this murder, being unaware then that the aristocrat in reality was his rival. While all this goes on Albin, the young innocuous nobleman from the country, asks Rollin: "Sagen Sie mir, Herr Rollin, spielt die Marquise oder ist sie wirklich so—ich kenne mich absolut nicht aus."

[31] *Ibid.*, p. 265. At the Berlin performance in the *Lessing Theater* (31 May 1930), however, the audience indeed intended to be part of the game which caused the only really improvised scene: the appearance of the *real* director Hans Hartung who shouted insults at the *real* audience!

[32] *Ibid.*, p. 303.

[33] Werner Kallmorgen, a German theater architect, cleverly remarked on this subject: "Das Schlagwort vom 'Totaltheater' das den Zuschauerraum unter Illusion setzt und das Publikum swingt, in der Garderobe seine Zivilkleider abzugeben und das dem Stück entsprechende Kostüm in Empfang zu nehmen." *Darmstädter Gespräch: Theater*, ed. Egon Vietta (Darmstadt, 1955), p. 23.

[34] The perspicacious Antonio Gramsci was already aware of the affinity of Pirandello's ideas with those of Evreinov. Yet these appear here not in their sociological aspect, e.g., masking or unmasking of character, as Gramsci saw them applied by Pirandello. Lacking any secondary implication they are transplanted into the atmosphere of theater itself and approach Huizinga's concept of play as set forth in his *Homo ludens*.

[35] From several quarters there has come recently a new appreciation of Schnitzler's importance as an innovator. Wolfgang Kayser thinks his significance for the *Teatro grottesco* may have been overlooked because of the emphasis put upon the works of Synge and Andreev (*Das Groteske*, Oldenburg, 1957, p. 219).

[36] Here I could not agree with R. J. Nelson (*Play within a Play* [New Haven: Yale University Press, 1958], p. 119 f.) who says of the play: "We do not have the mingling of the real and the unreal, their perplexing fusion as in Pirandello and much twentieth century drama." The mingling is quite obvious, but it happens *on* the stage.

To this Rollin, Schnitzler's poet, answers: "Und was ich hier so eigen-
tümlich finde ist, daß alle scheinbaren Unterschiede sozusagen auf-
gehoben sind. Wirklichkeit geht in Spiel über—Spiel in Wirklichkeit." [37] This is Schnitzler's formula. He presents such a situation
*on* the stage, whereas Pirandello, going a step further, has it engulf
the real audience as well, which thus becomes part of the play. With
Pirandello, then, Albin's question about the reality of the goings on
is asked by the *real* audience. That is, in his play a step is taken
which is decisive and which does not aim at re-establishing mere
theatricality, whether or not the play was written in reaction to contemporary emphasis on staging. In connection with Pirandello, Francis
Fergusson remarked on the "curious convention-of-no-convention" of the
fourth wall, and said: "This is a pretense which it is difficult to maintain;
and side by side with modern realism many dramatic forms have
flourished which frankly accepted the stage as such and the audience as
extremely present." [38] But Pirandello conceived of the audience as extremely present to such a degree that it is in reality no longer there; it
is no longer watching but participating and transcending its status of
audience.

In an address delivered before the *Libre Esthétique* of Brussels, André
Gide, elaborating on the relationship of life to theater and the role of
the mask in it, stated: *"Où est le masque?—Dans la salle? ou sur la
scène?—Dans le théâtre? ou dans la vie?—Il n'est jamais qu'ici ou que
là."* [39] This kaleidoscopic aspect of the mask is indeed one of the central
problems of Pirandello's theater. Yet in his *Teatro sul teatro* trilogy he
is no longer content to apply this principle in its social implications as
he did in many of his other plays, or to translate it into the world of
art as in the posthumous and fragmentary "myth" of art *I giganti della
montagna.* Here he wants to achieve a forcible fusion of the two states:
the mask becomes the absolute principle itself.

According to Bergson any emancipation of means becomes comical;
and that is exactly where the situation leads. Léon Régis exploited it
as such in his comedy *Brout.*[40] There, a Monsieur Brout coming from
Chinon visits a theater in Paris and ends up on the stage instead of in
the audience. This happens because upon his entering the theater in the
first act he sees on the stage a deceiving replica of an audience, and the
stage manager, quickly sensing his chance with Brout, goads him into
sitting on the stage. From that bewildering experience on, Brout is no

[37] *Der grüne Kakadu,* ed. Schinnerer (New York: Appleton, 1938), pp. 36-37.
[38] "The Theatricality of Shaw and Pirandello," *Partisan Review,* XVI (1949), 589.
[39] "L'Évolution du théâtre," delivered 25 March 1904 in *Nouveaux Prétextes* (Paris,
1930), p. 19. As to Pirandello's use of the mask as symbol, see also Ulrich Leo,
"Pirandello. Kunsttheorie und Maskensymbol," *DVLG,* XI (1933).
[40] Cf. Karl Vossler, "Zeit- und Raumordnungen der Bühnendichtung," in *Aus der
romanischen Welt* (Karlsruhe, 1948).

longer capable of carrying out his business because he immediately sees the histrionic act and buffoonery, the inextricable mixture of theater and reality, of essence and appearance, in whatever he does; so that in the last act, having lost his faith in reality, he becomes a politician.

We may argue that such a rapprochement of theater and life, of stage and audience, is nothing new, and we may point above all to Baroque theater practice. Yet it is small wonder that an age, so deeply rooted in an antithetical *Weltanschauung* for which everything terrestrial was *nur ein Gleichnis* and by which human life and existence were seen as *el gran teatro del mundo,* should find its most congenial expression in the medium of theater; and it is, furthermore, small wonder that an age whose basic principle and experience was that of theatricality should make use of the form of theater to its ultimate resources. Thus the Baroque age pursued the subtle possibilities of a myriad of kaleidoscopic reflections of essence and appearance, of *Sein* and *Schein,* gliding and blending relentlessly into one another, yet never being one. The artists drew again and again upon the theme of life as bounding, extending over into the domain of play, of theater, and upon the motif of illusion becoming reality.[41]

It is hardly astonishing that the playwrights, too, exploited this situation so propitious to their medium. We may think of Ben Jonson's *Every Man out of His Humour* in which two spectators, one taking the side of the audience, the other that of the poet, accompany every turn of the action with their comment. Or we may point to his *Bartholomew Fair* where the stage-keeper tells the audience what to expect, and the prompter enters a pact with an audience of not too highly valued mental capacities. Yet these plays are for the most part literary-satirical comedies deriding an average audience. This is brought out especially in *The Staple of News,* which is no longer didactic, but indulges in a series of derisive taunts at the audience, represented by four personifications who accompany the piece with the most barbarous and disgraceful comment. Jonson here, as in *Magnetic Lady,* objectively represents the audience. However, the asides of these spectator-personifications form only a frame within which the real play goes on, and they merely create a reflective attitude on the part of the audience. These endeavors are a far cry from the taking of the audience into the play and from being merely suggestive of such a direction.

Even Beaumont-Fletcher's all-out satire *The Knight of the Burning Pestle,* where the commentators are not personifications, but are drawn

---

[41] Cf. Quevedo, *Doctrina de Epicteto* XIX (*Obras,* Madrid, 1877, III, 395): "No olvides que es comedia nuestra vida,/Y teatro de farsa el mundo todo,/Que muda el aparato por instantes,/Y que todos en él somos farsantes." Further, Lope de Vega's *Lo fingido verdadero,* Jean Rotrou's *Le véritable Saint Genest,* etc. On this subject in general see Jean Rousset's excellent work *La Littérature de l'âge baroque en France. Circé et Paon* (Paris, 1953).

from the parterre to partake in the play, observes a strict separation of the fictive from the real audience. And there are two further aspects which differentiate it from a theatrical modern play: the characters of the frame piece never talk to the main actors, even though they at times parenthetically address remarks to them, nor do they talk to Ralph once he has assumed his role. They are always answered by the speaker of the prologue or by a supernumerary. By thus keeping the inner and outer plays separate, there is maintained a considerable degree of clarity.

The major difference, then, between such plays and contemporary ones which make an all-out effort at theatricality seems to be that the plays just spoken of make the audience exactly aware of the two worlds, theater and life, stage and audience. They draw upon theatricality to a high degree, but in doing so they only render the audience more conscious of the antinomy of the whole, without a thought of its elimination. Only German romantics like Ludwig Tieck, who owed their success largely to their excellent (or was it indeed?) knowledge of the Elizabethans, went a step further.[42] A discussion of the German romantic theater in this respect goes beyond the limits of this paper. It may be stated, however, that plays like Tieck's *Der gestiefelte Kater* and *Die verkehrte Welt* with their exaggeration of technique originated (and were only possible) under circumstances far removed from the theater. His satirical tendencies, overdeveloped as they were, led him far from any real and workable theater. This seems also to have been Friedrich Schlegel's point when he broke the not too surprising news, in remarking on *Der gestiefelte Kater*, that the cat was as if strolling on the roof of dramatic art.[43] For Tieck the mode of theatrically is only the container which best suits his ideas; he is not concerned with subtleties. The Elizabethans, on the other hand, by playing on the complexities of the stage-audience relationship (and far from blurring and effacing it) made the audience critically aware of its existence.

On our modern stage, in comparison, the audience is to be made part and parcel of the whole performance; it is to be dragged, as it were, into the play. With this we move toward the concept of theater as a rite, as the liturgical celebration of a community; indeed a situation not unlike the one from which theater originally sprang. Thus, in the Twenties, Hanns Johst wrote in Germany: "Das kommende Theater wird Kult werden müssen oder das Theater hat seine Sendung, seinen lebendigen Ideengehalt abgeschlossen." [44] A few years later, the then German *Reichsdramaturg* Schlösser, carrying on from there, stated pathetically:

[42] It is not wholly without reason that critics have attempted to establish parallels between Tieck and Pirandello. Cf. G. Mazzoni, "Pirandello e 'Il gatto con gli stivali,'" in *Il Messaggero* (Roma, 10.8.1938).

[43] *Athenäumsfragmente*, Nr. 307.

[44] "Vom neuen Drama," in *Ich glaube! Bekenntnisse* (München, 1928), p. 36.

"Die Sehnsucht geht nach einem die historischen Vorgänge zur mystisch allgemeingültigen eindeutigen Überwirklichkeit steigernden Drama." [45] More recently, Mario Apollonio, although not at all of the same ilk as these predecessors, concluded a *compte rendu* on the state of theater in postwar Italy along the same lines: "Occorrerà, al teatro di domani, che la festa dello spettacolo sia l'occasione di un religioso ritrovamento concorde della verità di tutti, il commento liturgico al rito del tempo, l'armonioso arco aperto sul tempo infinito della vita morale." [46]

In reality, however, such a concept of theater as performance of a mystic rite still has the aspect of a forcible fusion of stage and audience. To achieve this, there are many other devices used in contemporary dramatic practice beyond those mentioned previously. One such further expedient which is apt to reduce aesthetic distance between stage and audience is the deliberate addressing of the real audience by the actors, not meant as a mere aside. This occurs, for example, in Wilder's *The Skin of Our Teeth* where, at the beginning of Act I, Sabina says to the audience: "Now that you audience are listening to this, too, I understand it a little better. I wish eleven o'clock were here; I don't want to be dragged through this whole play again." [47] The same happens in Act III when Mr. Antrobus explains to the audience that some actors who were to appear in the last act have been taken ill.[48] Perhaps it is not astonishing that the audience doomed the play when it was first presented in 1942. Plays like those of Wilder are for a rather sophisticated audience; but even with such a one there always arises the question as to how long it can, or is willing to, stand such repeated pointers which try to tell it: "See, we're playing!" Pirandello went through a similar experience with his *Sei personaggi* when, on the opening night in the *Teatro del Valle* in Rome, shouting and rioting broke out after the show, and he hurriedly scrambled into a taxi leaving the scene amidst shouts of "buffone!" and "manicomio!"

A further practice of contemporary theater affecting aesthetic distance is the breaking up of the one-level performance achieved by remarks of the actors on the actual performing while it is going on, switching thus from the world of appearance to the world and level of essence. So in *The Skin of Our Teeth*, Sabina, during Henry's quarrel with Mr. Antrobus in Act III, cries out: "Stop! Stop! Don't play this scene. You know what happened last night. Stop the play. Last night you almost strangled him. You became a regular savage. Stop it!" [49] Brecht achieved

---

[45] R. Schlösser, *Das Volk und seine Bühne* (Berlin, n.d. [1935]), p. 55.
[46] "Il teatro," in *Dopo il diluvio,* ed. Dino Terra (Milano, 1947), p. 342.
[47] Thornton Wilder, *The Skin of Our Teeth* (New York: Harper, 1942), p. 13.
[48] Interesting is a faint resemblance to Giordano Bruno's *Candelaio,* where the speaker of the *Antiprologo* leaves hurriedly after expressing doubts that the play will get off the ground because of the troubles some actors are beset with.
[49] P. 130.

the square, so to speak, of this device. In the fifth scene of his "Volks-
stück" *Herr Puntila und sein Knecht Matti* the servant Matti proposes
a stratagem to Eva to save her from having to marry the Attaché. In
order to show that he and the landed proprietor's daughter are intimates,
Matti first suggests addressing her by her first name in the Attaché's
presence. When she asks Matti how he would go about this, he says: " 'Die
Bluse ist im Genick nicht zu, Eva.' " Eva, really reaching to her back,
replies: "Sie ist doch zu, ach so, jetzt haben Sie schon gespielt!" [50] Interesting and indicative of Brecht's idea of theater and acting is his use,
in a stage direction of the same play, of the expression "Theater spielend"
in the pejorative sense of "feigning."

Another means of reducing aesthetic distance is the conscious evocation
of an atmosphere of suspension between essence and appearance, between the world of the stage and real life. We find an example of this
at the end of Pirandello's *Questa sera si recita a soggetto*. There Mommina, after having sung an aria from the *Trovatore* to her children,
collapses and falls "dead" in their presence. The children suspect nothing since they believe this belongs to the role their mother was just
reciting; but Mommina does not get up even after the actors of the
play one level more external than hers come onto the stage and wish
her to. They, then, become afraid she may be dead in all "reality." The
same atmosphere of suspense and interpenetration of essence and appearance, of play and "reality," we find in André Obey's *Maria* where,
in Act II, Jeanne is introduced who is first supposed to marry and then
to die, as the stage manager tells the audience. But it is Maria who in
"reality" takes the deadly poison and provides the spectacular finale.
Although this play was inspired by Faulkner, it is hardly conceivable
without Pirandello, as Joseph Gregor has already pointed out.

A major practice of contemporary theater which tends to reduce
aesthetic distance is the use of a narrator or a commentator. Although
he is in many cases employed to provide an increased sense of theatricality, his functions involve more than that. This is especially true of
Wilder's *Our Town* where he has a triple function: as stage manager
he addresses both actors and audience, and he also participates as stage
manager-clergyman in the play within the play. Another example is
Tennessee Williams' narrator of *The Glass Menagerie* who, from the
beginning, clearly tells the audience: "I am the narrator of the play,
and also a character in it." [51] Here, as in Wilder's play, the narrator,
at home in both worlds of stage and audience, constitutes a suggestive
link between the two realms. That again raises the audience from its
status of merely assisting at a performance. This, however, is an ex-

[50] *Herr Puntila und sein Knecht Matti,* in *Versuche 22-24* (Berlin, 1950), p. 38.
[51] Tennessee Williams, *The Glass Menagerie* (New York: New Directions, 1940), p. 5.

pedient to be adopted too easily, and in many second-rate plays it is devoid of any deeper sense and is nothing more than the skillful use of a theatrical device.[52]

There seem to be conflicting opinions on the use of the narrator. Melchinger sees Shaw's *Saint Joan* as the prototype, yet the device was used by Cocteau in *Les Mariés de la Tour Eiffel,* and Wedekind and Schnitzler must also be thought of in this connection. Again, to point out influences here and "firsts" means little to the point of irrelevance in an essentially undramatic theater whose development was bound to go in this direction.

The use of the narrator finally leads us to a form of theater which relies on this expedient as a means of subsistence: the so-called epic theater of Bertolt Brecht.[53] This also can be discussed only in its major implications within the frame of the present study. Brecht wants to overdistance in order to prevent any *Einfühlung,* any empathy, on the part of actors and audience. This he calls: "Die Aufgabe der Illusion zugunsten der Diskutierbarkeit." [54] Consequently, he rewrote some parts of *Mutter Courage* after the Zürich production because the audience had "identified" itself with the heroine, in spite of the usual precautions he had taken in this respect. How problematic such provisions still remain is shown by another instance even more indicative of the audience's usual "resistance" and immunity to such measures because it occurred at one of the performances of Brecht's own *Berliner Ensemble.* If anywhere, it is here that the ultimate realization of the Brechtian *Verfremdungseffekt* should be achieved; but it was precisely here that a worker, queried on the performance of Brecht's adaptation of the Gorki novel *Die Mutter,* hardly testified to the effectiveness of even the most orthodox staging of an orthodox play.[55] How the *Verfremdungseffekt* is to be achieved by the actor Brecht discusses in his essay *Die Straßenszene,* the gist of which is that the actor's business is not very different from that of an eyewitness of a traffic accident who demonstrates to a quickly gathering crowd how the accident, of which he was the sole witness, occurred. With Brecht, the anti-Stanislavsky *par excellence,* the actor has become, then, a teacher with a pointer, a *philologus in actu;* he "is" not King Lear, but he "demonstrates" King Lear.

But, we might ask, does the audience need this pointer? Can we speak

[52] Cf. also John Gassner, "Forms of Modern Drama," in *Comparative Literature,* VII (1955), 143: "This 'willed' and cultivated theatricalism suggests, if it does not invariably succumb to, a schizoid and Alexandrian sensibility."

[53] With Brecht the term "epic" has retained little of its original implications but stands as a synonym for antidramatic and antiemotional.

[54] "Das moderne Theater ist das epische Theater," in *Schriften zum Theater,* p. 23.

[55] "Hans Garbe über die Aufführung," in *Theaterarbeit,* ed. Helene Weigel (Düsseldorf, 1952), pp. 168-170.

of a complete illusion in the theater?[56] We know that the actor plays, that he derives the impelling force of his play exactly from the tension between essence and appearance; and with all our knowledge of modern psychology we hardly expect any direct feelings from the actor. We know there cannot be any identification of the acting with the normal personality. What Brecht emphasizes is the age-old distinction between two types of acting already known to Plato: the *Rhapsodos* on the one hand and, on the other, the actor whose performance involves a measure of identification with the character. To say, however, that only one of these is the "true" one amounts to an arbitrary pronouncement; for, after all, even the actor who seems to identify himself with the character he represents is only giving his interpretation of that character. He remains, ultimately, always psychologically differentiated from that character, so much so that his drive to play comes precisely from the subtle interrelationship between the acting and the normal personality. What we witness, then, is not *the* Hamlet, but X's Hamlet and Y's Hamlet which are the result not of *possible* "identification," but of wanted identification. The degree to which the actor allows a rapprochement between his acting and his normal personality is his own, and to determine it from the outset means to abolish the tension from which he derives his drive to play.[57]

All Brecht achieves with this rigorous demand is a loss of distance through overdistancing. What we get, then, is a theater from which all tension and antinomy have been removed, and which is demonstrating situations of a mere factual nature and relationship. Although Brecht solemnly states that it is not at all his intention to emigrate from the *Reich des Wohlgefälligen*,[58] one can hardly conceive of his *Lehrstück* as a pleasant diversion. Here theater is turned into an institution for the presentation of painless, spoon-fed, and "guided" historical, at times possibly also ideological, information, not to speak of an institution for the mentally retarded. What is left of the art value of such an institution is questionable, although Brecht describes his epic theater as highly artistic.

This "demonstrating" aspect which is valid for the world of the actor

---

[56] Cf. Stendhal, who has his *Romantique* say: "Il me semble que ces moments d'*illusion parfaite* sont plus fréquents qu'on ne le croit en général, et surtout qu'on ne l'admet pour vrai dans les discussions littéraires. Mais ces moments durent infiniment peu, par exemple une demi-seconde, ou un quart de seconde. On oublie bien vite Manlius pour ne voir que Talma." *Racine et Shakespeare* (Paris, 1925), I, 17.

[57] It is this aspect which does not at all exist for Brecht, and which he wholly mistakes. In his "Verfremdungseffekte in der chinesischen Schauspielkunst" (*Schriften*, p. 79) he states that the actor who has achieved complete identification would need no more art than the cashier, doctor, or general whom he represents needed in real life. But it is exactly the *degree* of identification, the subtle play of the antinomies, from which the drive to play originates!

[58] "Kleines Organon für das Theater," in *Schriften*, p. 130.

is that also for the audience: it, too, is supposed to learn something conducive to social action. It is not to be entertained, or, rather, the "entertainment" is to be of a special sort. In comparing the "dramatic form" of theater with his "epic form," Brecht says that in the latter the audience would be *gegenübergesetzt*, as far as its relationship to the stage goes. This is misleading and also rather doubtful; for in the same comparison Brecht admits that, whereas the "dramatic form" would allow the audience to have feelings ("ermöglicht ihm Gefühle"), the "epic form" forced decisions from the audience ("erzwingt von ihm Entscheidungen").[59] This is directly solicited by the epilogue of *Der gute Mensch von Sezuan:* "Verehrtes Publikum, los, such dir selbst den Schluß Es muß ein guter da sein, muß, muß, muß!" [60]

We only have to consider similar forms of such a theater to become aware of its primarily indoctrinating character (which also explains its constant haranguing of the audience and its intention to destroy aesthetic distance). In this connection Brecht's association with Karl Kraus has been pointed out. Many of Kraus's accomplishments were indeed of the same intent; arousing the audience and influencing its thought. Kraus openly advocated this practice, as is shown by his "political theater" *Die Unüberwindlichen,* or the "Martian tragedy" *Die letzten Tage der Menschheit* with its contemporary historical characters and its documentary use of official speeches. Such a form of theater has been repeatedly experimented with. Interestingly enough, though hardly surprising, it has always flourished as the medium of more or less radical and militant political ideologies interested in getting across an idea to the point of indoctrination. Thus, in Mussolini's Italy Giovacchino Forzano wrote several plays of this kind, always keeping in mind the "actuality" of the relevant theme, and in Germany as well "living history" was recommended for the stage of the *Thingspiel.*

Close to Brecht's concept of the *Lehrstück* are, furthermore, the diverse kinds of documentary drama in its varying degrees, such as that fostered by the American *Federal Theatre* of the Thirties featuring "living newspapers," or, more recently, Piscator's adaptation of Tolstoi's *War and Peace* in Germany.

Brecht claims to follow Chinese theater practice with his *Verfremdungseffekt*, yet we may wonder whether he has not mistaken an historically developed situation for something merely technical which can be transplanted without its original situation. Although he sees this problem, the solution he offers is hardly convincing, and Melchinger even charges him with an "intentional will to misunderstanding," [61] for the Chinese actor would be unthinkable without ritual and myth. Yet

---

[59] "Das moderne Theater ist das epische Theater," in *Schriften,* p. 19.

[60] *Versuche 27-32,* Heft 12 (Berlin, 1953), 106.

[61] *Theater der Gegenwart* (Frankfurt/M-Hamburg, 1956), p. 179.

the idea of the *Lehrstück* seems to us to have a much greater flaw, and that is the not uncommon practice at present of mistaking literature for the handmaiden of history. Lessing, in taking issue with an article of the *Journal Encyclopédique* in his *Hamburgische Dramaturgie* (XIX), said it was assumed without reason that one of the purposes of theater was to retain the memory of great men; for such purposes we would have history. Furthermore, he stated that through theater we should learn not what this or that single individual *did*, but rather what every man of a certain character under certain given circumstances would do[62]; and finally, following Aristotle, that the intention of tragedy was far more philosophical than that of history. This in the end, then, means no more and no less than that the poet is not the resurrection angel of history (Hebbel). At the root of this criticism lies the basic incompatibility of poetry in the widest sense and history, of historical truth and poetical truth.

Thus, Brecht's *Lehrstück* as well as the documentary drama really fall outside of theater proper, for what is true for tragedy holds as well for drama. In fact, this raises the question, what documentary drama, or even drama written with the intent to document something (be that true or distorted history, which ultimately does not matter, for it is the intent which matters, and, after all, what *is* "true" history?), has to do with art. Between both forms of theater lies the whole span from the *factual* to the *ideal* (Dilthey). Yet the position Brecht takes can be well understood, for it is Aristotle who implies that the poet should not be bound so much by historical truth as by its transcending qualities. That is, the δυνατά of history are by no means the *conditio sine qua non* for the theater, though they may be used, but rather the δυνατά of a higher level,[63] those that have made their way from the *factual* to the *ideal*. And Brecht, after all, makes it clear that his is *eine nichtaristotelische Dramatik*. But what, we may ask, is there left for any *Dramatik*, be it Aristotelian or non-Aristotelian, by mere history? By this we do not want to conceive of history as being a cut and dried matter, but what really does its inherent factual truth (if there is one) have to do with that of poetry in the widest sense? [64]

---

[62] To prevent thus an audience from seeing certain things because they are not conducive to an ideal world seems to mistake the mission and sense of theater. Cf. Pascal's negative position in this respect in the oft quoted fragment No. 11 (Brunschvicg) of the *Pensées*, and also Molière's comment in the *Préface* of 1669 to *Tartuffe*. Furthermore, the Encyclical of Pope Pius XII *Miranda prorsus* with which Guido Calogero takes issue in this sense ("La libertà di vedere. Considerazioni sulla natura dello spettacolo," in *Il Ponte*, XIII, 1957, 1191-98).

[63] Cf. Friedrich Schlegel (*Prosaische Jugendschriften*, II, 218): "Was in der Poesie geschieht, geschieht nie, oder immer. Sonst ist es keine rechte Poesie. Man darf nicht glauben sollen, daß es jetzt wirklich geschehe."

[64] Cf. Wilhelm Dilthey (*Das Erlebnis und die Dichtung* [Göttingen, n.d.], p. 118, et passim): "Der Vorgang, in dem ... die poetische Welt entsteht und

## IV

Hand in hand and parallel with the destruction of aesthetic distance from within the play goes the destruction also of spatial distance between stage and spectator. By this we refer to modern attempts to abolish the proscenium arch,[65] the most conspicuous one of which is the creation of the arena-type theater, be it in huge or small dimensions.

The very name *arena,* however, in its *pars pro toto* nature suggesting the origin of this architectural form, points to purposes diametrically opposed to the demands of theater. The term *arena* (L. for *sand*), originally denoting the central space of an amphitheater which was covered with sand, clearly indicates the nature of the spectacles given there, which were of the show and gladiator type, intended to be seen in the round and from steps more steeply arranged than those of theaters.[66] Thus, any attempt to use the arena form for theater mistakes the basic character of theater which draws upon the two opposites of stage and audience.[67] The actor can have but one face, but one opposite. Theater is in this way basically different from the art of dancing, for which either orchestra or arena were the congenial form. Modern advocates of the arena-type theater always quote ancient Greek theater practice, yet in none of the Greek theaters was the audience seated completely around the orchestra. Even in Epidauros, where the spectator rows go beyond the half circle of 180°, the whole of the theater is based upon the vis-à-vis of actor and audience. Polycletus, though leading the half round of the θέατρον beyond 180°, was far from conceiving any play in the round. This is shown by the fact that the θέατρον does not have a single radius (although the orchestra itself is a circle), but is constructed around three centerpoints: only the eight middle sections have a common centerpoint, whereas the radius of the outer end sections is about 3.5 m. greater.[68] That is, this curve has been chosen so that the spectators of the outer sections do not have to turn their heads to see

ein einzelnes d i c h t e r i s c h e s W e r k s i c h b i l d e t, empfängt sein Gesetz aus einem Verhalten zur Lebenswirklichkeit, das vom Verhältnis der Erfahrungselemente zum Zusammenhang der Erkenntnis ganz verschieden ist." [Spacing as in text.]

[65] Cf. Marinetti (*Manifesto del teatro futurista sintetico*, p. 19): "Eliminare il preconcetto della ribalta lanciando delle reti di sensazioni tra palcoscenico e pubblico."

[66] Even where the name was retained for open air theaters as in Italy in the eighteenth and nineteenth centuries, it always denoted a theater in the half round (Cf. the *Arena Nazionale* of Florence, the *Arena del Sole* in Bologna, etc.).

[67] Cf. Melchinger, p. 36; also Hélène Leclerc, who speaks of the "deux cellules initiales du théâtre: la scène et la salle, la place de jeu et le groupement des spectateurs." ("Autour d'une exposition," *RHT*, II [1950], 303.)

[68] Other Greek theaters had adopted similar solutions to allow a frontal view. One such is the Theater of Dionysos in Athens, which uses the tangent instead of the elliptic form of Epidauros. For respective dates see Wilhelm Dörpfeld and Emil Reisch, *Das griechische Theater* (Athens, 1896), p. 120 ff., and p. 169 ff.

the play. It is obvious from this that the architect had in mind a "frontal" approach. Otherwise, he could as well have let his θέατρον follow only one centerpoint, leaving the audience of the outer sections to view the acting from behind. This, however, is the very fact which modern propagators of the play in the round not only do not want to avoid, but ardently advocate.

Epidauros had three centerpoints and two different radiuses. The point where the sight lines of all spectators meet and merge thus extends itself from the centerpoint of the orchestra toward the skene: the place where the performance could best be seen by all spectators. The theater, thus, was erected (and Dörpfeld assumes this to be true of all Greek theaters) for performances taking place between the center of the orchestra and the proscenium, the actors being, therefore, "οἱ ἐπὶ σκηνῆς." This saved Greek audiences from viewing the backs of their actors, quite unlike the circus atmosphere of the modern theater in the round. It seems, therefore, hardly understandable that Greek theater practice could, in all seriousness, be called upon to justify a play in the round.

Whatever earlier performances may have been like, a play in the orchestra was a foregone conclusion when the structure following the Lycurgan theater was completed in Athens[69] with an important innovation: the action now is transferred to a stage. This is a fundamental change and constitutes an incisive turn in the destiny of theater: audience and actors are now facing one another, the chorus as intermediary having been removed. This change seems to pay tribute to the essence of theater which is, in fact, a vis-à-vis, a *Gegenüber*. Propagators of the arena-type theater, therefore, apparently attempt to defend their form by relying upon historically shaky positions. Moreover, the aesthetic effect of theater in the round is in no way touched by the rather controversial question of its use, or the use of a similar form, historically. The fact is, the evolution of theater went the way it did; therefore, if such a form as the theater in the round is genuine, it will have to stand or fall on its own merits.[70]

---

[69] T. B. L. Webster (*Greek Theatre Production* [London: Methuen, 1956], p. 22) gives for this the *terminus post quem* as 320/10 and the *terminus ante quem* as 156/5.

[70] Cf. Glenn Hughes, *The Penthouse Theatre* (Seattle: University of Washington Press, 1950), p. 9: "If the comedian has, during many centuries [sic], in several countries, performed successfully in a circle, then why not draw a circle and put him in it? That is, a modern comedian—not a traditional clown. Not Scaramouche, but Nick Potter." Yet, this is, alas, not such an undisputed conclusion that by dint of it we can confine Nick Potter to a circle! Cf. Emil Staiger, "Vom Pathos," *Trivium*, II (1944), 87: "Neuerdings gibt es Dramaturgen, welche die Rampe beseitigen und die Bühnenspiele lieber in einer Art Arena oder dann in einem Raum aufführen möchten, der innigeren Kontakt erlaubt. Das zeugt von einem völligen Mißverständnis der dramatischen Kunst."—Even Thomas Mann (who, indicatively, never viewed theater with a gentle eye) is among the "abolitionists." So he tells us ("Versuch über das Theater," written 1910; in *Rede und Antwort*, Berlin, 1922, p. 61): "Die konkrete Erscheinung des Volkstheaters ist selbstverständlich das Massentheater, dessen Zuschauerraum den Typus

Modern stage design has offered *mille e tre* solutions to bring about the activation of the audience, and only the most conspicuous ones can be mentioned here. The basic type, of course, is the *arena,* and most of the solutions offered derive from that form. Apollinaire, in the prologue of *Les Mamelles de Tirésias,* already speaks of a "théâtre rond à deux scènes / Une au centre l'autre formant comme un anneau / Autour des spectateurs." By 1927, Walter Gropius, then director of the *Bauhaus* in Dessau, had given a tangible example of such a stage in his project of a *Totaltheater* for Piscator.[71] In this design the audience was to be made part of the scene through projections of films on the ceiling and on screens distributed throughout the audience. Furthermore, the circular front stage (occupying the same position as the orchestra in a Greek theater) and part of the orchestra seats were to be made mobile so that the circular front stage could be revolved a complete 180° to the center of the audience, thus forming there an arena. This leads to a total elimination of aesthetic distance, imposing the play atmosphere upon the audience to such an extent that any psychologically differentiated process of thinking and appreciation on its part is made impossible. A complete identification of space is achieved and the words "audience" and "stage" become synonymous.

This combined solution of the *Totaltheater* filiated other forms which realized only one of the aspects of Gropius' mammoth plan. Thus, in the theater in the round there is no ramp of any sort: one step from the first seating row is "stage." This reminds one of the manège of a circus, except that there one does not sit so close to events the outcome of which may not be the expected,[72] and the modern spectator in such institutions in the round can no longer rely on Partridge's last resort: "And if it was really a ghost, it could do one no harm at such a distance." But distance is something which precisely is avoided in such theaters with the express

---

des Zirkus-Amphitheaters wieder [sic!] wird annehmen müssen, und dessen Bühne nicht die unseres Halbtheaters bleiben kann." We are somewhat surprised at this "wieder," for where have amphitheaters in antiquity been built and used for plays? Were the *coliseum* in Rome, the *Arena* in Verona built for theater or for circus?—Mann modified his rigid first stand somewhat in his later Heidelberg speech of 1929, but his basic view on the function of theater remained the same. (Cf. "Rede über das Theater zur Eröffnung der Heidelberger Festspiele," in *Altes und Neues,* Frankfurt/M, 1953, pp. 342, 352.)

[71] Walter Gropius, "vom modernen theaterbau, unter berücksichtigung des piscator-theater-neubaues in berlin," *Berliner Tageblatt,* 2 Nov. 1927.

[72] The difference between circus and theater from the point of view of reality has been discussed by Céline Arnauld ("Le Cirque, art nouveau," in *L'Esprit Nouveau. Revue Internationale d'Esthétique,* I, n.d.). Cf. p. 98: "On a tendence à rapprocher le cirque du théâtre. Selon moi, c'est une vue des plus fausses. Le cirque est un spectacle fait de réalités. Le théâtre, au contraire, ne vit que de fictions. . . . Au cirque, la crainte que nous ressentons devant certains exercices dangereux est une crainte *réelle* provoquée par un danger réel. Sur la scène, tout est fiction, et il faut une âme naïve pour oublier que tout cela n'est qu'un jeu."

purpose of making any psychologically differentiated situation impossible.[73]

Other stage forms conceived along the principle of audience activation try to encircle the audience. One example of this is the theater with a tripartite stage: a main stage and two lateral stages closing in on the audience. In Europe, Van de Velde has experimented with it since 1914, and Auguste Perret adopted it for his model at a 1925 exposition. A more recent development[74] added a fourth "lobby-stage," encircling the audience completely. Consequently, the seats here have become revolving ones to enable the audience to face either stage. Permitting simultaneous acting as they do, these stages are close relatives of the medieval simultaneous stage. Yet there is an important difference: simultaneous acting in a three quarter or a full circle is not the same as that presented frontally, as was the medieval custom! Significantly, earlier attempts at simultaneous acting still retained the frontal approach. So Cochin's *Projet d'une salle de spectacle pour le nouveau théâtre de comédie* of 1765, or Cosimo Morelli's theater in Imola of 1779, both essentially growing out of the Palladian stage architecture with its three openings as exemplified in the *Teatro Olimpico* of Vicenza. Other designs can only be pointed out: Norman Bel Geddes' "space theater" in 1924 for New York, or that of Ottmar Schubert in 1937;[75] Werner Frey's and Jacques Schrader's *Mehrzwecktheater* for Basel in 1953, and, finally, the recent project of an "all-round" theater with a "panorama stage" of André Perrottet von Laban and Eya and Martin Burckhardt.[76]

If we regard all these innovations in stage design against the fourth wall convention, the *scène encadrée* (which in many cases were and are still "projects"), as a reaction against a loss of contact with this very *scène encadrée*,[77] why, then, does this happen today? Does the cause of this loss of contact not lie too deep for a mere change in the outer form of theater to remedy? Such a contact can never be one sought on the basis of a psychologically undifferentiated atmosphere between stage and audience, since it eliminates a priori the tension between the two cells of theater, and therewith their very existence. Does a remedy, then, not

[73] Cf. Glenn Hughes, p. 24 f.: "It has been our observation that at Penthouse plays people in the first three rows are really *in* the play [sic!]. With the fourth row they begin to feel themselves outside it. And we must not succumb to the temptation to enlarge our audience." Yet, in the same pamphlet (p. 51) the author says: "The theatre, any theatre, lives by illusion," which strikes us as a *contradictio in adjecto*. How can the arena-type theater with all its anti-illusion measures possibly *create* "illusion?" It is one of the very forms which are used to destroy "illusion!"

[74] An example of this type is the theater of Baylor University by P. Baker.

[75] See *Der Architekt* (1955), No. 4, pp. 129-131.

[76] See *Darmstädter Gespräch 1955; Theater*, p. 95.

[77] See Hélène Leclerc, p. 304: "C'est en réaction contre cette forme et cette perte de contact que s'orientent toutes les recherches actuelles. Quand le genre du spectacle fait encore préférer la 'scène encadrée,' tous les efforts des architectes tendent vers l'adoucissement de la liaison entre scene et salle."

lie first and foremost in the very vehicle of theater, its repertoire? Do not the playwrights rather than the architects have the primary responsibility here? For theater receives its tension (and thus contact) through the representation of its themes eternally conflicting with the world as it is. Thus Melchinger states: *"Die Identität von Schauspielern und Publikum gründet sich im Widerspruch."* [78] It is rather here that we see the possibility of achieving a contact, and not in the mere technical solution of fencing in the audience like a herd of intellectual sheep. For theater derives its essence and lifeblood from this reaction, and were we ever to succeed, as the philosopher Reinhold Schneider observed at the recent Darmstadt Theater Congress, in transforming human existence into a solved equation, then the drama would be dead.

## V

In reply to a discussion question brought up originally by Friedrich Dürrenmatt at the Darmstadt Congress on Theater in 1955 as to whether today's world could still be represented by the theater, Brecht sent a short message from Berlin saying, yes, it could be represented on the stage, but only if it were conceived as *veränderbar*, as changeable. In this statement, besides being seen again as a revolt against the *Sosein*, theater is also thought of as a means of changing the world in a particular sense. As to the nature of this particular sense there can be little doubt, since the connection is quite evident with the Marxian idea that the philosophers have only interpreted the world, but that the task is to change it. Another sentence of the same message, however, abandons the general tone of Marxist doctrine given to it and gets at the heart of the matter. There Brecht concludes that in an age whose science knows how to alter nature to such a degree that the world almost appears inhabitable, man may no longer be described to man as a victim, as an object in an unknown yet fixed and immutable world; and a little further we read the statement: *"Vom Standpunkt eines Spielballs aus sind die Bewegungsgesetze kaum konzipierbar."* [79]

This puts the finger on the central issue, and also clearly states the dilemma; that is: can the modern playwright really represent this world of ours while being part of it? We do not want to drive home the obvious; yes, he can. Molière was part of his own world, so were Shakespeare, Goldoni, and Schiller. The question lies apparently with the artist's conscience. May not the "peculiar" way which he chooses to represent this world he lives in be a consequence of the knowledge (made objectively clear or not) that he also is a *Spielball*, a playing ball? Does the playwright, thus refusing to represent this world in terms of *as if*,

---

[78] Melchinger, p. 110. Melchinger sees *Widerspruch* even as the primary impulse of all art.

[79] Brecht, *Schriften zum Theater*, p. 8.

not state that he as a *fixum* is gone as well? And in doing so he is consequently interrupting the show of his *as if* world in order to question his own representation, showing in such wise the very questionability of his art, though still using it as a medium. Thus, the destruction of illusion, of aesthetic distance, does not appear to be merely a gimmick in the sense of the *épater le bourgeois* of yore, but seems to have a deeper reason and meaning: that of a *sincérité truquée.*

Thomas Mann clearly pronounced on this crisis of the artist's conscience[80] when he doubted whether the play of art is still allowed, given the present state of our consciousness, our perception, our knowledge, and our sense of truth, and whether it is still spiritually possible and can be taken seriously. Furthermore, when he questions whether the work of art as such, closed in itself, self-sufficient and harmonious, has any legitimate relation to the complete uncertainty, the problematical nature and the chaos of our social situation; and, finally, whether all appearance, even the most beautiful one, and exactly the most beautiful one, has not become a lie in our day.

The sometimes painfully felt emphasis upon theatricality, done often in such an obvious way that one at times has the feeling the emancipation of the means is being done for the sake of the means themselves, might thus also be taken as a defense of the playwright who by no means wants to be suspected of believing his own make-believe.[81] For a mere destroying of illusion such heavy guns are not necessary, for nowadays Fielding's Partridges are few and far between. The phenomenon of destruction of aesthetic distance may accordingly be the expression of an awareness on the existential level of the questionability of a specific art form as handed down to us by times with an outlook and relation to the world very different from ours. There may be more reasons for this change in approach, and there certainly are as with any complex phenomenon, but this one seems to us to be of central concern.

The playwright himself assumes his audience will no longer accept theater as theater, that it is too aware of the theater as being a "swindle," not real (and here, not only the play, but also the playing of the actor is involved). Therefore, the playwright too wishes to make known his awareness of the unrealness of theater by analytically dissecting it, by playing with it, or making fun of it; and it is quite indicative that in a

---

[80] Thomas Mann, *Entstehung des Dr. Faustus.*

[81] This concern was expressed directly by E. A. Winds, a German theater superintendent, in a Q and A discussion with Brecht. There, Winds calls attention to the de-emphasizing of the *as if* character of theater in Brecht's work as being important for modern theater since it rescued it in the eyes of the audience: "Denn es ist kein Zweifel, daß der Zuschauer und Zuhörer im Theater heutzutage der Illusion des 'als ob,' die von ihm verlangt wird, nämlich Schauspieler und darzustellende Rolle in ihrer subjektiven Ausdeutung als identisch zu empfinden, nicht mehr in allen Teilen zu folgen bereit ist. . . . Es scheint mir . . . eine Frage der Existenzberechtigung des Theaters unserer Zeit." (*Schriften zum Theater*, p. 238.)

great many such plays this aesthetic problem occupies a central position: theater within the theater. But by this analytical approach, by this making fun, by establishing a sort of rapport between himself and the audience rather than between his art and the audience, the playwright possibly still hopes to reinforce the truth of his story. Perhaps there is an effort on the part of the playwright to reaffirm the truth of art to life again by making fun of art as art.

As the situation stands, modern theater does its best to be "not debtor to the old" (although in some quarters it explicitly tells us it is), and it is yet doubtful whether it can be "creditor to the new." The spectator has been "liberated" from any fixed viewpoint, as the cubists proudly used to claim; yet his freedom has proved to be more of a "Greek gift" than one by which he is enabled to perceive new values, new values which always will have to be conveyed in terms of art. The basic relativity, heterogeneousness, and insecurity of these times should thus certainly be represented, but *within* the form of art and not as principle *of* that form of art. That is, in Brecht's very words, the dynamics of representation should not be mistaken for the dynamics of the matter to be represented.

# Piscator's Political Theater

## by Ernst Schumacher

The "proletarian theater" was founded by Erwin Piscator together with Hermann Schüller in March, 1919, in Berlin. Piscator, in his book *The Political Theater*, which appeared in 1929, emphasized that his stage had only its name in common with the proletarian theater of the "League for Proletarian Culture" under the direction of Arthur Holitscher, Ludwig Rubiner, Rudolf Leonhard, Alfons Goldschmidt, and Karlheinz Martin. This distinction was inappropriate.

The first version of the "Program of the Proletarian Theater" was just as Messianic and sentimental as that of Rubiner, Goldschmidt, and other left-wing theater people, while the second version proceeded on the following basis: "We banned the word 'art' radically from our program; our 'plays' were proclamations with which we endeavored to intervene in contemporary events, to act 'politically.'"

In the programmatic introductions and commentaries we read, among other things: "The subordination of every artistic intention to the revolutionary goal: conscious emphasis and propagation of the idea of class struggle." In all questions of style the determining question must always be: "Will the gigantic circle of the proletarian audience gain by it? Or will they be bored or confused and infected by bourgeois ideas? *Revolutionary* art can only proceed out of the spirit of the revolutionary working class." They derived from this the demand that the style which was to govern the actor as well as the author and director must be of a "completely concrete nature."

Whatever is said, must be said artlessly, without experimentation, smoothly and not in an "expressionist" manner, determined by a simple, unconcealed revolutionary purpose and will. Consequently all neoromantic, expressionist styles and problems and their like, which proceed out of the individual anarchic need of the artist, are excluded from the very beginning.

The proletarian theater must gradually be able to do without the bourgeois professional actor. The proletarian actor must not become ab-

"Piscator's Political Theater." Translated by J. F. Sammons. From *Die dramatischen Versuche Bertolt Brechts, 1918-1933* (East Berlin: Rütten und Loening, 1955).

sorbed in his role. He must make everything an expression of the proletarian idea. The author, on the other hand, must be "the crystallization point of the proletarian cultural will, the catalyst for the worker's urge for comprehension."

> The other task of the proletarian theater consists in exercising its propagandistic and educational effect upon the masses of those who are still politically undecided or indifferent or who have not yet understood that bourgeois art and this kind of "enjoyment" cannot be taken over into a proletarian state.

Here are contained in essence all the theses of the revolutionary "objectivity" (*Sachlichkeit*) which was to govern aesthetics and practice of the [German] radical left in the Twenties. First of all one can here point to the agreement with the international *Proletkult* group, that the task of literature and art lies in "direct action," in the organization of proletarian forces and proletarian life as a whole. A. Lunacharsky made the following restriction in 1919: "Art is above all things the organization of emotional attitudes of individuals or of groups, classes, whole nations, and so forth. Proletarian art is the expression for the process of organizing this emotional life." Correspondingly, as we have noted, the partisans of the "proletarian theater" in Germany had spoken primarily of the task of encouraging the proletarian feeling, of awakening it and developing it. In the *Proclamation of the Executive Committee of the Provisional International Bureau for Proletarian Culture* of September, 1920, we read, on the other hand, that the purpose of the proletarian cultural movement is to arm the proletariat with new knowledge, to organize its movements through the new art, to fill its life with the proletarian, Communist spirit.

A. Bogdanov declared in 1920 in his essay *What is Proletarian Literature?*: "Today poetry and literature are in any case the most widespread and effective means for the education of the urban population, that is, the introduction of the individual into the system of social relations." Correspondingly he characterized the proletarian writers as "organizers," as "representatives of the general tasks, of the *general* will of the community itself, of its *general* power." If the proletarian writer is intimately involved with the community, then he can become "the organizer of its forces and its consciousness in artistic form." In an essay "Art and the Proletariat" in *The Red Banner*, Bogdanov similarly called the artist an "organizer of the living forces of the great community."

These and similar theorems of the *Proletkult* group tended in practice to transfer artistic impulses (in the theater, dramatic impulses) into direct political action under the leadership of the literati and practicing artists. *The Red Banner* in 1919 already had pointed out the dangers of such artistic political activism. It wrote:

The mistake of the League for Proletarian Culture lies in its pretension of making a revolution by its activity, of being able to lead the fight for freedom of the proletariat by its efforts. . . . But the opinion that the value of art consists in being a part of the proletarian fight for freedom, that in other words it can replace the revolution, the class struggle, is a great error.

Piscator was one of the liveliest and most persistent advocates of the "direct action" of literature, and especially when the "proletarian theater" had finally failed because of the revocation of his license in 1921. Piscator used the expression "direct action" in the theater on the occasion of the staging of the revue *Red Rumble (Roter Rummel)* before the Reichstag elections of 1924. Thus it was not the primary task of the theater to create art, but to carry on political propaganda, as had already been stated in the program of 1919. Therefore Piscator pleaded for a "tendentious drama" through which enlightenment, knowledge, and comprehension were to be communicated. "Direct action" demanded a "revolutionary professional theater," the duty of which should be the political enlightenment of the masses (in contrast to the proletarian lay theater which was to penetrate the working class as a whole with propaganda).

But "direct action" could not be satisfied with enlightening the masses politically while they remained purely passive. It was necessary to include the masses actively in the stage action. The boundary between audience and stage had to be removed to a great extent. Piscator believed he could bring this about in two ways. On the one hand, through the stage action; by staging the masses, the masses were to be activated and enlightened. "No longer the individual with his private, personal fate, but the times themselves, the fate of the masses is the *heroic factor of the new drama.*" The intention was to show "the reciprocal effect between the great human and superhuman factors and the individual or class." Piscator called "the basic idea of all stage action the enhancement of private scenes with historical relevance." With this, Piscator continued, "nothing else can be meant but enhancement to political, economic, and social relevance. Through them we brought the stage in contact with life." That this view was undialectical is obvious. The private sphere, taken concretely, contains within it the "political, economic, and social" aspect, or, expressed more precisely, it is an expression of it.

But to the presentation of the masses on the stage was to be added the cooperation of the masses. This was achieved by the direction. We shall speak about the methods later. Piscator saw the ideal of "direct theater" fulfilled in the production of the documentary drama *In Spite of Everything (Trotz alledem)*, the content of which was the revolution of 1918, describing the fate of Rosa Luxemburg and Karl Liebknecht. This political revue was given in Berlin's *Grosses Schauspielhaus* on

June 12, 1925. The proletarian mass organizations furnished the audience. Piscator claimed: "The masses took over the direction." *The Red Banner* wrote: "The masses began to act, too," and continued: "The theater had become reality for them, and soon it was no longer stage versus audience, but a *single* great audience, a *single* great battlefield, *one single* demonstration. It was this unity which on that evening finally produced proof of the agitative power of political theater." Piscator expressed his goal as follows:

> The removal of the boundary between stage and audience, the hauling in of each individual member of the audience into the action first welds the audience entirely into a mass for which collectivism is not an acquired concept, but an experienced reality, when it is their distresses, their longings, their hopes, their sufferings and joys to which the stage of the political theater gives voice, expression, and form.

In this formulation, the danger of "direct literature" and especially the theater becomes clear: the stage and the experience communicated by it as a substitute for the collectivism lacking in reality, as a substitute for an experience of the masses which in the real world, in political life, does not happen even to the revolutionary party. The stage becomes, as in the bourgeois theater, a place where the inadequacy felt in reality disappears, where the negative complexes can be swept out of sight. The hard, weary skirmishing which is full of sacrifices and often seemingly useless is forgotten, and is replaced by a flight into autosuggestion: everything is going to be all right; it's coming along; we'll make it. It is the substitution for the real class struggle by the demonstration of a copy on the stage. It was certainly not a matter of chance when in September, 1930, *The Left Turn* (*Die Linkskurve*), the organ of the League of Proletarian and Revolutionary Writers, impressed by the real effects of this political art, especially the political theater, recalled that the proletarian class must concentrate its energies primarily upon the economic and political struggle. . . .

The dangerous tendencies which lay hidden in the theory of "direct action" in art and literature, namely the claim of being able to enlighten, mobilize, organize, even lead the masses in this way, had been seen by Lenin long before the First World War, when he wrote his essay *Party Organization and Party Literature*. As much as he pleaded for a true party character in literature, he stressed at the same time: "Literature must be a *part* of the general proletarian cause, a little 'cog in the wheel' in the one great unified mechanism which is driven by the whole class-conscious vanguard of the whole working class." To be sure, this essay was not published in German until 1929.

If Piscator saw his task as one of enlightening the masses politically and schooling them for the class struggle, then it was obvious that he should deal with contemporary materials. Already in the "Proletarian Theater" in 1920-21 Piscator declared: "My idea in those days was a much closer connection with journalism, with day-to-day affairs." He defended his "contemporary theater" as follows: "A contemporization of all mankind has taken place. . . . It [literature] must be real, real to the last detail, true to the point of ruthlessness if it wants only to mirror this life. But how much truer and more real must it be if it wants to intervene in this life as a moving force." And in another place: the theater in all times "stood or fell with its 'contemporaneity.'" The epoch itself, "the times themselves," should become visible on the stage. With Paquet's *Flags (Fahnen)* in the Berlin *Zentraltheater* in 1924 Piscator believed he for his part had "crossed the threshold from the theater of art to the theater of the age." *Flags* dealt with the trial of the Chicago anarchists in 1889.

But the content of the times is at its most contemporary in journalistic reporting, in documents. Repeatedly Piscator emphasized his close relationship to journalism. Now the historical drama was to be a "political document of its epoch," not "the tragedy of fate of some hero." Thus— as Piscator wrote—history does not become the background, but political reality does. "It is not the inner arc of the dramatic event which is essential, but the epic course of the epoch from its roots until its last effects are represented as exactly and as comprehensively as possible. Drama is only important to us insofar as it can be documented." Piscator claimed that it was from the document alone that the artistic effect obtained "at the same time an unsuspected intensification." Thus the highest form of the drama was the "documentary drama," in which "the connection between the stage action and the great historically effective forces" was created. Piscator considered the revue *In Spite of Everything* and Alexei Tolstoy's *Rasputin* of 1927-28 successful in this regard.

Here Piscator's efforts resemble those in Soviet Russia during the first years after the revolution. Piscator's theories were anticipated by Kerzhentsev in all essential points. For example, Kerzhentsev was also for a "fusion of audience and stage," which could best take place in a kind of circus. The audience should be included in the action as players. Piscator in his book *The Political Theater* also refers to Kerzhentsev along with Bogdanov, Diebold, Jhering, Kerr, and Anna Siemsen. But while Piscator was endeavoring to create mass theater in Germany in Kerzhentsev's sense, this movement had already passed its peak in Russia. In its place came the mass film of Eisenstein, Pudovkin, and other directors. If the mass theater in revolutionary Russia had a real basis in the masses, in Germany it remained a formal, isolated experiment.

The dramatic form of the representation of historical events and the expansion of every individual fate to a mass fate of the epoch was necessarily epic. The "epic course of the epoch from its roots to its last effects" could only be produced in a juxtaposition and succession of scenes and

tableaux. The dramatic form becomes reportorial. Piscator saw the first
success of the "consistent attempt to interrupt the scheme of the dramatic
action and put the epic course of the material in its place" in the production of Paquet's *Flags* in 1924. For the first time a play had the subtitle of "Epic Drama." Piscator said that Paquet had attempted "to lay
bare the roots of the case in the epic elaboration of the material" and
had represented the "essential social and economic background." Piscator
summed up: "Thus, in a certain sense, *Flags* represented the first Marxist
drama, and that production the first attempt to comprehend the materialistic motive forces." The "scientific penetration of the material" in a
Marxist sense could only be brought about in the form of epic theater.
To support the claim that "the communication of a certain perception
in the philosophy of history, as is provided by the purely historical
truths," can only be represented by a succession of stations, episodes, extracts, sketches, and tableaux out of history, Piscator referred to the works
and experiences of Döblin, Joyce, and Dos Passos in the field of the
novel and to Brecht as well as to his own work in the area of the drama.
This is not uninteresting, because here Piscator has unconsciously confirmed his agreement with undialectical, essentially mechanical materialism—with mere sociology.

The philosophical method of these writers at this time was mechanical
materialism, or the naïve realism which takes reality as its objective.
This view of the world hindered the above-named writers from penetrating to the foundation of the social process. Thus they restricted
themselves to reproducing the "thing in itself" as it appears to the undialectical observer. It remained essentially a mere description of the
behavior of human beings in certain situations, a spontaneous regis-
tration of social or natural phenomena, a journalistic reporting. With
even the most exact description of the events, their meaning still remained opaque. The method was at bottom naturalistic, except that it
was less primitive.

. . .

Now if Piscator similarly spoke up for the principle of reporting, of an
epic succession of tableaux and stations, of the accumulation of documentation, then this is essentially based on the same insufficiency in the
philosophical method. Like Dos Passos, who is his closest relative in the
epic area, Piscator was unable to grasp concretely the subjective factor
of history: the functioning, active human being, the Marxist class fighter
in a political sense, both as an individual and as the product of his class
and the class struggle. The sociological schematization made him appear
only as an abstract in this or that form—above all as part of an anony-
mous mass. The process itself is no less abstractly comprehended. It was
not the result of the action of real living people but something me-

chanical, which therefore could only be developed mechanically in precisely this epic, serial, montage form—not in a living way.

We cannot investigate here how Piscator, in his attempt to justify this
theory, could attract Brecht as he did, because first the methodological
means which Piscator used to realize his theory must be listed. In Piscator's opinion, contemporization and documentation as well as the epic
form called for "montage" in direction and production. For a "release
from the petrified architecture of the old naturalist form of the drama,"
for the expansion and deepening of individual fate into that of the
community of the epoch, Piscator required technology. "The new
dramatic principle with expansion of materials into space and time required an enlargement and improvement of the apparatus." Against
Stanislavsky's naturalism Piscator declared: "It is not accidental that the
spiritual metamorphosis of the theater comes at the same time as the
technical transformation of its equipment."

According to Piscator only an intensified application of technological
means enabled the overcoming of the political problems and their introduction to the masses as a means of agitation. Piscator went in for
the "autonomous acting scaffold." "With this construction we hope to
show that the problem of the individual's position in society does not
have to be represented separate from it, but that his fate is imbedded in
its political and social structure."

In this regard, Piscator had the support of *The Red Banner*. It vouched
for Piscator in 1927 on the occasion of his production of Toller's *Hurray,
We Live (Hoppla, wir leben)*:

> How can one in our age of proletarian revolution and imperialist reaction
> make a theatrical presentation? *Only* by exploding the previous bourgeois,
> private word-theater with the *application of the greatest technological
> means,* in order to awaken this age of technological achievement to life.
> Out of this political will of the proletarian, revolutionary director arises
> the *new content of the theater.* This content, which cannot be presented
> with the meager means of the traditional bourgeois stage, demands the
> *new form* and is working it out. Piscator's achievements as a director are
> determined by the new content, the new theme.

This critique was of course absolutely wrong. The point of it was that
only the director creates the play, as Piscator himself later formulated
it. According to this critique the content was to be found in the technological form of Piscator's stage, which leads to empty formalism, even
if it does have a revolutionary appearance. . . .

The new form first arose through the use of projections. These were
initially utilized in the "epic drama" *Flags* in 1924. Boards were set up to
the right and left of the stage. The text projected on them, according
to Piscator, drew the moral from the action, expanded the material
beyond the stage, and illuminated the background of the action. It

turned out to be a "pedagogical principle" which was used in almost all subsequent productions. From the projections came the use of film. Piscator differentiated between the didactic film, which instructed the audience about the material, the dramatic film, which was a scenic substitute, and the commentary film, which according to Diebold had taken the place of the ancient chorus. Through the film, according to Piscator, "the whole drama was lifted out of its original plane onto the higher plane of the didactic drama (tendentious drama)." The film was first used in *In Spite of Everything* (1925), then again in *Rasputin* (1927). Heinz Hilpert and Julius Bab in a discussion in the *Berliner Volksbühne* in November, 1927, declared against the use of the film in the theater, because it weakens the effect of the drama.

In *Rasputin* the segmented globe stage as a "symbol of the world" was used for the first time. "The *idea of the globe* became urgent in me, upon which all events unfold in the closest entanglement and in mutual dependence." In the segments, as they opened, various historical situations with well-known political personalities were shown. At the same time film strips commented on the events. . . . In 1925 already Piscator had used what he termed the *Praktikabel* as a basic form of stage construction—a terrace-like irregular structure which possessed a flat incline on one side, steps and pedestals on the other, and stood on a revolving stage. A further innovation was the moving belt which was used in the dramatization of *The Good Soldier Schweik* (*Der brave Soldat Schwejk*), in order to make Schweik's marches possible. Alongside of it the stage decorations turned in the opposite direction.

As far as the decorations were concerned, it was Piscator's goal that "in place of static decoration the dynamics of a real stage construction should take place before the eyes of the audience." The decorative element was to lose its autonomy by being included in the movement of the stage. Piscator reached this goal best, according to the opinion of *The Red Banner,* in the production of Friedrich Wolf's Chinese play *Tai Yang Awakens* (*Tai Yang erwacht*) in 1931. Here the "stage-decorations had been divested of their formal character" and become an ingredient of the revolutionary action. The stage constructions of John Heartfield served, as did the whole stage apparatus, for the "reportorial corroboration of the facts" of the revolutionary events in China from 1925 to 1927. In the production of *The Emperor's Coolie* (*Des Kaisers Kuli*) by Theodor Plivier (performed on August 29, 1930, in the Lessing Theater, Berlin), Piscator had used still another means for the fusion of stage and audience, of theater and reality. He directed "coolies" into the audience who then hurried upon the stage. Besides this he used a "narrator," who commented on the course of the Battle of the Skagerrak, which was illustrated by film diagrams.

These technical innovations, the efforts to bring to the stage the life of reality and to include the masses in the action were actually not as new as it seemed in Germany. Piscator only imitated extensively what Tairov and Meyerhold had demonstrated years before in the Soviet Union and in Germany itself. While Piscator still celebrated triumphs in Germany, the Russian proletariat had already turned away from this "unchained" and "dynamic" theater because it recognized that it was at bottom only a variation of bourgeois illusionism.

Just as Tairov and Meyerhold remained basically bourgeois directors, Piscator, in the rigorous insistence upon his will as the director and in the subordination of the play as written to the direction, agreed with the formal experimenters of the bourgeois theater in Germany at the beginning of the Twenties. He defended himself by saying that this attitude was not artistically but philosophically determined; indeed, he set his view of directing equal to "scientific analysis" in the Marxist sense. But his practice surrendered the theater to formal technical externalities. The "materialist" Piscator fulfilled the demand of the "idealist" Schiller, that the form must destroy the content.

The primacy of direction was shown most clearly by his treatment of classical works on the stage. Meyerhold and Tairov fulfilled therein the demand of Kerzhentsev for "deformation," a "direct distortion of the author's intention." Piscator is quite their equal, as is shown by his production of Schiller's *The Robbers* (*Die Räuber,* 1926), which was one of the false, superficial contemporizations well-known from the beginning of the Twenties (Ziegel in Hamburg), even if he dressed it up in a revolutionary costume. The purely mechanical compression of reality in and by the stage apparatus finally led not only to an elimination of the poetic content of a work of art, even to its destruction, but also produced basically the same reaction in the audience as was evoked in the bourgeois theater by other means and other subjects.

Piscator had proclaimed: "The theater should no longer have a merely emotional effect on the audience, no longer speculate on their emotional preparedness—it appeals quite consciously to reason. It should communicate not only uplift, enthusiasm, thrill, but also enlightenment, knowledge, comprehension." But, with the growth of the technical apparatus, the "furioso of action," which had called forth a "human shock" in *In Spite of Everything* turned increasingly into an intensification of the emotional element, such as the bourgeois theater in its way was no longer able to produce. Under the confusing impression transmitted by the technical stage construction and its functioning, the consciousness of the audience, especially the proletarian audience, had to receive short shrift, despite the mass of material to be communicated. At this point it is not uninteresting that Piscator repeatedly complained about the lack of support from the workers' organizations. This was due not only to a lack of means, but also to the fact that Piscator's theater was basically not a proletarian theater, but like Meyerhold's and Tairov's in Russia a radically left, petty bourgeois theater, which received its ideal support chiefly from intellectuals and working circles strongly interested in art, but obtained its material aid from the capitalists.

It is precisely the inclusion of the audience in the stage action, the removal of the separation between theater and reality, such as Piscator strove for, which made the illusion of the audience complete. For the spectator no possibility at all remained to think things over correctly, because too much reality, and indeed uncommunicated reality which had not gone through a real artistic medium, stormed in on him. The actor, too, did not have the opportunity to develop that inner distance from the role which Piscator considered suitable to the new age.

Before summing up, let us refer to a few basic pronouncements of Piscator which show the limitations of his Marxist world view. Piscator spoke of an "epoch of classicism" with its correspondence to the "great personality"; of an "epoch of aestheticism," which saw its "eternal plane" in the "intensification into beauty"; of a "moral age" with the absolute value of the "ethical"; of an "epoch of idealism" with its urge toward the "sublime."

To these "epochs" Piscator opposed the "fateful forces of our epoch": "economics and politics and, as the result of both, society." Piscator here has obviously taken over schematic concepts of bourgeois sociology and aesthetics and given them a vulgar-Marxist answer. According to him, history acquires a materialistic basis only in our epoch, but this in Piscator's terms is absolutely mechanical. The basic element of history, the activity of the human being, does not appear in Piscator's thought. Society is presented only as result and product, not as an active element. This coarse, undialectical materialism, which partly transforms itself into idealism, found its fulfillment in the following formulation: "We cannot allow either ideal, ethical, or moral impulses to break into the scene when its real motive forces are political, economic, and social."

In summary, it can be said that Piscator acquired the materialistic, dialectical method only schematically. This failing prevented him from really penetrating into the essence of the history which he wanted to represent artistically. To be sure, he used the terminology of scientific socialism, but numerous pronouncements and his methods of representation on the stage prove that he comprehended class history more as a mechanical construction than as a dialectical process. This proceeded from the negation of his original class position, that of the petty bourgeoisie. Recognizing and feeling the individualism of the bourgeois world as unfruitful, moved by the great revolutionary, collectivist wave which ended the imperialist war, he fell into the extreme of an undialectical view of the masses, and thus of collectivism. The subjective factor of history, the active human being in his effort to come to terms with nature and other individuals—the motor of all history—disappeared behind the sociological concepts community, process, revolution. In addition he had the genuinely petty bourgeois need to make himself the schoolmaster of the slowly, incompletely, and wrongly reacting masses, and of the vanguard leading them. The real socialist impetus which animates petty bourgeois people of Piscator's type, became an almost Messianic urge to instruct and lead the masses, which led to an under-estimate of the political organization and the fact that the true instruction of the masses and the education of the proletariat take place on the economic and political battlefield of the class struggle.

# On the Artistic Originality
# of Bertolt Brecht's Drama

## by I. Fradkin

Bertolt Brecht is not only one of the most prominent writers of the twentieth century, but one of the most important representatives of socialist realism in foreign literature. . . . Brecht's theses entitled "Socialist Realism in the Theater" (as yet unpublished) have been preserved in his literary legacy:

1. Socialist realism is a true-to-fact representation of life and human relations by means of an art derived from socialist attitudes. This representation facilitates penetration to the essence of social processes and stimulates intellectual responses of a socialist kind. The pleasure every art form should give—in social-realistic art—is above all pleasure derived from the awareness that society effectively determines (*meistert*) the fate of man.

2. A work of art, created on the model of socialist realism, reveals the dialectical laws of social development, the knowledge of which helps society to determine the fate of man. It offers the pleasure of discovering and observing the operation of these laws.

3. A work of art, created on the model of socialist realism, shows characters and events as historically determined, subject to change, and contradictory by their very nature. This marks a decisive turning point for art: serious efforts are needed to discover and master new expressive methods.

4. A work of art, created on the model of socialist realism, expresses the point of view of the working class and is directed toward all people of good will. It draws a picture of the world for them and reveals the tasks of the working class, whose self-determined goal is to show that, as a result of the creation of a society free from exploitation, human creative possibilities (*Produktivität*) will develop in dimensions unheard of until now.[1]

"On the Artistic Originality of Bertolt Brecht's Drama." Translated by Ruth Crego. From *Voprosy Literatury* (Moscow), December, 1958, pp. 70-79.

[1] I consider it my duty to express my gratitude to Käthe Rülicke, Brecht's disciple and co-worker, who placed a typed copy of the above theses at my disposal.

97

The above-mentioned theses require some explanatory remarks. First of all, it is obvious that they point beyond the interests of the theater. They have a broader meaning and refer to all kinds and genres of literature and art. It should also be noted that Brecht left us a rough working draft, not designed for publication in such a form. Several thoughts are merely hinted at in passing and can be correctly understood and interpreted only in the context of Brecht's other theoretical observations and studies, and the body of his complete works.

A good part of Brecht's theses define the most general characteristics of the method of socialist realism. Thus for example, he points to an accurate ("true-to-fact") representation of life as the essence of this method; to the educative influence in a socialist spirit exerted by it ("it stimulates intellectual impulses of a socialist kind"); its party-mindedness ("it expresses the point of view of the working class"), etc. But along with such incontestable features of socialist realism, Brecht's theses also contain some points of emphasis and definitions which, although they do not contain anything unusual or absolutely new, in any case reflect individual characteristics of his creative mind.

Above all, Brecht recurrently stresses in his theses an *antifatalistic* element. In his opinion, one of the major tasks of the literature and art of socialist realism is to awaken in people consciousness of their own strength. A man should understand and be deeply convinced that there is no inevitability in this world which predetermines his *fate*; that everything depends on himself alone; and that there are no powers (whether divine providence or fate) uncontrolled by him or external to human society. . . .

Arguing against the narrow fatalism widespread throughout the contemporary capitalist world, Brecht comes to the conclusion that the products of socialist realism should stimulate intellectual activity and lead to the *recognition* of the natural process of social development. The knowledge of these dialectical processes secures the people's confidence in the historical conditioning of existing social relations, and, consequently, in their *mutability*.

This confidence in the fact that an unfair social order and a world of exploitation and persecution is neither stable nor eternal destroys the power of fatalistic superstitions over the minds and souls of men and opens the road to social *action*. In this way, the art of socialist realism—this is one of the major ideas of Brecht—should inspire the aspiration to revolutionary reconstruction, to *changing the world,* society, and man. . . .

Brecht feels that socialist realism, aspiring to be an active weapon for the socialist reconstruction of life, can accomplish absolutely new social tasks never known before in the history of world art . . . by supplying the arsenal of art with new expressive methods. For this reason, Brecht stresses in his theses the need for *artistic innovation* as one of the basic and unavoidable features of socialist realism. . . .

. . .

Brecht stepped resolutely on the road leading to socialist realism in the second half of the Twenties. The year 1926 had a special, critical meaning for his ideological and artistic development. At that time Brecht's close contact with the proletarian revolutionary movement and the German Communist party was established. Having come to the conclusion that his future creative work would come to a dead halt without a firm grounding in Marxist theory, he enthusiastically studied the classical works of scientific socialism and in October 1926 devoted his vacation to a thorough study of Marx's *Kapital*.

In the same year (1926) Brecht laid the foundation for his theory of the "epic theater." The term itself and the initial idea for this theory were born in March; in July, its basic contours had already taken shape.[2] In April, Brecht reworked his comedy *A Man's a Man* for the last (the seventh) time, and it was first performed at the end of the year. Henceforth, Brecht always considered that comedy his first work which met the conditions of "epic theater."

It can be stated with assurance that the theory of the "epic theater" and the aesthetic principles associated with it, which from that moment were for the most part actually embodied in Brecht's creative practices, were formulated simultaneously with his active participation in the proletarian class war and with the study of Marxism-Leninism. If the Marxist world view, which Brecht approached at that very time, posed new social tasks for him as an artist, the theory of the "epic theater" was, as he suggested, the key to accomplishing those tasks; it was for Brecht a means to fulfill what he himself, proceeding on the basis of Marxist-Leninist doctrine, wanted art to achieve. . . .

. . .

In all his works, Brecht tirelessly condemns deceit as a weapon of the exploiting classes. A lie is always resourceful: it emerges in imposing dress, in a cloak of pretty words, together with skillful demagogy; it attempts to arouse and manipulate the dark emotions and instincts stripped of rational control; the lie is unselfishness itself, indeed self-effacing altruism, but when unmasked and pinned to the wall, in self-defense it calls itself a "good," "holy," "saving" lie. . . . But Brecht, dedicated to a sober and severe truth without verbal decorations and

[2] Elisabeth Hauptmann, "Notizen über Brechts Arbeit (1926)" in *Bertolt Brecht, Sinn und Form* (Zweites Sonderheft [East Berlin: Rütten und Loening, 1957]), pp. 241-243.

suspicious feelings (because of their "good origins") unfailingly exposes every pose of social deceit and the machinations of the most "ideal" lie. Every kind of appeal to universal, classless, moral categories, which soar above the "vain and earthly," always elicits from him an ironically skeptical grin and a sharp, infallibly aimed response. Brecht often clothes this response in the dress of parody. . . .

In the play *The Roundheads and the Peakheads* the subject matter of Shakespeare's comedy *Measure for Measure* is parodied. The landlord Emanuel de Guzman seduces the peasant girl Nana, who later becomes a prostitute and ends up in the brothel of Mme. Kornamontis. Moreover, a civil war blazes up in the country and the peasants revolt against the landlords. A certain Angelo Iberin, adventurer and demagogue, appears on the scene in the role of the "savior of the fatherland," propagates racial terror and blames the representatives of the racial minority, the so-called *Peakheads,* rather than the landlords for the peasants' misfortunes. In order to smooth over class contradictions and direct the people's wrath into another channel, he demonstrates the new justice of the *Roundheads* and sentences the Peakhead de Guzman to death "for the seduction of a Roundhead girl." But Iberin's right-hand man, the commandant of the concentration camp, the Roundhead Sasarante, promises to spare the life of the sentenced man under the condition that the latter's sister Isabella, a Peakhead, young virgin and novice in a convent, meet him (Sasarante) at night. Isabella is forced to comply, but by virtue of her innocence not knowing how she should conduct herself at the rendezvous, she goes to the brothel for advice, and Mme. Kornamontis advises Isabella to send Nana, whom "it would cost nothing," in her place. Protecting the honor and innocence of the landlord's sister, the peasant girl, suitably compensated, takes upon herself the outrages of Sasarante and a camp guard. De Guzman in his turn also finds himself a proxy: Nana's father, Callas, a tenant of de Guzman, agrees to go to the scaffold in place of his landlord, if in return he will release him from two years of rent. In conclusion, the viceroy, having returned to the country, announces the pardon of both de Guzman and Callas. . . .

The plots of both Shakespeare's comedy and Brecht's play are very similar; but at the same time a completely different syndrome of ideas is implied within the framework of two such similar fables. Shakespeare, the humanist of the era of the Renaissance, composed a passionate hymn to universally significant, lofty passions and moral concepts—love, honor, justice. He glorifies love as a feeling organically inherent to the nature of man, unconquerable, selfless, and free; he glorifies the honor of women, to which force or compulsion to love is the vilest outrage; he glorifies justice, by which retribution is rendered in full measure to any hypocrite or violator, however high a social position he may occupy, according to the enormity of the crime he has committed.

Keeping the plot outline of Shakespeare's comedy almost intact, Brecht parodies all its elements. Impure and self-seeking love unites Nana with de Guzman—blackmail on one hand, material calculation on the other. Isabella does not turn to a priest for advice but to the owner of a brothel. Not the loving, abandoned wife goes to the rendezvous in place of Isabella, but a prostitute whom she hires . . . and so on. And all these parodied situations taken together emphasize and strengthen Brecht's ideologically tinged message, the red thread woven through the entire play. Brecht refuses to recognize universal meaning free of class distinctions in the feelings or moral categories advertised in bourgeois society.

Love? A free, selfless feeling? Yes, it should be like that, but in a world of exploitation, where poor people can support themselves only by selling their labor, their skills, their bodies—in such a world even love has long since become a commodity, an object one buys and sells. Honor? It is all very well for the rich to talk about it. What could be a more pleasant complement to plenty of food, warm clothes, and a good roof over one's head? But honor cannot replace them. Impartial and equal justice for all? Granted. But, on the other hand, Iberin would have paid heavily if Isabella, a "well-born child," had turned out to be the victim of his lackey's lust. And why does the rape of the peasant girl, the tenant's daughter, go unpunished?

Such are the thoughts which Brecht attempts to stimulate and undoubtedly does stimulate in his readers and audiences by means of a reconception in parody of a traditional subject; using this method, he develops and sharpens their sociocritical thinking . . .

On the basis of the preceding comments a few conclusions can be drawn regarding the character and functions of the elements of parody in Brecht's drama. One should state first of all that Brecht's parody is a form of social satire, and its object is not essentially literature, but bourgeois society. . . .

Brecht's parody has nothing in common with the narrow conception of parody as mere "literary imitation." His parody has gone far beyond the limits of purely literary arguments and conflicts of various artistic tastes and styles, and its purpose is not at all to debunk this or that classic work. If Brecht in some way parodies Shakespeare, Goethe, or Schiller, it is by no means with the intention of discrediting or disparaging these writers (whom, by the way, he highly respects—particularly the first two. For himself he sets a completely different task. . . .

With the growth of bourgeois society, well-defined concepts of certain universal and absolute virtues and ethical categories (honor, justice, truth, the good, etc.) meaningful to all peoples and divorced from all sociohistorical conditions, have developed and been widely accepted. These categories have gradually become traditional and begun to be taken for granted as fixed and indisputable. They have been cultivated and propagated over a number of generations, with all the means for forming public opinion at the disposal of the ruling classes. And they are frequently substantiated by references to the popular works of the classics, which as a result are forcibly lowered to the level of bourgeois banality and triteness. Millions of readers and spectators have known Shakespeare, Goethe, and Schiller from school days but from standard reading texts and even more important, by way of monstrously sterile interpretations of the representatives of public education.

Brecht tended to borrow subjects so often and, moreover, to parody them because he found this a profitable and very flexible way to stimulate the revolutionary awareness of the masses. Forcing the spectator by means of parody to reconsider critically the common concepts which he has learned in school, Brecht leads him *"via* literature" to a critical re-examination of the bases of bourgeois morality and ideology.

·   ·   ·

Not so long ago some critics in the German Democratic Republic doubted whether Brecht was a realist. Six or seven years ago [1951-52] his name was often dangerously linked with the word "formalism." Indeed, is a work truly realistic which tells about people who live in a country not to be found on any geographical map; people who belong to two human races unknown to science? What kind of realism is it, when in one play a dead man is interrogated, and in another, Buddhist gods spend the night in a prostitute's shack? It remains unclear at least why the same critics were not suspicious of the realistic nature of *Gulliver's Travels* (in which horses establish their own state), *Faust* (with the help of dark powers, an old man is rejuvenated), [Balzac's] *La Peau de chagrin* (the length of the hero's life is determined by the size of a shrinking piece of leather), and so on?

Today there is no particular need to defend Brecht from accusations of formalism; in the German Democratic Republic the voices of those critics who advanced such incriminations have long since grown silent, and their reproaches have been replaced by the general recognition of Brecht as a remarkable representative of socialist realism. The reproaches were at the time caused by fear of artistic innovation, and the suspicion —peculiar to dogmatic criticism—of everything that led even to the smallest digression from the usual and "approved" formats. And really, what other reasons can there be to label Brecht a formalist if one does not consider experiments with new methods of artistic communication a formalist crime?

For Brecht, beginning in the mid-Twenties, it was always an inflexible truth that except for the innovation of ideas—that is, except for new, socialist content—there is not and cannot be real aesthetic innovation. For him the social content of art came first, and his creative experiments

—as we have tried to show in this article—were always directed toward meaningful form, that is, toward expressive means capable of communicating the new, socialist ideas of his work in the best and most organic way. Brecht criticized formalism harshly, treating it as a reactionary attempt to give life to the corpse of old, deceitful bourgeois ideas by means of rouge, powder, and other superficially formal, pseudo-inventive devices. "They have tried," Brecht wrote in an unpublished fragment *What Is Formalism?* "to make the old palatable again somehow, by way of formal 'renovation'; the shabby old trousers have been made over!—They're no warmer for all that, but they look nicer and warmer. . . ." [3]

Thus Brecht was uncompromising with formalism as one of the harmful varieties of social deceit, but he by no means considered aesthetic innovation on the basis of a progressive world view "formalistic" and did not intend to renounce new form.

There is an article by Brecht called "On the Range and Variety of the Realist Way of Writing." In this article he comes out strongly against the tendency to narrow the concept of realism; against reducing realism to a compressed enumeration of some kind of obligatory, formal demands; against its identification exclusively with the style of one or a group of writers, all similar to one another. "Realism," Brecht writes, "presupposes latitude, not limitation. Reality itself is broad, varied, contradictory. . . . Truth can be concealed in many ways and communicated in many ways. We determine our aesthetic, just like our ethic, according to the demands of the struggle." [4]

Brecht shows that such writers as Dickens, Grimmelshausen, Cervantes, Swift, Tolstoy, Voltaire, Balzac, and Hašek are all undoubtedly realists, but nevertheless all different. The experience of several of these writers—Brecht emphasizes—testifies that realism does not exclude the creation of characters and situations which are improbable from the point of view of ordinary plausibility, and that fantasy and invention are completely legitimate methods for a realistic artist. What is important is that reality be correctly understood and accurately represented. But the forms of representation can be various, and exclusive rights should not be granted to any one form, however good it may be.

Brecht's judgments about fantasy and invention as fully acceptable and legitimate forms of realism correspond in many ways to the thoughts of outstanding Soviet writers, masters and theorists of socialist realism—M. Gorky, V. Mayakovsky, and others. . . .

The artistic devices and forms of socialist realism . . . comprise the major and distinguishing uniqueness of Brecht's artistic style. Using

[3] Brechtarchiv, Ms. No. 03/040. I would like to express my gratitude to Wolfgang Pintzka, Brecht's disciple and co-worker, who placed the photostats of much material from the Brechtarchiv at my disposal.

[4] Cf. *Neue Deutsche Literatur* (East Berlin: Aufbau-Verlag, 1954[5]), pp. 106-107.

philosophical fantasy and invention widely in his work, Brecht often stresses the advantages he sees in these forms of art: they help the reader and spectator work out conclusions and generalizations. Brecht found these forms particularly useful in accomplishing the propagandistic and didactic tasks of the art of socialist realism.

Brecht treated his own works with integrity and responsibility. He was ready to rewrite endlessly and correct everything which concerned the logic of the fable or truth of the characters and accuracy of social circumstances. He listened to comments regarding these aspects with great interest, attention, and gratitude. But he was absolutely indifferent when historical anachronisms or inaccurately represented local realities were pointed out to him. He did not aspire to "historical concreteness" in the narrow sense of the term, or to everyday lifelikeness. "The action takes place in the province Setzuan, but it could take place wherever man exploits man," Brecht remarks in one of his plays. It is important to him that, even if they are not inhabitants of the province Setzuan but, let us say, citizens of the United States of America or of Japan, readers and spectators can break out of narrow, local-historical conditions and, for themselves, draw social conclusions and a motivation to act from the play. According to Brecht, the element of abstraction is necessary in order to fulfil successfully the instructive functions of his plays.

"Instructive," "enlightening," "teacher"—we do not repeat these words by chance. Of all the philosophical and artistic traditions of the past which every writer to some degree emulates and reinterprets for himself, the traditions of the Enlightenment, the traditions of Voltaire, Swift, Diderot, Lessing, and Goethe are closest of all to Brecht's creative practice and theoretical views.

This is clearly seen in the predominant role of the rational principle in his artistic method. Brecht in his plays, just like Voltaire in his philosophical narratives or Swift in *Gulliver's Travels* and *Tale of a Tub,* is primarily a propagandist of defined philosophical and sociopolitical ideas; he subordinates the choice of his subjects and symbols to these ideas. Like certain realists of the Age of Reason, he avoids—in order to allow the generalizing, deductive reasoning of the spectator to expand— the presentation of concrete, everyday details. . . . Brecht portrays ancient Georgia or China under Chiang-Kai-Shek with as little attention to ethnographic, geographic, or historical accuracy as Voltaire portrays the "Bulgarian" army in his *Candide,* or the countries through which the heroes of the *Princess of Babylon* travel.

The tendency to philosophical fantasy also links Brecht with the men of the Enlightenment. Like Swift, Voltaire, Montesquieu, and to some degree Lessing, Brecht often transfers the action of his works to exotic settings—India, China, Mongolia, ancient Rome, medieval Georgia, Japan, the goldbearing Klondike, and so on. In these exotic settings, the philosophical idea of the play, freed from the fetters of familiar and customary existence, achieves universality more readily. Subjects in exotic dress more easily take on the form of a "parable"—one of Brecht's favorite genres which, as we know, was not alien to the men of the Enlightenment.

Brecht's theoretical positions and his concept of the epic theater also, in their bases, approach the aesthetic of the Enlightenment. Brecht calls his epic theater the theater of the "age of science," and in that term the mentality of the Enlightenment is clearly felt. The principle by which Brecht turns the uncontrolled, elemental "emotions" of the actor into a symbol or an execution "from the inside" has its immediate antecedents in the ideas of Diderot's *Paradoxe sur le Comédien.*

Very often, Brecht finds a starting point for his theoretical constructions in Lessing's *Hamburgische Dramaturgie* and in the correspondence and aesthetic studies of Goethe and Schiller. A comparative analysis along these lines could lead to truly striking discoveries. . . .

Of course, the difference in epochs and ideas led Brecht to adapt certain aesthetic tenets of the Enlightenment to completely different ends; he put them into artistic practice in a completely different way and drew absolutely different conclusions from similar premises. For this reason it would be somewhat rash to identify Brecht with the representative men of the eighteenth century. Similarities as well as contrasts converge in the fact that Brecht is—if one can express it this way—a "socialist teacher." This profoundly original and unique characteristic of Brecht's artistic method, reinforced by his almost unequaled talents, determines to a significant degree that eminent position which his work occupies among the varied forms and artistic styles of universal, social-realistic art.

# Brecht's Dramatic Theory

## by Hans Egon Holthusen

Brecht's theory of the theater is world-famous today, but un-fortunately all too often misunderstood, thoughtlessly parroted and applied to literary phenomena which have little or nothing to do with Brecht's world. His theory evolved out of constant practical experience with the stage and with living actors and directors. Its basic ideas were already extensively developed at the end of the Twenties; they can be found in postscripts and notes to various plays of that period, for example, *The Threepenny Opera, Mahagonny,* and *A Man's a Man.* But in later years, sometimes in notes but also in independent theoretical tracts, they were extended, refined, corrected, and altered in a number of points.

About 1930 he put all his emphasis on the concept "epic theater." "The modern theater," we read in the notes to *Mahagonny,* "is epic theater." Neither the phrase nor the idea is original with the author of this apodictic sentence. When Brecht traveled from Munich to Berlin in 1924, the word "epic" was already current there in certain revo-lutionary experiments on the stage. Wedekind, Döblin, Paul Zech, and Alfons Paquet had prepared the ground for him. Piscator, long before, had begun to translate new poetic impulses into a new technique of stage direction. Epic theater was in the air, and not only in Berlin. Stravinsky's *History of a Soldier* had been written as early as 1918; Pirandello started at the beginning of the Twenties to propagate a new critical and analytic method of acting; in France it was Paul Claudel who, influenced by the Japanese noh play, developed, together with Darius Milhaud, a new operatic style in his "Christophe Colomb" (published 1929), a combination of reportage and discussion in place of the old form of pathos and illusion.[1] Brecht's theoretical achievement was that he was able to combine the different innovations which were emerging in various places, tie them in with Marxist ideas, and thus systematize them. In the notes to *Mahagonny,* a schematic table using key words

"Brecht's Dramatic Theory." Translated by J. F. Sammons. From *Merkur,* XV (1961), 520-531. Reprinted by permission of the author and *Merkur.*

[1] For details, see John Willett, *The Theatre of Bertolt Brecht* (New York: New Directions, 1959), pp. 106 ff.

compares the traditional, "dramatic" form of theater with the epic. "Experience" and "Conception of the World," "Suggestion" and "Argument," "Feeling" and "Reason" are contrasted with each other; whereas the dramatic theater "involves the member of the audience in an action on the stage" and "consumes his activity," the epic theater makes him an "observer" and "awakens his activity." The former treats the human being as a "fixed entity," as "unalterable," the latter comprehends him as an "object of investigation," as "alterable and changing," in short, as a "process." Of the reactionary stage one may say: "Thought determines being"; of the progressive, "Social being determines thought." From these ideological principles, however, follows a new law of form. While the dramatic theater believes in the "inevitability of development," epic theater progresses in "leaps"; the former sets up "one scene for the other," the latter "each scene for itself." To this we may add a parallel passage from the *Little Organon for the Theater* of 1948:

> Since the public is not invited to throw itself into the fable as though into a river, in order to let itself be tossed indeterminately back and forth, the individual events must be tied together in such a way that the knots are strikingly noticeable: the events must not follow upon one another imperceptibly, but rather one must be able to pass judgment in the midst of them. . . . The parts of the fable, therefore, are to be carefully set off against one another by giving them their own structure, that of a play within the play.

Other utterances of those years—of which the notes to the Berlin production of *A Man's a Man*, with Peter Lorre in the leading role (1931), are especially penetrating—are concerned with the "new art of acting" corresponding to the epic theater. The manner of speaking should be "analyzed according to gesture," and the effort of the epic actor should be "to make certain events among human beings striking," "to posit human beings as environment." The actor should not be "a single unalterable figure, but rather a constantly changing figure who becomes clearer 'through the way in which he changes.' " In place of "empathy" the demonstration of patterns of behavior under certain social conditions is required. In the expression "to make striking," not only the desire for a critical and didactic style is evident, but also the pleasure in the drastically imitative in its most naïve form. According to Brecht and many of his contemporaries, certain qualities that have degenerated through the centuries of classical and postclassical theater because of nothing but "empathy" and pretentious subjectivity, are now to be reawakened to life, by reverting to the original urge for play and imitation in the human being, who acts out before other human beings what he has observed about people. An element of the *commedia dell' arte* is to come into play again—sprightliness, drollery, improvisation—but not without a deeper critical meaning. The two actors whom the young Brecht admired perhaps most profoundly were Charlie Chaplin and Karl Valentin.

The word "alienation" (*Verfremdung*) does not appear before 1936 in a Brecht text. Not until the notes to the play *The Roundheads and the Peakheads* (*Die Rundköpfe und die Spitzköpfe*) is it used for the first time. This play, which is artistically not very important and which introduces itself with aggressive irony as a "fairy tale of horror," was written in the years 1931-34, attacked Hitler's racial policies, and attempted to expose them as a maneuver to veil the reality of the class struggle. It was given its first performance on November 4, 1935, in Copenhagen. The notes (undated in the Suhrkamp edition of 1957) contain a description of this performance, and were therefore probably written down toward the end of 1936. Here we find the following explanation under the key word "alienation": "Certain events of the play—by means of inscriptions, interpolations of music and noise, and the technique of the actor—should be elevated (alienated) out of the realm of the ordinary, natural, or expected, and function as scenes complete in themselves." A series of examples from the Copenhagen production follows.

The concept of "alienation" was not invented by Brecht either. It is a translation of the Russian word *ostrannenie,* which the aesthetician Victor Shklovsky, one of the leading representatives of Russian formalism, had already suggested in 1917 in an essay on "Art as Artifice," in order to denote the transformation of an "ordinary" or "automatic" perception into a poetically felt, poetically visionary perception. This essay has been reprinted several times, e.g., in Shklovsky's book *On the Theory of Prose* (Moscow, 1925), which is considered a chief work of the formalist school, and one may assume that even in the years of officially prescribed "socialist realism" the concept *ostrannenie* was not forgotten in Russia. In 1935 on his way from Denmark Brecht spent a short while in Moscow, and at this opportunity—so one may guess along with the English writer John Willett[2]—the word must have come to his ears and struck him as a brilliant definition of his own favorite idea. At the same time he was able to see a living example of the new acting technique in the person of the Chinese actor Mei Lan Fang, who knew how to produce a scene in a critical, aloof manner without make-up, costume or lighting. The predilection for the Chinese theater which had already been awakened in him was thus reinforced. How much he admired it is apparent in an essay of 1936 on "The Alienation Effect in the Acting Art of the Chinese." In 1940, in "A Little Description of a New Technique of Acting" he was to say: "The Chinese art of acting is masterly in its treatment of gesture. By openly observing his own movements the Chinese actor arrives at the A-Effect."

Alienation, in the sense in which Shklovsky used the word, denotes a

[2] John Willett, *op. cit.,* pp. 179 ff.

purely aesthetic process: an act of the imagination which, at least from the time of Romanticism, has generally been regarded as valid (more or less) and has been described by numerous writers and theoreticians of the last century and a half. Shelley, for example, attempts to describe the act this way: poetry makes familiar objects to be as if they were not familiar. Schopenhauer, Hofmannsthal, T. S. Eliot, and others have expressed themselves similarly. In making the concept his own, Brecht gives it a new interpretation: he divests it of its romantic, monologic character and applies it to the area of human society.

Brecht's purpose is expressed simply by rejecting the word "imagine" (*einbilden*); instead of it he prefers the older "portray" (*abbilden*). Reality, always understood as social reality, and art belong together most intimately; art is a critical reproduction of reality. The alienation effect, to be sure, is the most eminent task of art, but art has no patent on it; it can be observed step by step in social reality as a "procedure of daily life": "For a man to see his mother as the wife of a man," so we read in a note to the "New Technique of Acting," "an A-Effect is necessary; it occurs, for example, if he acquires a stepfather. If a person sees his teacher oppressed by a bailiff, an A-Effect arises; the teacher is torn out of a context in which he appears big, and transferred into a context in which he appears small." But art has the task of appealing to critical thought and thus to the will by the intentional production of such effects: "We make something natural incomprehensible in a certain way, but only in order to make it all the more comprehensible afterwards. In order for something known to become perceived it must cease to be ordinary; one must break with the habitual notion that the thing in question requires no elucidation." Here the disinterested astonishment of the aesthetically moved person has been transformed; he is trained to become dialectically alert with an essentially social concern. When Brecht says: "A thing which has not been changed for a long time appears to be unchangeable," one is to deduce that it can be changed as soon as it has been frightened out of its naturalness by alienation, i.e., detected in its historical dependence. It is not an accident that "alienation" (*Verfremdung*) reminds us so conspicuously of the concept "estrangement" (*Entfremdung*) created by Hegel and borrowed by Marx. Estrangement primarily and taken quite generally means the disharmony which always reappears between the world as it has come to be and the pressing forces of historical progress. Then, however, in its specifically Marxist interpretation, it comes to mean the state of progressive deterioration and oppression into which the human being must fall when he has no share of the means of production controlled by the capitalist system, sees himself degraded to a commodity, and no longer disposes over himself and his life. Alienation is thus no more than a portrayal of estrangement, i.e., making estrangement "striking." There is no doubt about its final goal: it is the removal of estrangement—it is revolution.

In the *Little Organon for the Theater* (1948) the fifty-year-old Brecht recapitulates the sum total of his theoretical insights and demands. Much that we know from earlier writings is repeated, sometimes with variations; some trains of thought already conceived in youthful years are expanded and deepened, others retracted, new things are added. By way of introduction the author speaks against a (bourgeois) "cult of beauty, which is practiced with a disinclination for learning and contempt for what is useful," and wants to have his theater understood as a "theater of the scientific age." In radical contradistinction to every idealist or existential, ontological or even neo-Thomist interpretation of the phenomenon of art, artistic achievement is here set upon an equal footing with scientific achievement and connected with the Hegelian-Marxist idea of progress. Art is in no way different from science—a mode of "emancipation out of nature into production"; it is the task of the one as well as of the other to make the planet on which we live "livable." "Science and art, however, are similar," so we read in the twentieth paragraph, "insofar as both exist to alleviate the life of men; the one is concerned with their sustenance, the other with their entertainment."

Science has the function of subduing and exploiting the realm of nature for the use of man, and recently, for about the last hundred years, of comprehending also the laws of social existence; art has the function of "involving itself in reality in order to be able to produce more effective portrayals of reality." Both assume a common concept of reality which will only admit that aspect of the world exhibiting historical progress. The idea which originated in Hegel's brain and was translated by Marx into the language of materialism should also rule on the stage and determine the gestic expression of the actor. "The actor must play the events as historical," Brecht had already demanded in his "New Technique of Acting":

> Historical events are unique, transitory events bound up with particular epochs. The behavior of the persons in them is not something purely human, unchangeable; it has obsolete aspects and aspects that can be made obsolete, and it is subject to the criticism of whatever epoch happens to follow. Constant development alienates us from the behavior of those born before us.

Development, progress, constant change of situation is the sense of world events: the playwright and the actor under his orders must "historicize" everything present, that is, make every situation comprehensible in its "historical relativity." In the *Little Organon* we find the concept of the "historical field":

> We need a theater which not only renders feelings, insights, and impulses possible—such as are permitted by the particular historical field of human relations in which the particular action takes place—but which uses and

engenders thoughts and feelings that play a role in the changing of the field itself.

This "historicizing" method is only another expression for alienation. The objections which must be raised by "bourgeois," indeed by any non-Marxist aesthetics against this schematicized view of the course of the world are obvious. In a reality regarded only historically, what has become of the mystery of the human individual with whom I can identify even though I am a member of a subsequent generation and live in radically different historical conditions? What has become of the "universal humanity" which clings to every immortal individual— which even after millenia is still directly manifest and moving? The young Brecht would have dismissed such questions cynically; the mature Brecht is too careful, too well-informed, one might almost say too learned to make light of them. In the "New Art of Acting" he attempts, in a clever, argumentative manner, to put even the "universally human" into an historical perspective. "Every step forward," we read there,

disposes of a step forward—precisely by progressing beyond it, that is to say, progressing over it—but uses it, too, and in a certain sense it remains preserved in human consciousness as a step forward, insofar as its effects remain in real life. An interesting generalization takes place here, a continuous process of abstraction. When we are able to share the emotions of other people, people of past ages, other classes, etc., in the works of art that have come down to us, then we must assume that we are participating in interests which are in fact universally human. These people of the past represented the interests of classes who led progress.

Not until the *Little Organon* does the author pose a question which is indeed quite difficult to answer in Marxist language, and it is this: "Where is the living man himself, the inimitable one, the one who is not quite the equivalent of his counterparts?"

The living! The inimitable! Can one—as a good Marxist—deal with it theoretically at all? From Brecht's last weeks of life remarks have been transmitted through conversations of acquaintances[3] which show how much this question disturbed him and how masterfully, indeed arbitrarily, he could tamper with his own theory when concerned with justifying the absolute predominance of the living. Discussing various questions that had to do with the rehearsal of his play *The Days of the Commune* (*Die Tage der Commune*), people very soon arrived at basic issues. One of Brecht's colleagues, Manfred Wekwerth, reports how much the playwright was concerned to save the affectively "concrete" aspect from the depredations of abstracting theory, and how well he himself

[3] M. Wekwerth, "Auffinden einer ästhetischen Kategorie" in *Bertolt Brecht, Sinn und Form* (Zweites Sonderheft [East Berlin: Ruetten und Loening, 1957]).

knew how to keep the abundance of meaning in reality accessible by means of a continual "dialectical" operation. "He spoke savagely," says Wekwerth, "of people trying to put the vital multiplicity, the innumerable shadings, the all-moving unrest of contradictions and absurdities into the same old slot." There can be no doubt against whom this thrust was directed: not so much against the "bourgeois" theater as against the wooden-headed simplicity of the Communist propaganda stage, here periphrastically called the "usual theater."

> Brecht noticed that I was making a note: "Draw a heavy line under *living*. There are blockheads who perpetually mistake the defunct for the living." He argued further that this stupidity is particularly well-entrenched in the usual theater; they have developed it into a trick of the trade to make a clean sweep of the irregularities, that is to say, the contradictions of a fable. But a place swept clean is also an empty place.

And shortly thereafter: "He considered philosophy relevant for the theater only insofar as it aided in a lively representation of social processes, no further." Philosophy as used here is of course only another expression for Marxism.

It is worth noting how a superior intelligence wrings a good measure of freedom from the cultural bureaucrats of a Communist regime—not by force, to be sure, but with Baal-like cunning. Of course, he could depend upon the extraordinary prestige of the Berlin Ensemble when he said, "There is no purely theoretical access to our manner of acting," and he could at any rate claim to be the better, i.e., shrewder Marxist. What was he trying to do? For him the "concrete" was always something "self-contradictory" through and through, and the sovereign contradiction in Marxist language, is called the "dialectical" principle. Brecht endeavored to make fools of the Marxist blockheads in Marx's name when he finally made the dialectical principle the uniquely valid maxim of his theater and reduced his whole theory to this one idea. To his friends he suggested the word "dialecticize" (*dialektisieren*) as a new, final synonym for alienation or creating epic theater. "The dialectical solution," he says, "is always the more vital, the more many-sided, the more naïve one." If people had believed that the dialectical or alienating presentation was an achievement of the critical consciousness, this crafty dialectician in the meantime had found reasons to declare quite simply the other side of the coin as decisive. "Dialecticizing," he now claims, "is in the last analysis a matter of feeling." What began as alienating irony now ends in praise of the value of the naïve. "Brecht was always inexorable against the more recent experiments of Marxist aesthetics," Wekwerth reports, "but now he caught it in its ignorance of the naïve: 'Those people seriously believe there are great beauties in art without the naïve. The naïve is an aesthetic category, the most concrete

one.' " Then is the naïve dialectically identical with the ironic? Or do
we have a new proof of Gottfried Benn's thesis that contemporary thought
is based on the "ambivalence of concepts," on the "fusion of everything
with its opposite"?

When Brecht wrote his theoretical summation, the *Little Organon*, he
had already written all his dramatic masterpieces, without exception.
He had accumulated such a fortune in practical experience that he was
hardly liable to allow ideological considerations to do violence to it
any longer. The whole presentation has a pleasantly relaxed effect; the
argument is calm, clever, and presented in fine, clear prose. The scan-
dalous genius of the Twenties has become a sage. His sense for purely
aesthetic values has energetically fought itself free and at the same time
refined itself; what he previously judged in terms of its dogmatic content
he now prefers to appreciate in its formal aspects. This is first apparent
in the novel definition of the theater as a "place of entertainment" and
of "pleasure," which is equivalent to a clean disavowal of his didactic
plays: "It [the theater] should not even be expected to teach, at least
nothing more useful than how one may move pleasurably, in a bodily
or mental sense." Here we are dealing with a formal retraction of an
earlier position: "Then let us withdraw, doubtless to everyone's regret,
our intention of emigrating out of the realm of the pleasurable, and
let us announce, even more to everyone's regret, our present intention of
settling in this realm."

The individual elements of the dramatic event now are also regarded
as essentially aesthetic phenomena. Particular emphasis is put upon the
concept of the "fable" (*Fabel*), which, unburdened of all contentual determinants, is described formally as "the totality of all gestic processes
containing the information and impulses which are supposed to create
the pleasure of the public." The fable, "the heart of the theatrical
production," is comprehended as an interplay of meanings in which it
is possible to control at will the degree of interest which they will gen-
erate; for the actor it is "in its totality the possibility of bringing together
what is contradictory, because the fable, as a limited event, yields a
certain meaning—that is, of many possible interests it satisfies only
certain ones." But the "gestic," to come to the second important concept
of this theory, is the "material" of the fable, or more exactly, it is the
area in which the fable is realized in scenes and materializes into action.
Scene and action are understood as an interconnected pair, and realization
considered with a view to the practical performability of what has been
written.

Brecht hardly ever speaks of "drama"—almost always only of "theater."
Like Aristotle, whom he enjoyed confronting critically, he wanted to
have the meaning and essence of the drama defined on the basis of the
"theatrical production," that is to say, of the performance. Max Kommerell has called tragedy as Aristotle understood it a "phenomenon of

life": the "why" of tragedy, catharsis, cannot be detached from its essence; only in the completed catharsis, i.e., the performance before the people, does it realize its entelechy.[4] For Brecht, although he had no patience with ritual purification, tragic truth and the like, the theater is still "engaged in reality," and is concerned with making "the portrayals retreat before that which is portrayed"; through gestic alienation it is supposed to achieve social effects, change the consciousness of the audience. But in the course of the years his concept of the gestic was also refined. The heavy-handed exaggeration which one could observe in Brecht's early plays (for example, the elephant scene in *A Man's a Man*) is no longer demanded; instead "elegance" is required, "strength and grace." The tone in which the *Little Organon* defines the "gestic area" as the "area of attitudes which the characters take toward one another" reminds one more of Goldoni than of the early Brecht. "The carriage of the body, melody of speaking, and facial expression are determined by a social 'gestus': the characters insult, compliment, instruct each other, etc." Everything seems to have become light and transparent, raised into an ideal and universal realm. The eternally imitative, the eternally comic is contrasted with the flat-footed triviality of "socialist realism" as well as with the clumsy "spiritual whey," as Brecht called it, of the bourgeois theater. In the sixty-sixth paragraph the author finally goes so far as to reduce the material content of a dramatic event to a so-called "basic gestus." Examples for such a basic gestus are: "Richard Gloucester woos the widow of his victim," or "God wagers with the Devil for Faust's soul," or "Woyzeck buys a cheap knife with which to kill his wife." "Basic gestus" denotes the core of a fable, explained as the "displaying" of a combination (conceived primarily in a social way) of "figures," although, to be sure, a purely social interpretation would be misleading— at least in the case of Faust. Basic gestus approximates the German equivalent of the English word "gist"—the core or main point of a thing or an argument.

It is true for Brecht, as for every arch-poet concerned with critical questions, that, strictly speaking, his theory of theater fits only his own work. Brecht is incomparable; he of course knew that and occasionally expressed it in mischievously provoking remarks. He calls his theater "thaëter" and the "gestic" or "alienating" music to be written for him he calls "misuc."[5] All of his work is to be different from anyone else's, a dialectical counterblow against the usual theater. In younger years, somewhat presumptuously certainly, he coined the phrase "non-Aristotelian theater," just as contemporary scholars were able to speak of a "non-Euclidean geometry" or a "nonclassical physics." He conceived his rebellion against the idea of fate as non-Aristotelian; in its place he

[4] Cf. Max Kommerell, *Lessing und Aristotles* (2d ed., Frankfurt-am-Main, 1957).

[5] Cf. Hanns Eisler, "Bertolt Brecht und die Musik" in *Bertolt Brecht, Sinn und Form* (Zweites Sonderheft [East Berlin: Rütten und Loening, 1957]), pp. 439 ff.

wanted to put the idea of a world made by men, and subject to alteration by men. Non-Aristotelian was his antipathy to the hero and the heroic, his crucially deep reservations about the tragic principle, his reverence for the "little fat god of fortune." Connected with all this is a deeply imbued resistance in younger years against the classical conception of dramatic fable. "A well-knit plot," so we read in Aristotle's *Poetics*, "consists in that it has neither an accidental beginning nor an accidental end." The young Brecht believed in a necessary course of dramatic action as little as he was able to believe in "fate." He insisted that one exhibit everything happening in a state open to discussion, that one must experiment with dramatic actions. Thus it was in his opinion not only possible, but even highly desirable, to write a play with two different endings. In *He Who Says Yes* and *He Who Says No* he gave an example.

By the time he was fifty years old, all of these views had lost much of their sharpness. Like other important revolutionaries of the early Twenties, such as for example Hindemith, or T. S. Eliot, or Karl Barth, Brecht, too, in mature years more or less revised the radical derring-do of his youth and sought a compromise with tradition. Thus in the *Little Organon* he speaks with visible respect for Aristotle and even attempts, with elegant legerdemain, to fasten upon him his own concept of "pleasure":

> When stating that the theater has emerged out of ritual, one is only saying that in the process of coming out it became theater; it probably did not retain the ritual intent of the mysteries, but rather the pleasure in it, pure and simple. And that catharsis of Aristotle, the purification through fear and pity, or from fear and pity, is a washing which is not only produced in a pleasant manner, but actually for the purpose of pleasure.

Now his unconditional attachment to the value and the sustaining function of the fable seems to connect him with Aristotle again. If one compares his art and theory with the theoretical and practical experiments of the so-called absurd theater, of the "antitheater" with its dissolution of plot from its youngest period, then he stands decisively on Aristotle's side. Also on Schiller's side, if you will, insofar as he agrees, as Brecht does, with the Aristotelian axiom that the "chief emphasis" in the drama lies "in the connection of events with each other."

In summary one may say that the theoretician Brecht succeeded brilliantly in connecting an historically determined *social* interest with a universally human *aesthetic* interest. "To entertain the children of the scientific age in a palpable manner and cheerfully": this, according to his definition, is the task of the arts. The system has its ideological rigidity: the social aspect is made absolute. Out of this rigidity its one-sidednesses, its blind spots can be explained—for example a certain helplessness before the mystery of the individual, the "inimitable one," above all, the naked incomprehension of all metaphysical experiences of the human soul, for which reason religious concern is listed together with the "expressions of bodily pain in illness" under the "private" attitudes (in paragraph sixty-one). It is well-known that an absolute concept of "society" implies an unconditional opposition to the concepts "being" and "existence," and vice versa. Two hostile conceptual languages have developed here which constantly endeavor to interfere with each other: one attempts to remind the human being of his trans-social immediacy to being, death, or transcendance; the other tries to expose the existential thinker as a mystic hostile to reason and progress, if not as an evil fascist, and his philosophical language as the superstructure of a certain sociological and historical situation. Corresponding to this conflict are two strictly opposed theories of the essence of art. If we listen to Heidegger, then art is "establishing truth in the work"; the art work "exposes in its way the being of that which is." For Brecht the proposition is valid that "truth is concrete"—a slogan which, painted on a piece of cardboard, he had hung over his desk for years. But for him thinking concretely means "turning things into history." Art, or more exactly, his theater, was to reveal the sense of historical, or more exactly, sociological and historical changes, and nothing else. But what in the theory can appear as total existential blindness and "obliviousness of being" (in Heidegger's sense), turns out to be in the poetic practice of the mature Brecht a fortunate dramaturgical principle for setting dramatic persons in motion, into conversation with each other, and bringing them to battle—people who know much more about themselves and their state of being in the world than is implicit in their sociological and historical situation. Death and love, nature and fellow feeling, and the unfathomable mystery of the world as a whole: all this is immediately given to them. To see these creatures act puts us in a position to *understand* an "historicized" process in a certain sense, as well as to *see through* it in a dreamlike manner. To use Brecht's own words from the *Organon*, it provides us with "the pleasure in the possibilities of change in all things."

# Brecht's *Galileo*

## by Günter Rohrmoser

There are three versions of *Galileo*. Brecht wrote the first in 1938-39 in Denmark; it was published by Suhrkamp as a theater script and performed in Zurich in 1943. The second, American version was written in 1945-46 during the translation of the play into English which Brecht undertook with Charles Laughton, who played Galileo in 1947 at Beverly Hills, California, and in 1948 at New York. Finally the third version, which is based upon the English one, was written during Brecht's rehearsals on the stage of the *Schiffbauerdamm Theater* in Berlin. The essential difference between the individual versions is the ending, which is concerned with judging the figure of Galileo, his submission to the Inquisition, and answer to the question about the beginning of modern times and a new age.

The 1938 version shows Galileo as an old man who outsmarts the Inquisition and, simulating blindness, completes his work and has the results smuggled out of the country by one of his pupils. Thus the cunning of reason triumphs also in the ethic of the scientist's political action, it is as far ahead of its century as his knowledge is, and causes a light to dawn in the darkness of his age. "I insist that this is a new age. If it looks like a blood-stained old hag, then that's what a new age looks like. The burst of light takes place in the deepest darkness." In the version of 1947 the last sentence, among others, has been deleted, just as in general the judgment upon Galileo has become harsher. Now he practices science like a vice, secretly and without any obligation to humanity. Galileo retracts his doctrines out of cowardice, and his contributions to the progress of science do not outweigh his failure to human society. Because of Galileo's failure in succumbing to sensual temptation, the new age, which emerges as a real possibility on the horizon of history, is no different from the dark ages of the past. Modern science, in itself an instrument of progress, transforms itself into a force for oppression in the hands of the rulers to whom Galileo has delivered himself.

"Brecht's *Galileo*" (abridged). Translated by J. F. Sammons. From *Das deutsche Drama vom Barock bis zur Gegenwart,* edited by Benno von Wiese (Düsseldorf: August Bagel Verlag, 1958). Reprinted by permission of August Bagel Verlag.

There is no possible doubt that Brecht altered his view of Galileo and the historical importance of his scientific discoveries under the influence of the atomic bomb, which was developed and first dropped on Hiroshima during the creation of *Galileo*. Brecht could not ignore the fact that the atomic bomb with its fateful possibilities was a product of the science founded by Galileo at the beginning of the scientific age. In 1938-39 German physicists succeeded in splitting the uranium atom; in 1945 the atomic age began to exhibit its destructive possibilities; and in 1945 Galileo answers the question, "Do you no longer believe that a new age has begun?" this way: "Quite. Be careful when you pass through Germany with the truth in your pocket."

In Brecht's notes to his *Galileo* of 1938 we read:

In the midst of the fast-growing darkness over a feverish world, surrounded by bloody deeds and no less bloody thoughts, by increasing barbarism which seems to be leading irresistibly to perhaps the greatest and most terrible war of all time, it is difficult to maintain an attitude proper for people on the threshold of a new and happy age. Does not everything indicate that night is coming, and nothing that a new age is beginning? Therefore should we not maintain an attitude proper for people heading into the night? Do I not already lie in bed thinking of the morning that has gone by in order not to think of the one coming? Is this not why I occupy myself with that epoch, the golden age of the arts and sciences of 300 years ago? I hope not.

These remarks are extraordinarily illuminating for Brecht's relationship to the hero of the play, as well as for the immediacy of the problem to which we owe its creation. It is true even in the earliest version that the perspective in which Bertolt Brecht views an event of the past is oriented to the present and its oppressive problems. But Brecht is by no means concerned with opposing to the night of barbarism threatening his own present a picture of an age in which, like the morning after a long night, an epoch of renewal and hope for mankind begins. For Brecht continues in his notes: "The symbols of morning and night are misleading. The fortunate ages do not come like the morning after a good night's sleep." Here Brecht is not only attacking the oversimplification of an image of history which separates epochs from one another like day and night, light and darkness, good and evil: rather he is questioning the total relevance to history of an analogy based upon a process of nature. What fascinates Brecht primarily in the historical problem of the beginning of a new age is the abstract aspect of a situation still concealing within itself all possibilities, and the courageous feeling of a man who has complete trust in the situation because he has not yet tested its strength against reality.

Beloved is the sense of beginning, the pioneer situation, thrilling the effect of the beginner's attitude, beloved the feeling of happiness of those who oil a new machine before it is to demonstrate its power, those who fill in a blank spot on an old map, those who dig the foundation of a new house, their house. The researcher who makes a discovery that changes everything knows this feeling—as well as the speaker who prepares a speech that will create a new situation.

It is clear that with these formulations Brecht is seeking a newly grounded ethos. It is to correspond to the spirit which animates the children of a scientific age, who in an almost sporting manner lay hold of the possibilities science and technology open up to them. This ethic is uninterested in the inner man and is directed completely toward the area where things can be made and manufactured. The satisfaction which this ethic supplies is the purely functional joy of being able to do well and easily what is possible. It is the ethic of the artist transferred to the area of technical manufacture and social practice. Technology and art have in common that they are both abstracted from a purpose determined by their content. They can be measured against this purpose, and indeed it is the reason for their existence.

It is self-evident that Marxist doctrine does not permit such a late bourgeois philosophy of *l'art pour l'art*. It insists that all forms of human activity—including technological and artistic activity—be subordinate to the Marxist's highest concern, the goal of the classless society. We owe Brecht's most exciting achievements to his inability to kill the artist in himself for the sake of blind obedience to the party line, and to his skill in extracting artistically the greatest use from the tension which resulted from it.

Galileo's life embraces a twofold responsibility: first to the work to be achieved, and then to the society to which this work is committed and which it seeks to serve. Can the two requirements be reconciled or do they stand in an irreconcilable contradiction to each other? If it is characteristic of a new age that society as a whole begins to move and the unquestioned oneness of the individual with its institutions begins to dissolve, then such a society offers Brecht an excellent model on which to demonstrate his basic propositions.

The shortest answer to the question of whether a new age has begun, which Brecht formulated in the Berlin text of 1955, is the one that causes the most torment and tension. It is all the more difficult to understand, as Galileo expounded shortly before the passing of judgment in his case:

As a scientist I had an almost unique opportunity. In my day astronomy emerged in the market place. At that particular time, had one man put up a fight, it would have had wide repercussions. If only I had resisted! If only the scientists could have developed something like the Hippocratic oath of the physicians, a vow to use their knowledge for the welfare of humanity alone. As it now stands, the best one can hope for is a race of inventive dwarfs who can be hired for anything.

But how does this obviously changing interpretation in the several versions relate to the artistic and dramatic structure of the work? If it were possible to interpret the play as a revue-like, "epic" chronicle striving for colorful details, our final judgment on Galileo's life would indeed be a matter of indifference. For then the structure of the play would pursue the theatrical goal of reproducing his biography as such. The same would be true if the play were concerned with the interpretive dramatization of a complex character. Both possibilities are rejected. In turning to history Brecht is concerned in substance with the basic historical and human problem of his own age, which he is certainly correct in calling a scientific one. Galileo does not interest him as a character, but as a case, although the individual vital substance of the hero is not sacrificed to an abstract scheme to the same extent as in the plays of a Marxist cast, the didactic plays. Galileo is "shown" in the concrete detail of his daily, even intimate life, because it is just exactly here that the characteristics clearly appear which explain his behavior in the great trans-personal, historically important decisions of his life. The importance the individual physiognomy of Galileo, who cannot be reduced to a social type, acquires for the answer to the question about the beginning of a new age (from a Marxist standpoint quite questionable in its estimate of the role of the great individual for the course of history) forbids us to interpret *Galileo* as a drama of modern science. From this standpoint Galileo would even be morally coresponsible for the terrors of the modern atomic age.

The arrangement and execution of the play permit us to interpret Galileo's behavior in recanting under pressure from the Inquisition in the sense of a rational cunning, which accommodates itself to the powerful only formally and seemingly, in order to be able to undermine their authority more effectively. For the fact that Galileo does not fear death under all circumstances, indeed is ready to face it if the execution of his experiments requires it, is proved by his attitude during the plague: he passionately continues his experiments despite constant mortal danger. He had proved repeatedly that he only judged the forces and powers of the world functionally, insofar as they were advantageous or detrimental to his researches. Decisive however is the way in which Brecht has Galileo's inner make-up determined by a hedonistic view of life and an obsessive joy in experimentation and discovery.

The new method is made possible by Galileo's driving interest in "alienating" the world, his childish joy in removing things from their familiar, traditional explanations in an act of amazed wonder and seeing them, as though for the first time, untouched and fresh from the moment of creation. The demand Brecht made of the theater in his *Little Organon*—namely, that the communication of the moral must give pleasure and that theater entertainment must instruct us about the methods in which the children of a scientific age acquire their sustenance—has, according to Brecht, entered history in the person of Galileo as a new possibility for the human being was realized by him. Teaching a new science in a new way, he practices a new human attitude in a world which he sees in a new way, a world which turns out to be both needful and capable of change.

Thus in the very first scene of the drama we read:

> On our continent a rumor has appeared: There are new continents. And since the time that our ships have been traveling to them, people have been saying all over the laughing continents: The much-feared ocean is a little pond. And a great desire to investigate the causes of all things has arisen—why the stone falls when one drops it, and how it rises when one throws it up. Every day something is found. Even men a hundred years old have boys shout into their ears what new things have been discovered. . . . Because where faith has been for a thousand years there is doubt now. . . . The most honored truths are being tapped on the shoulder; that which was never doubted is being doubted now.

Brecht's extraordinary closeness to the position which he expresses in these sentences is immediately clear. To this extent the life of Galileo is a key to the interpretation of the total phenomenon Bertolt Brecht.

The responsibility for future, unforeseeable possibilities with which Galileo is burdened is not only historically an anachronism, but also disguises, perhaps consciously, the problem of the play. The suspense, the dramatic substance lives on the open dialectic with which the question of the beginning of a new age is put. From Brecht's humane, even radically anthropological position the question of a new age is identical with the possibility of developing a new type of human existence and establishing it in the face of the resistant tradition. Time and man stand in a dialectical union which cannot be dissolved one-sidedly in a moralistic way. If Galileo had resisted the Inquisition and had been prepared to stand up for truth with the sacrifice of his life, then he would have been able to aid progress as well as reaction. The solution to this question is dependent upon another: namely whether—and how far—the new method and attitude to things already represented an element of general social practice. If it does, then Galileo's insistence could have meant *its* final victory. If, on the other hand, the new truth had not yet entered the general consciousness, then one would have to see a meaningful action in Galileo's self-preservation. There can be no abstract yard-

stick here, unless one were to judge *post eventum,* which would be
nothing other than making the outcome of an historical experiment the
basis for its moral justification. Only the atomic bomb motivates in-
ternally the judgment which Galileo makes over himself. The suspense
increasing from scene to scene is not immanent in the course of the
play, but is the result of the contrast between the possibilities apparent
in the described events and the actual outcome which contradicts the
expectations that were called forth. The scene showing the effect of his
step among his pupils allows us to recognize the method according to
which the whole play is constructed. The audience knows that what
Galileo does will be decisive for the fate of truth in the historical world.
Truth itself is not in question, but rather the possibility of its establishing itself in the historical process. Galileo—like no one else in
previous history—seems to have the chance of bringing about a turning
point of epoch-making importance. By letting tense expectation, triumphant exultation, deep depression, and shocked despair among the
pupils follow directly upon one another, Brecht succeeds in transforming
the drama of the historical decision into a perceptible scenic movement.
The "basic gestus" articulates with dialectical and most extreme intensity the meaning of this event which determines the coming centuries.
No talk of epic theater ought to obscure our eye for the mastery with
which Brecht forms the dialectic of thought. "Unhappy is the land that
breeds no hero!" "Unhappy is the land that needs a hero!" Set up this
way, the problem no longer permits of a moral solution.

Galileo cannot fulfill the historical heroic role in which his pupils
would like to see him, because he is unable to transcend, and hopelessly
falls victim to, the law of human frailty. He could have overcome the
limitation of action forced upon him by social determinants with the
sacrifice of his life. His pupils call him "winebibber" and "glutton" and
fail to recognize that without the joy in good food Galileo would never
have possessed the weakness of pursuing the vice of his thirst for knowledge so intemperately. That one person can at the same time discover
and suppress the truth, this contradiction is grounded in the structure
of a newly beginning epoch which must first establish itself against the
traditions. Its knowledge does not correspond to its ability. The church,
which here represents all authority but is by no means polemically presented, takes this inability into account.

One problem remains remarkably unclear in Brecht's play: the relationship of the truth of Christianity to the church which is supposed to
represent truth in the scientific age, or its relationship to the truth of
these sciences and especially to their instrinsic claim upon men not
directly concerned in the work of science and its discoveries. The question is not one of the truth of revelation, but of the conformity of revelation to the Aristotelian view of the world and the need to secure the
authority of the papal throne through this view. The historical Galileo

probably used his Biblical faith in creation in his fight against the presumptions of a formal tradition; Brecht makes no use of it, because for him the refutation of Aristotelian astronomy involves a denial of the Biblical faith in creation. "The heavens, it appears, are empty. People are laughing with delight because of this." For Brecht, the change in the comprehension of truth itself comes with the new method and its application, represents the newly discovered possibility of changing the sociological, historical world by means of revolutionary intervention. Since Brecht views the process from the end, backwards—from the atomic bomb, from the transformation of liberation into destruction—the reasons with which the representatives of the Church opposed the teachers of the new truth become more valid for him. The formula that the Church defended its order only for the sake of its sovereignty is too simple; instead history has taught that the Church hierarchy could be of the opinion, and not only out of self-interest, that it must protect men from the terrible possibilities to which they would be exposed on the new path. His undogmatic position permits Brecht to show masterfully a picture of the situation in which it is obvious how even the Church, in itself the force for the preservation of the old, acquires an interest in the new and cannot escape the force of the changing course of history.

A runaway monk—who, after Galileo abjures the truth, returns to the bosom of the Church—belongs to Galileo's most intimate pupils, and a cardinal favorable to the new sciences ascends the papal throne. Brecht, the epic narrator of the plot, who judges by hindsight, lets us know that at no time was Galileo's life in serious danger; bold, decisive behavior would have saved him from the torture.

What has Brecht achieved dramaturgically with this device? The event acquires the depth of tragedy in its perspective backward. Galileo's failure is based upon a false assumption; he could have avoided his renunciation of truth. If Galileo had been right, the catastrophe for which humanity was to pay with infinite suffering would not have seemed unavoidable. Brecht does not make an argument for a tragic view of history out of his insight into the objective senselessness of the situation. When he calls the attention of the audience to the fact that the tragic process taking place before its eyes would have taken another course if Galileo had been conscious of the strength of his position, he calls upon the audience to apply this consideration to the historical situation of the present. Whether or not this hope is based upon a false assumption is a matter of indifference for the effect of the play. Through the magic of the theater, the artful interplay of varying interpretations and perspectives changes the laborious profundity of speculation upon the philosophy of history into the cheerful surface of scenic and balladesque events. It is a triumph of Brecht's sovereign mastery of his means, that he does not need to interrupt the immediacy of the stage action with extraneous elements in order to make the didactic meaning transparent. The commentary has been absorbed into the text, and only the dynamic tension between the scenes produces the drama and its meaning. It would overstep the limits of our discussion if we attempted to show in detail how Brecht integrates the interpretation into the events so that the course of events becomes a commentary to what is happening. The pleasurable representation of thinking makes thinking itself a pleasure. The thesis to be demonstrated depends, to be sure, upon the premise that stupidity is the archenemy of mankind. But thinking does not take place in a vacuum that is withdrawn from history and its vicissitudes.

The abandonment of the traditional division into acts, the substitution of a loose succession of scenes which seems to be based only upon chronological order corresponds to the necessity of bringing together all the evidence which enables the audience to pass judgment on the case. The various and surprising points of view serve as an exercise in the dialectical way of looking at things which for its part determines the arrangement and construction of the scenes.

The artistic method which Brecht follows in *Galileo* does not develop suspense out of what is represented, but rather out of the relationship in which the mode of representation stands to the factual events. Traditional drama tends to concentrate on elements advancing the action; Brecht, however, assumes the "epic" narrative attitude of a painter of mores concerned with completeness of material. But the completeness is that of a prosecuting attorney who makes his plea for a just verdict. The oversimplified idea which people have of the founder of a new epoch and of the epoch itself is destroyed by new arguments stressing the complexity of the matter, and the members of the audience, called as witnesses, are driven to a reconsideration of the case, even seduced into it by the force of scenic suggestion.

While traditional drama developed its specifically dramatic quality out of the suspense of the process of actively and passively overcoming a given contradiction, Brecht's dramaturgy proves how impossible it is to stop the dialectic of the whole process by a one-sided solution that transcends history. It is not consistent with Marxist doctrine that Brecht permits his Galileo to be an individual, a "hero," and accords to him such a decisive role for the course of history. Rather, the part played by Marxist theory in Galileo's life is limited to the extent to which it calls attention to the truth of contradiction and its dialectical force in moving history. In the rest of Brecht's late plays, written primarily during his exile, he deals as a rule with truth as it is or ought to be, in similes disguised as parables. The playwright communicates morality didactically or narratively in such a form that the comprehended truth can intervene effectively in the world. The theme of *Galileo* is the process of discovering truth.

The dramatic weakness of the late plays such as *The Caucasian Chalk Circle* and *The Good Woman of Setzuan* is connected with their problematic relationship to Marxist doctrine. They are plays of great theatrical effectiveness, but are dramatic only in a derived sense. The exemplary function they serve in displaying the role that cunning and goodness play in the historical process stands only in a loose relation to the conditions of the concrete social and historical situation in which the events, which have been turned into a paradigm, transpire. The parabolic content consists in the transtemporal, transhistorical meaning which the application of the doctrine to any and all historical situations of man permits. The trial forming the center of the stage action in *The Caucasian Chalk Circle* has no contemporary referent, indeed avoids any and transfers the event into the legendary past. *The Good Woman of Setzuan*, finally, demonstrates the impossibility of being good and staying alive at the same time so impressively that one is tempted to look for the failing in the structure of the world itself. It is not a question of changing the world but of adapting to the world as it is. No process is set in motion, but rather a condition is revealed. The revelation of the truth masked in the parable takes place in sententiously pointed remarks which are directed straight at the audience, and justification in the dramatic action itself remains accidental and not very convincing. The question of how the possibilities of mankind relate basically to the necessities of history is not even put. But it is given in the life of Galileo. Indeed, one can characterize the real message of the play by saying that history is basically open in its outcome and that its course is exposed to so many surprises that the activity of man is needed if the destiny of mankind is to be achieved.

Galileo's failure illustrates a fundamental failing of the Marxist historical dialectic. The materialistic view of history is in principle incapable of producing an ethic of political action. In it situations are not foreseen in which the spontaneous intervention of the individual is required in order to give to the movement of history a direction toward the human *telos*. Galileo does not betray materialism, but betrays rather his humane and social intention just because he is a consistent materialist. This is the source of the ambiguous light in which he appears in the play. It can be understood both as an accusation and as a defense. The autobiographical substance as well as the unsettled question of the extent of the individual's importance for the outcome of historical processes contribute to this ambiguity. The contradiction to the official doctrine in which Brecht finds himself in this question (it is most closely connected with the moral heritage of his late-bourgeois origins) to be sure contributes to the aesthetic quality, but on the other hand makes it almost impossible to determine the specific character of the work. It is not a tragedy, because the final result of the historical experiment still lies in the future. It cannot be interpreted as history, either, because of its forceful contemporary reference. It cannot be counted among the parable plays, because the figure of Galileo and his fate are inseparably bound to concrete history. We cannot speak at all of a "didactic play" because the "example" has a character of inimitable uniqueness which is not transferable or even applicable. In a peculiar manner the life of Galileo unites all these characteristics so that they are metamorphosed into a new form of drama. The diverging aspects are unified by the double function of the dialectic: as artistic play and as a method of overcoming the world historically.

The inconclusiveness of historical experiments transforms the dialectic into a kind of artistry; and the fate that hangs over all events calls the artist back into history, in order to use the dialectic desperately, but not without hope, in the fight for the final achievement of a free society planned for human beings and their needs. The epic elements of Brecht's theater serve to regain the original drama of a man who refuses to accept passively an uncomprehended fate. He tries to withstand it by thinking and acting. Like a second Oedipus the human being himself discovers the solution to the riddle with which the sphinx of history challenges him.

Brecht's drama communicates something of the cheerful and courageous attitude of the Enlightenment which, aware of the regressive character of one-sided progress, holds undeviatingly to progress itself and its necessity. Brecht's theater is no longer a moralistic place, but a school and courtroom in which things are accounted for: what has been gained and lost is remembered and, above all, new steps forward are practiced. Progress consists not in progress, but in progressing. This is why the Galileo of the third version is right in answering affirmatively the question about the beginning of a new age. His sensuality was not the cause of his failure—it was only a part of it—but rather a lack of knowledge concerning the importance of the demand made by the unique moment. He risked his life during the plague and endangered what he had gained by submitting to the Inquisition when history was waiting only for a sign from him.

Brecht's drama is a question which becomes a demand. Who will make up for what has been let slip? Or is it already too late? The question might be asked of Brecht whether the truth to which he refers possesses enough authority to justify the sacrifice of a human being for it. This question seems to be the inevitable result of the play and of pursuing its problems.

# Brecht's Split Characters and His Sense of the Tragic

## by Walter H. Sokel

The theme of the split personality is a striking phenomenon in Brecht's dramatic work. It occurs in *A Man's a Man*. The ballet *The Seven Deadly Sins* and the two major plays *The Good Woman of Setzuan* and *Puntila* are built around this theme. Indirectly schizoid behavior forms an essential aspect of *Mother Courage* and an important one in *Galileo*. The theme of the split personality is one of Brecht's major devices for expressing one of his basic concerns. A proper understanding of it will shed light on his deep-seated though oft-denied sense of the tragic and on the relationship between that and his political utopianism.

According to Martin Esslin, the theme of the split personality expresses a conflict in Brecht between reason and instinct, prudent self-preservation and romantic self-abandonment. This conflict provides the creative tension nourishing his work. Brecht, according to Esslin, was in both camps simultaneously, and his fundamental ambivalence serves as a clue to his entire personality. Esslin's brief analysis supplies a starting point from which we can push further the exploration of the problem of the split character and its relation to the sense of the tragic, to utopianism, and Communism in Brecht's mature work. The plays of his mature period in which schizophrenia, or more accurately the splitting of the self, forms the basic pattern will provide the material for our investigation.

Shen Te, the good woman of Setzuan, invents the person of her cousin Shui Ta, a hard-hearted, level-headed businessman, whose guise she assumes from time to time, even as the civilized Dr. Jekyll turns into the monstrous Mr. Hyde. As Shen Te she cannot bear the sight of suffering and shares her possessions with the poor whom she allows to exploit her. Her goodness is not a moral duty but a spontaneous expression of her nature. For her to be kind is pleasurable, to be unkind

"Brecht's Split Characters and His Sense of the Tragic." From the forthcoming book by Walter H. Sokel on problems of modern German literature, to be published in Munich. Printed by permission of the author.

is effort and pain. As for Brecht generally, goodness is here identical with the pleasure principle. However, in contrast to Freud, Brecht aligns morality with pleasure. Morality is altruism and generosity, and these do not result from the conquest of selfishness. On the contrary, they are the spontaneous outflow of human instinct. For human beings it is an easy thing to be good. Conversely, evil, meanness, ruthlessness involve effort and self-conquest; they are difficult to achieve because they fly in the face of human nature.

Brecht's vision stands in striking contrast not only to Freudian but to the traditional and conventional view of morality in general. In it egotism is strenuous to assert and involves self-sacrifice, while altruism is simple self-fulfillment.

Brecht opposes to the pleasure principle not the demands of morality —these are consonant with pleasure—but the necessity of self-preservation or, in Freudian terms, the reality principle. He effects a new twist in the old conflict between desire and duty characteristic of classical French and German drama. In the classical drama desire or the natural caters to the self and its passions while duty demands sacrifice of the self to the law of altruism and humanity. In the Brechtian play desire serves humanity as well as the self and its passions, but duty or restraint is exercised to help the self survive. Shen Te would like to give all her possessions away to make everyone happy because her nature thrives on giving. But her other self Shui Ta is compelled to be calculating, mean, and profit-minded in order to save Shen Te's property and thereby to make it possible for her to indulge her generosity in the future. As Shui Ta she denies her nature, in order to fulfill it as Shen Te. As Shui Ta she must exploit and deceive her lover, to whom—as Shen Te— she gives herself without reservations. As Shui Ta she adjusts to and manipulates her environment which victimizes Shen Te. As Shui Ta she assures her survival which Shen Te recklessly endangers. As Shui Ta she safeguards her livelihood but cripples her life; as Shen Te she fulfills her life but forfeits her livelihood. Making a living swallows living; livelihood devours life. The means defeat the end they are to serve.

This is the Brechtian sense of tragedy. It is expressed in the schizophrenia of his split characters, and Mr. Peachum sums it up in *The Threepenny Opera*:

> Who would not like to be a good and kindly person?
> . . . But circumstance won't have it so!

The natural instinct of man to be good, kind, generous, loving, free and easy is constantly thwarted by circumstances, by the harsh necessities of survival in a competitive world.

The tragic element in Brecht appears in two guises: as the inevitable clash between desire and fact and as the paradox of ends and means.

These are two sides of the same coin. Shen Te's wish to be generous must employ Shui Ta's profiteering meanness, or else she would be deprived of the means to be good. Her calculating self alone can insure the survival of her charitable self. For, left alone with her goodness, she would soon squander her money and become a pauper. Helpless to do good she would also cease to be good. Brecht holds with Aristotle that only in action can morality be realized. However, by trying to protect the means for the exercise of her goodness Shen Te must transform herself into the heartless entrepreneur and hated exploiter Shui Ta and so cease to be good. Praised by gods and men for her goodness as Shen Te, she stands accused of cruelty and wickedness as Shui Ta. Yet without Shui Ta's cruelty Shen Te's goodness would be completely ineffectual and therefore nonexistent. In order to realize his goodness man must renounce his goodness. His tragedy is that he can never effectively be what he naturally is.

This tragic dilemma appears in Brecht's play in three forms: generosity and sympathy toward all fellow men; sexual love as spontaneous affection and surrender without questions asked; and maternal love. As Shui Ta she knows the worthlessness of her charming but rascally lover Sun. But with her emotional feminine self, as Shen Te, she cannot give up the physical passion and tenderness that bind her to him. In Shen Te's love the drive for self-fulfillment and the need for self-preservation clash in hopeless combat that can never be decided.

As an expectant mother Shen Te affirms Shui Ta's ruthless capitalist career. Precisely because she loves her child she must deny herself pity and consideration of the children of others. She must assure the security of her own child and therefore turn her back on the misery of other children. This tragic dilemma is clearly imposed by society. Social conditions twist the natural goodness of human beings into its opposite. Shen Te's first thought as an expectant mother is to picture her son as a pioneer and benefactor of mankind. But the shock of seeing a child searching for food in the garbage cans makes her resolved that her child must be spared the lot of want and poverty. She vows to marshal the ferocity of a tigress to protect her child in this cruel and competitive world. And so Shen Te changes more resolutely than ever into Shui Ta.

Yet the schizophrenic split not only cripples and distorts human nature; it is futile in the bargain. It is inadequate and doomed to heartache and failure. Shen Te seeks to make sure that her son will never know of her other self, Shui Ta. She is deeply ashamed of this other side of her self. But it is this odious and despised Shui Ta self that has to secure the foundations for her child's happiness. Her child is to know nothing of Shui Ta. Thereby Shen Te denies the true understanding of reality to the very child whom she wishes to raise as a future hero and leader of mankind. He is to grow up in ignorance of the true nature of his mother, who withholds from him one half of her self and indeed the effective, functioning, providing part of her self. He is condemned to grow up ignorant of the means that are to secure his own life, ignorant of reality itself.

Consequently, the split imposed on Shen Te is more than a split between goodness and meanness, generosity and egotism, expansiveness and self-contraction, spontaneity and calculation, end and means. It is a division between intelligence and stupidity, understanding and ignorance. A dialectical reversal takes place. The calculating rationality of Shui Ta leads to its opposite—ignorance and irrational myth-making. Shui Ta who embodies the rational self of Shen Te must be concealed from sight. Rationality is hidden beneath a myth that denies its existence. Thus a split within human consciousness, within the awareness and understanding of the world becomes necessary. Ashamed of our acts, our feelings pretend that our acts do not exist. The life and happiness of the new generation is to rest on a fraud. The myth of a world without Shui Ta, i.e., without exploitation, competition, and evil is to hide reality from Shen Te's offspring. Reality is prettified; a fraud is perpetrated for the sake of love. Instead of coming to grips with the tragic problem of human life Shen Te decrees that there is no problem.

When she contemplates resorting to the idealizing fraud against her own child, Shen Te joins the ideology of the gods in the play. In these gods Brecht satirizes the fraudulence and self-deception of idealism divorced from action. The gods acquit Shen Te of the crimes of Shui Ta and proclaim her moral victory. Their verdict is that Shen Te, despite her split, is truly good. Yet this well-meaning and high-sounding confirmation is meaningless, since Shen Ta has to remain on earth and continue to face the dilemma of condemning goodness to impotence and wiping it out in the process of making it potent. The choice between defeat and self-defeat will continue to plague the good person. The gods have only two answers to this dilemma, neither of which is a true answer: the moral imperative "be good" which is empty of content since it fails to take notice of the all-important question of how the command is to be implemented; and the rosy clouds on which, in the end, they escape from mortal view, while down on earth distraught Shen Te lifts her arms despairingly after them.

Shen Te, unlike Puntila and Mother Courage, realizes the futility of self-deception. Unlike the gods on whom Brecht pours his sarcasm she is unable to preserve the utopian optimism which ignores the split between good intentions and evil means. Shen Te cannot, in the end, share the ideology of the gods that she herself had hoped to foist on her son —the ideology of idealism which evades and suppresses the truth. Because Shen Te does not succumb to the fraudulent idealism of the gods she, unlike them, is not a comic but a tragic figure. In her final despairing gesture she represents humanity in its tragic greatness: impotent, helplessly caught in the web of circumstances, in the perennial frustration of human aspirations, but honestly facing the truth instead of hiding behind make-believe, and therefore great.

In *Puntila* the relationship between the split personality and tragedy differs only slightly from that in *The Good Woman of Setzuan*. Puntila, the Finnish estate owner, generous, charming, ebullient, kind and witty when drunk, but tight-fisted, dry, stiff, unfriendly, and dull when sober is like Shen Te a character with tragic overtones. He desperately wants to be good, kindly, spontaneous, friends with everyone. He wants to live free of conventions and class distinctions by the pure exercise of his innate human vitality and conviviality. The conditional in Mr. Peachum's question, "Who would not like to be a good and kindly person?" applies to Puntila even more than to Shen Te. For Shen Te is good but has to act cruelly, while Puntila would like to be good and can achieve his wish only in the utopian state of intoxication. Shen Te's tragedy is that she cannot be in action what she is by nature. Puntila's dilemma is that he cannot be at all what he wishes to be, except in moments of drunken escape.

The reason for Puntila's frustration is circumstance—but circumstance that has shaped character so completely that the two have become one. Puntila is so thoroughly the product of his class, with its conventions and economic interests, that he can be freely human only in his fantasy world under the influence of liquor. Written in 1940, about one year after *The Good Woman of Setzuan*, *Puntila* reverses the relationship between the two sides of the split personality in the earlier play. Kindness, which in Shen Te is human nature, appears in *Puntila* as a mere wish dream of drunken sentimentality, while meanness, in Shui Ta a requirement imposed by circumstances, is in *Puntila* equated with human nature. The underlying assumptions of *Puntila* no longer call Rousseau to mind, but Marx. In *Puntila* human nature is not a given endowment but a product of class conditions and social circumstances. The universally human spontaneity, good fellowship, and expansiveness exist only as a romantic dream that can never come true (at any rate not without a radical change of social institutions).

On this impossibility, however, on the unreal utopian quality of human goodness, both plays are agreed. In the final analysis Shen Te too can merely *wish* to be good. For Brecht, as for Aristotle, ethics is defined by action, and being denied the possibility of doing good without the debilitating compromise with evil Shen Te like Puntila cannot *be* good. Ultimately Shen Te's tragedy and Puntila's dilemma are the same—the permanent frustration of the wish to be truly human. The same holds true of Mother Courage, who because of her material circumstances cannot fulfill her natural maternal love and has to sacrifice her children's lives to her livelihood.

In *Puntila* the permanent and tragic failure to realize one's human potential appears as Puntila's failure to break through the wall of human isolation to a friendship outside and beyond the barriers of class and status. Puntila woos his chauffeur Matti and craves for his friendship. He fails because the walls of class interest prove to be the true condition of man. When Puntila is sober he is a class snob and exploiter, and the thought of friendship with his chauffeur appears absurd to him. Conversely, too, to Matti's class-conscious rationality the intoxicated Puntila's romantic enthusiasms appear unreal and ridiculous. The practical impossibility, the purely romantic and imaginary nature, of the master's wish for human fraternity and unconditioned love, is shown most vividly when Puntila seeks to marry his daughter Eva to Matti. Eva, though romantically in love with the chauffeur, could never be a good and useful wife to him, because her class education and background have made her incapable of performing the chores which the wife of a working man has to perform.

The tragic element in *Puntila* does not lie in human reason, which on both sides accepts the class conflict as inevitable, but in the aspirations, the emotions, the wish dreams of men and women. The drunken Puntila longs for Matti's friendship, but his outstretched arms are not accepted by his realistic chauffeur, who knows that Puntila's circumstances are stronger than his dream. Eva's sexual craving for Matti's manliness and Puntila's brides, who against their reason wish to believe in the drunken lord's promises of love only to be rebuffed in grim and sober reality, supply variations of Puntila's own tragedy. The dream of human goodness and fraternity remains fantastic and utopian on the Finnish estate as in Mr. Peachum's London slums, in Shen Te's poverty-stricken China as in Mother Courage's war-ravaged Europe.

The tragic element in Brecht's plays seems to be brought about by social circumstances. The plays imply the possibility of a nontragic world, which a fundamental change of circumstances might attain. Brecht found Marxist Communism to be the instrument of such a change. *Puntila* ends with Matti's refusal to have any dealing with the ruling class. Only the elimination of the class society can provide the foundation for genuinely human relationships. Here seems to lie the clear Brechtian answer to the tragic split between human aspirations and circumstances. The revolution will achieve the dream of human goodness.

Yet is Brecht's answer really so clear beneath the surface? Is it as simple as it appears? Matti's tough unsentimental Marxist simplicity offers as little comfort to Puntila's dilemma as the gods offer to Shen Te. Puntila remains pathetic and Shen Te remains tragic. We see the tragic element in Puntila less clearly than in Shen Te because the automatism with which he changes from one side of his split self to the other is grotesque and lacks the dignity and nobility which the lucid awareness of her dilemma bestow on Shen Te. Yet, like Shen Te and

Mother Courage, Puntila partakes of the tragic because he himself forever defeats his deepest wish. Even as Shen Te in the guise of Shui Ta defeats herself, and Courage the businesswoman defeats Courage the mother, so the sober, practical estate owner and boss Puntila forever defeats the drunken, genial, quixotic Puntila's search for human brotherhood.

Brecht's plays of the split character are akin to Greek tragedies, insofar as they show an external necessity acting in and by the individual as a destructive barrier to his desire. The threat of starvation forces Mother Courage to support a war which devours her children one by one. Like the fate in Greek tragedy, economic necessity leaves her a desolate Niobe in the end. Yet this economic fate worked through her own actions. If Puntila realized his utopian longings in earnest he would be unable to run an efficient estate and keep his family's financial and social position. The necessity of status frustrates the cravings of his natural self. Matti never ceases to point out the quixotic nature of Puntila's dreams, and if Puntila were not split, but permanently drunk, he would be another Don Quixote with class-conscious Matti as his Sancho Panza. The necessity of choosing Shui Ta's means defeats Shen Te's ends. In all these cases one pattern of Greek tragedy prevails: Necessity, the condition of human existence, defeats the aspirations, nobility, and greatness of man. The split nature of his protagonists serves Brecht as his device for presenting this tragic pattern.

Our analysis has now come up against an interesting contradiction between Brechtian practice and theory. In his practice as a playwright one discovers strong affinities to the oldest form of tragedy. In his theory Brecht consistently attacked "the Aristotelian theater," i.e., the whole Attic tradition of tragedy to which his own plays show remarkable similarities. How can we account for this contradiction?

First we must remember that Brecht the theoretician ignored the tragic and heroic elements which inspired Brecht the poet and playwright. The tragic and heroic vein in Brecht results not only in such unforgettable creations as Mother Courage, Kattrin, her daughter, Shen Te, Puntila, but it also enabled him to write the one classic tragedy of Communism which world literature possesses: *The Measures Taken*. Secondly, however, there are at least three fundamental features which distinguish Brechtian plays from classical tragedies.

1. Brecht does not involve the spectator in the plot of his plays to the same extent that classical drama involves him. Classical dramas build up to a tragic fall or denouement. The plot keeps the spectator in suspense, and in it the chief meaning of the play is to be found. In Brecht's plays the plot loses its central importance. There is in these plays neither a development toward the tragic event, as in *Macbeth*, nor a development toward a tragic revelation, as in *Oedipus*. Instead Brecht demonstrates a tragic situation; he holds it up to our inspection. Of all Brecht's plays

*Mother Courage,* by its structure, comes closest to the traditional pattern of European tragedy.

2. Brecht does not present the tragic individual and the tragic instance or particular fate with which the spectator identifies and which moves him to pity and fear. Instead he presents the tragic case, the tragic problem *per se,* which the spectator is to understand, to reflect upon, to draw conclusions from. Brecht's theoretical writings lead us to believe that there is a hard-and-fast distinction between his epic and intellectual (or "cool") theater and the "Aristotelian" emotional and plot-centered drama. Actually there are many fine shadings and transitions from this type of play to the classical drama. Mother Courage, Kattrin, Shen Te undoubtedly move us emotionally as characters in Aristotelian drama do, while Galileo and Puntila conform much more accurately to the Brechtian ideal of the intellectual, "cool" theater. But in any event Brecht, in definite and sharp contrast to traditional Western tragedy, does not begin with the individual but with the problem. A comparison between traditional and Brechtian titles of plays can elucidate this difference. The main characters of classical dramas are first and foremost individuals who act out particular tragic destinies or stories before our eyes. Their proper names are identical with the titles of the plays in which they occur: Oedipus, Antigone, Medea, Hamlet, Macbeth, Othello, Phedra, Mary Stuart—these titles show the emphasis on the individual and his particular fate. Brecht's protagonists on the other hand are exemplifications of human problems; they are primarily not individuals but dilemmas. They are types: the courageous mother able to profit from and survive social disaster at a terrible price; the good person who wants to do good and must search for the means which prevent her from being good; the rich man and master who wishes to be the friend of the poor man and servant but cannot attain his goal; the scientist and searcher after truth who also wants to live and to live well and must consequently compromise his ideal. The titles of Brecht's plays indicate this problem-and-function-centered approach: *The Good Woman of Setzuan; Mother Courage* who, as one passage in the play explicitly tells us, is called "Courage" because she represents the courage the little people need in order to survive the catastrophes prepared for them by the great ones in the world. Even where proper names do occur in the titles they are combined with or expressive of the function of the name-bearer. The original German title literally translated *Master Puntila and his Servant Matti* neatly sums up the theme of that play; Galileo's name serves as an archetypal synonym of the scientist and searcher after truth.

Since Brecht starts not with an individual fate but with a general problem acted out before us by his characters, his plays are akin to comedy as well as tragedy. Apart from the humor and wit of Brecht's plays their structure, and functionalism, and the typicality of their characters link them to comedy. With comedy, especially Molière's type of comedy, the Brecht play shares its appeal to the detached critical spirit and nonserious peripheral role of the plot which is too unimportant to involve the spectator emotionally. But unlike comedy and more like tragedy it shows the defeat of aspirations which represent the best in man. This intimate mixture of comedy and tragedy, the ironic subordination of plot, the preoccupation with problems rather than individuals unite Brecht with the spirit of the whole experimental theater of the twentieth century, with Pirandello, Schnitzler, Camus, Beckett, Ionesco, Genet.

The third element that distinguishes Brecht from the tragic tradition of Europe at the same time, however, excludes him likewise from the contemporary experimental French theater with its emphasis on the absurd. For in his mature plays Brecht implies that the tragic predicament of man is not inexorable but that it can and should be remedied. Tragedy is part not of human nature but of circumstances, and circumstances can be altered. The questioning epilogue of *The Good Woman of Setzuan;* Matti's propagandist oration at the end of *Puntila;* even Kattrin's heroic action of human solidarity with its successful outcome set in instructive contrast to her mother's defeated profit-and-adjustment-minded mentality—all these exhibit a social didactic optimism that belies the tragic spirit. Man's tragic condition is not inexorable. Social action can overcome it.

Is this optimism, then, the final meaning of Brecht's mature plays in which schizophrenia reveals man's tragic condition? Certainly *The Good Woman of Setzuan,* for example, shows the cause of tragedy to lie in social circumstances. Yet this play also shows that tragedy results from the contradictory relationship between ends and means. Can Communism, the instrument of social change Brecht envisaged, be exempt from this tragic contradiction? Can Communism overcome the tragic condition of man? *The Measures Taken,* the play in which Brecht made Communism the protagonist, gives a negative answer. Communism is not exempt from the tragic contradiction between ends and means; it cannot overcome the tragic condition of man. On the contrary, Communism is for Brecht the tragic hero par excellence.

*The Measures Taken,* the play of Communism, deals with the same basic problem as *The Good Woman of Setzuan.* It shows that Communists are doomed to suffer the same tragic split as Shen Te, the good woman of Setzuan. The Young Comrade in *The Measures Taken,* like all Communists, has joined the movement to help eliminate misery and unhappiness on earth. The Communists' motives are the same as Shen Te's—goodness, generosity, the spontaneous wish to help one's fellowmen. But like Shen Te the Communists, in order to make their wish come true, must disguise their original self and assume the mask of ruthless, heartless schemers, as Shen Te must hide her self in the mask of Shui Ta to procure the means that will enable her to do good. Shen Te in the guise of Shui Ta must suppress the spontaneous stirrings of love, pity, and kindliness so as to acquire the means for them. The Communists, too, must squelch their compassion, rebellion, and indignation which brought them into the movement, to prepare in their shifting and difficult day-to-day work the conditions that will make their movement victorious. Shen Te's goodness squanders her money and threatens to make her goodness impossible in the future. The Young Comrade's outbursts of compassion and rebelliousness endanger the movement and threaten to make its further clandestine labor impossible. Shen Te's Shui Ta self must liquidate the Shen Te self in order to realize Shen Te's goals. The Communists must silence and kill the Young Comrade in order to realize his objectives at some future date. They execute him with his consent. The Young Comrade is the natural and spontaneous part of the self; the Four Agitators who murder him are the planning and deliberate Shui Ta part of the self which must suppress and kill goodness in order to prepare its actualization. In *The Measures Taken* as in *The Good Woman of Setzuan* man's natural wish for goodness clashes with circumstances. In *The Measures Taken* the persecution of Communism by the authorities and the fact that it has to work clandestinely and by clever strategy and compromise provide the same kind of limiting circumstances which the capitalist system provides in *The Good Woman of Setzuan.* The inhibition of the direct fulfillment of the wish by circumstances causes the split in the self, expressed in both plays by the mask which Shen Te and the Communists have to don to hide their real face. The mask symbolizes, and is the suppression of, the true self and the assumption of a pseudo-self, of a character opposite that of the true self. The pseudo-self has to deny, oppose, and even kill the true self in order to protect and realize *its* aspirations. The means deny the end which they alone can bring about. The Young Comrade has to be killed by his fellow Communists the moment he takes off his mask and reveals his true face. If he is not killed, his cause—Communism —is lost. The paradox of this relationship in which the pseudo-self must destroy the true self in order to fulfill it constitutes the essence of tragedy in Brecht's work. It is primarily the tragedy of those who, like Brecht himself, seek to eliminate tragedy from this world.

In his tragedy of Communism Brecht affirms the iron law of circumstance which kills the impulse of the human heart. In speeches patterned on Greek choral passages he celebrates the heart-inhibiting split between feeling and action. In his later plays he deplores the split and, implicitly or explicitly, condemns the circumstances which make the split necessary. Finally, in *The Caucasian Chalk Circle,* he presents characters who no longer need the split, whose behavior is the direct expression of their feelings. The relationship between *The Measures Taken* and the group of late plays might be illuminated by comparing the two contradictory responses a Greek tragedy such as *Prometheus Bound* or *Oedipus* can elicit. Some see in these plays an affirmation of necessity, a celebration of the fateful power in the universe which cuts down the individual and forces him to bow to it. Others may see the opposite in these plays—a rebellious sympathy with the individual's aspirations, a lamentation of his tragic failure and doom. In *The Measures Taken* Brecht would conform to the first, in the later plays to the second response. In this shift an important instance of Brecht's general shift from the nihilism and vitalistic fascination with which crime, violence, and conflict imbued the young Brecht (*Baal, In the Swamp, The Threepenny Opera*) to the more mellow humanist view of the mature Brecht can be seen. With its double heritage of apocalyptic mysticism and Western humanism, Communism was able to accommodate both tendencies in Brecht. However, with this shift from the romantic mystique of violence to the mellow humanism of his later period the role and function of Communism in Brecht's work also shifted. In the early period he faced the harsh, naked truth within Communism: its suppression of goodness in the name of goodness, its imprisonment of human nature for the sake of liberating human nature. He presented the cruel discrepancy between ends and means with an austere realism that disdained all glossing over. In his later period he either eliminated Communism from his works—which show the curse to which Communism is also heir, restricted to pre-Communist environments—or, as in *The Caucasian Chalk Circle,* he lifted Communism from reality to a utopian plane, an idyllic realm in which a rosy glow of human wisdom and kindness dissolves all contradictions. With regard to Communism, Brecht in his late period adopted the attitude of the gods whom he satirized in *The Good Woman of Setzuan.* He removed Communism from the real world with its grim schizophrenic split to the rosy clouds of fantasy and fairy tale, in which alone, as in Puntila's state of inebriation, wish and fact, ends and means, harmonize.

# Mother Courage
# and Her Children

## by Franz Norbert Mennemeier

Brecht approached his actual object in roundabout ways only. His epic theater, whose declared goal it is to provide today's "scientific age" with a theatrical pleasure suitable to it (cf. *Little Organon*), is a theater of parables and similes, of masques and fairy tales. Almost always the action takes place in far-away settings, in India, China, Japan, exotic lands out of which all temporal references have been carefully removed. Even a distinctly modern city like Chicago—the plays *In the Swamp* and *St. Joan of the Stockyards* take place there—appears in Brecht as a poetic medium furnished with the sensational features of imaginary "roaring Twenties." The classical drama of Bolshevism, Brecht's *The Measures Taken*, has modern China as a setting; nevertheless all tangible sense of the present has been banished from it, which supplied official party criticism with a welcome excuse to reproach the author of the embarrassingly explicit play with a lack of dialectical maturity. Brecht's political satire on Hitler's rise to power, published from his posthumous papers, *The Resistible Rise of Arturo Ui,* detonates its contemporary explosives ineffectively because of an all too indirect beginning, and must have recourse to interposed explanatory texts to remain at all comprehensible in its contemporary references. The same criticism holds true for the plays *The Roundheads and the Peakheads* and *Schweik in the Second World War,* examples of tendentious political literature seeking to intervene in the historical situation directly, but unwilling or unable to express itself directly. But the contemporary piece which renounces the poetic mask, the play *The Private Life of the Master Race,* has not gained by the direct approach to its theme; on the contrary, except for a few impressive scenes, the work belongs to Bert Brecht's weakest. Thus we see, remarkably enough, that Brecht, who as no other author bases his theoretical position on Marxism-Leninism

"Mother Courage and Her Children" (abridged). Translated by J. F. Sammons. From *Das deutsche Drama vom Barock bis zur Gegenwart,* edited by Benno von Wiese (Düsseldorf: August Bagel Verlag, 1958). Reprinted by permission of August Bagel Verlag.

understood as a science, in his poetic practice is the more convincing the more he is able to do without the concrete contemporaneity of the scientific age, the more his material permits him to express himself by allusion. Brecht was a Marxist—it would be foolish to attempt to set up a secret, "true" Brecht: the poet, versus a "false" Brecht: the ideologist under duress. Nonetheless, the remarkably fascinating, indeed "literary" style of Brecht which generously incorporates the literatures of all nations and times, and his joy in the historically given subject and its critically attentive "making" (and therewith the form of Brecht's writing) are clearly determined by requirements that are only distantly concerned with the goals of the class struggle, but much more with aesthetic truth and the artistic and intellectual pleasure arising from it.

Brecht's best-known and most successful play and the classic example of epic theater, *Mother Courage,* along with *The Caucasian Chalk Circle* and *The Good Woman of Setzuan,* enables the audience to regard its own times in the alienating mirror of the past with anger, emotion, and enjoyment. The play, written for the man of today overshadowed by the terror of "scientific" wars, in its subtitle feigns a pleasant walk through far-distant history: it reads, *A Chronicle of the Thirty Years' War.*

## The Great Capitulation

The figure of Mother Courage, who has little more in common with Grimmelshausen's tramp than her name, her business sense and her numerous legitimate and illegitimate husbands, shows Brecht at the peak of his skill at characterization. The basic experience of the young Brecht, noticeable everywhere even before the confrontation with Marxism beginning in 1926, was the insignificance of the individual oppressed by biological and sociological processes. "One is none," we read in the comedy *A Man's a Man,* which presents with bitter irony the functional, infinitely exchangeable character of a man. In the plays of that period, in which the motif of "agreement" and of "extinction" play a central role, all the actors, as it were, wear masks; they are formless and faceless beings, "empty pages on which the revolution writes its instructions" (*The Measures Taken*). The later Brecht did not give up his view, which a priori excluded any playwriting centered around characterological problems and excluded tragedy as well as the battle between fate and the individual; but he corrected it. In exile Brecht created figures of flesh and blood, figures which were no longer the emblems of sociological forces, but living beings existing in terms of yes and no. Galileo, greedy for truth and the pleasures of the table; Puntila, who becomes a human being only during his recurrent periods of drunkenness every year; the judge Adzak with his peasant cleverness, "corrupted" equally by a willingness to take bribes and by his healthy sense of justice; the delight-

ful, coarse Grusche, a genius of practical humaneness—these, like Mother
Courage, no longer are mere sounding boards of their respective social
classes and situations; they are intriguing individual phenomena of
human existence. If Brecht also gave them a critical contour, a sociological "gestus," nonetheless he did not alienate them completely. Instead
of interfering with dramatic experience in this play, Brecht, by the conception of his main character, only made it more varied and, in the
final analysis, more intense—for experiences do not consist only of
feelings.

Mother Courage is a complex figure. Brecht correctly resisted anyone
presenting her primarily as a mother who, "like Niobe," is unable "to
protect her children from the vicissitudes of war." For the playwright,
Mother Courage is the "merchant-mother," "a great living contradiction
who is disfigured and deformed beyond recognition." In the scene on the
battlefield she is "truly the hyena." In her "antitheses in all their
abruptness and incompatibility" are united. The play does not intend to
display "the indestructibility of a vital person afflicted by the iniquities
of war" as in *Schweik* but, on the contrary, the destructibility of even
the most energetic human being. Therein lies her deeply moving tragedy
for the audience: "that here a fearful contradiction survived that destroyed a human being, a contradiction that could be resolved, but only
by society itself and in long, terrible battles" ("Mother Courage Presented
in Two Ways," [1951].[1]

Of course, this last remark makes it immediately clear that the later
attempt to establish the guilt of Mother Courage as a false sense of class
consciousness and a criminal, active promotion of the war collapses in
the face of the realistic ambiguity of the play. Although the eagerness
of Mother Courage to "turn a penny" in the midst of dissolution offends
the sensitive observer, although the religious war unleashed by the "big
boys" is exposed in its commercial reality with aggressive ardor, still one
does not experience the action of *Mother Courage* primarily as an historical event belonging to "an historical and transitory epoch," and thus
an epoch to be overcome with energy and cunning, as Brecht claims.
Rather, one experiences the action as a representation of the inhuman,
unfeeling state of this world, against which there is no rebellion for the
individual. Of course one may, along with Brecht, nourish in a quiet
corner of one's heart the hope that some miraculous day war and destruction may be counted as "history," as a result of a pacifist transformation of the human race. It seems to be not without importance
that the much-maligned instigators of the catastrophe in the play never
become dramatically tangible themselves: they emerge in their conversations as mere schemata, rhetorical, quasi-popular scapegoats of a
world-wide catastrophe swallowing up the guilty and innocent, the evil

[1] Published in [periodical] *Aufbau* [East Berlin], 1955, XI, together with other pieces
made the title "Die Dialektik auf dem Theater" (pp. 1019-1024).

and virtuous, the stupid and intelligent, the angry and resigned with the same terrible indifference.

Two songs, above all, illuminate the "philosophical" basic gestus of the play: Mother Courage's "Song of the Great Capitulation" in the fourth scene and the "Song of the Wise and Good." The first song, functioning as advice to the young, brawling soldier and connected in this way to external dramatic action, is a lyrical résumé of the scene: it points to the inner structure of the whole drama at the same time. In the temporal stream of epic theater there is a momentary intimation of a life beyond oppression as a utopia. The prerequisite for an alteration of existing conditions would be the "great" anger. Clearly people do not feel such anger. Behind the promisingly wild, revolutionary saber rattling of the soldier cheated of his tip a very "small" anger becomes quickly visible. The whistle of a subordinate officer is sufficient to restore in the mechanism order and obedience that have been briefly disturbed and to nip in the bud the rebellious impulse of the soldier inexperienced in reunuciation. But Mother Courage is experienced. Her "Song of the Great Capitulation," full of maternal sympathy for the "little" capitulation of the soldier, describes the course of life as inevitable disillusionment of all individual impulse to "higher things," as the inevitable erosion of all personal desires for happiness. The picture of the music band recurring in the refrain, in which one winds up marching, "keeping in step, now fast, now slow / And piping out our little spiel," underlines the gray opportunism, the wretched "accommodation to people" to which the human being is reduced by the process of existence. The pious proverb ("Man proposes, God disposes"), turned by Brecht into its opposite by a slight twist, a mere change of punctuation and stress ("Man proposes: God disposes"), recurs also from stanza to stanza, summoning up the picture of a world in which small, human plans collapse because the whole lacks planning and guidance. The poem drags along with it, like a heap of old rubbish, the devalued slogans of petty-bourgeois, pious activity ("All or nothing," "I am the master of my fate," "You can't hold a good man down," "Where there's a will there's a way").

The theme of the Great Capitulation is also treated in the "Song of the Wise and Good," which the cook and Mother Courage sing when the sutler woman's business has been totally ruined by plague and famine, and nothing remains but beggary. In altered form the song appeared already in *The Threepenny Opera*: there it occupies a somewhat inorganic position within the dramatic context. The charm of the passage in the drama at hand lies in the natural interaction of the lyric and dramatic planes. From stanza to stanza, the text of the song is more advanced than interrupted by the home-baked reflections of the cook— a chanting, logically inarticulate sing-song in prose. These reflections have a semipublic character; they are asides, as it were, and, sanctioned by a "public" verse form, combine impressively into an emotional whole with the message of the song. For Brecht, the virtuoso of language, it is a masterly achievement of alienation. The popular ballad form expands into an unspeakably melancholy, subtly humorous litany of the despoiled creature and of the senselessness of human effort. It is a song sung as though from a distance and still of a direct, elementary expressive power. The song was awkward for Marxist critics because of its apathetic character (cf. the interpretation by Hans Mayer in *Theaterarbeit*, pp. 250 ff.). Here a deep, pessimistic side of Brecht, associated with death and transitoriness, becomes visible; a "Biblical" sadness wells up, which again and again thwarted his stubbornly maintained faith in progress; it is this sadness to which Brecht owes his best inspirations.

Despite the melancholy, a subtle humor carries through the song that is itself highly novel within the framework of the popular ballad. Bert Brecht permeates and alienates the elementary lyricism of the lament with a surface structure of logic. The cook must apply his song about the person of great virtue to his own particular case. In this process comical "leaps" occur, which reflect the absurdity of all attempts to bring sense into the senseless and chaotic course of the world. Right at the beginning, after the "great men" are named "who were brought low," the cook proceeds: "So you can see that we're good folk, too, and have a hard time getting by." The "too" attempts, among other things, to force the two separate ideas together conceptually. But, as everyone knows, the cook does not belong among those for whom the "virtues" listed in the poem have become dangerous—i.e., "daring," "honesty," "wisdom," "unselfishness," etc. He is by no means "too bad for this world" (to quote *The Threepenny Opera*), and the word "decent" with which he describes himself is in fact a decorative epithet for the *Pfeifenpieter*. To give another example: in the fourth stanza it has just been reported how St. Martin and the poor man "froze" as a result of the excessive altruism of the former—"Better for you if you have none!"—there the cook unconcernedly intones further: "That's how it is! We're good, we stick together. . . . And so, as the song says, we sink lower and lower." This lamenting, lyrical, reflective style, which makes the inexactitude of popular reasoning fruitful for artistic purposes, usually serves Brecht as a means of social criticism. But in the song under discussion it seems to be concerned to make language itself relative. It is "alienated" to the chatter that is not only the jargon of a cook but represents the speech of even the most intelligent man when he becomes conscious of the extent of the catastrophe of life. The concepts of virtue in the song, moreover, are not exempted from the process of alienation. The poem uses them as formulas emptied of meaning, as moral *topoi* connected with semilegendary, semihistorical personages (the "wise" Solomon, the "daring" Caesar, etc.). Like the song of the Great Capitulation, the "Song of the Wise and Good" also emphasizes the speed of decay: "But ere night came and day did go / This fact was clear to everyone: / It was his wisdom that had brought him low." The moralizing scheme suited to the popular ballad style reveals a deeper metaphysical meaning. Behind the rational, pragmatic appeal to morality and the argument of morality, the natural sound of existence is hidden: lament for the transitoriness of what exists and the insignificance of human works, the good as well as the bad.

With the symbol of the wagon the play illustrates a tendency to destruction which is rooted in life and not to be overcome in spite of all activity. Throughout all the scenes Mother Courage's wagon is to be seen, reflecting the questionable prosperity of its owner and her restless life exhausting itself necessarily in the confused course of her business. At the end it rolls across the stage as a ragged, dilapidated cart, with Mother Courage as a lonely dray animal in front: there is no difference any more between the means and the purpose of existence—a hopeless position.

## The Courage of Poor People

With this background in mind, it is no longer possible to interpret sociologically the "poor folks" who command the scene in the play, quite apart from the fact that Mother Courage is no "proletarian" but rather a businesswoman, temporarily even a rich one. In a world threatened by plague, hunger, and death, even the rich people are poor people, whether they know it or not. The radical skepticism exhibited by the play makes it understandable, too, that for Brecht so-called world history can have no autonomous meaning. Brecht does not only create the effect of catastrophe in the misery of little people to shed light, for the sake of justice, on an area of universal history usually forgotten by historiography; he is also concerned to expose critically the true essence of "monumental" history. Monumental history, which reckons its purposes out beyond the little history of men, according to the presentation in the play is perverted history. When the army chaplain on the occasion of General Tilly's burial speaks of the "historic moment" of the event, Mother Courage answers: "It's historic to me, all right, because they punched my daughter in the eye." At the beginning of the same scene the report of Tilly's "heroic death" is ironically mixed in with the ordinary, fussy chatter of Mother Courage taking inventory. Just like the cook, whose critical remarks on great politics are a sort of sounding board for Bert Brecht's materialistic philosophy of history, so Mother Courage repeatedly expresses her contempt for the "brass hats" and their warlike intentions garnished with ideology: "Oh, yes, to hear the big fellows talk, they're fighting for their beliefs and so on, but if you look into it, you find they're not that silly; they do want to make a profit on the deal. So you and I back them up!" In another place Mother Courage holds forth on the exploitative character of public concepts of morality: "Any place there are such great virtues, it proves that something's rotten there. . . . In a good country such virtues wouldn't be needed. We could all be cowards and relax." As the quoted sentences show, Mother Courage's dislike of the great, to be sure, is mixed with sympathy. A more or less secret concord exists between the great and the little people: business. "Business" in Brecht's play is the expression for the corrupted state of (present) history and for the "participation" of people in it, to which one must immediately add that participation has the mark of self-defense and of elementary control of existence, not of ethical guilt. Participation is the true "courage" of Mother Courage. In it is rooted that "terrible contradiction" of the most stirring, most many-sided of Bert Brecht's heroines. If the author in the newly published edition of 1957 altered the end of the text and has Mother Courage, who has just lost her third child and has been reduced to beggary, now say as her last line: "I must get back into business," it is consistent with the sense of the play, and it has the flavor of true tragedy—whether one interprets the sentence according to Marx or not.

Mother Courage cannot keep herself out of the war that is destroying her. Most of the time she is blind to the contradiction in her situation; she is adapted to it. The strength of Mother Courage is rooted in being adapted, in her conformity which is restricted by no alien, "higher" ideology. When in the eighth scene, as peace has temporarily "broken out," the army chaplain angrily calls Mother Courage, who is lamenting the threatening ruin, a "hyena of the battlefield," it rings false and bathetic. Because in contrast to the clergyman, who is not adapted but certainly compromised, who seeks to live off the "business" and at the same time to keep aloof from it, Mother Courage has recognized, if not the danger, then at least the inevitability of business and the identity of peace and war grounded in the mercantile sphere. For Mother Courage there is no difference between business (-war) and ideology; the business *is* her ideology: "I won't have my war all spoiled for me! Destroys the weak, does it? Well, what does peace do for 'em? Huh?" Only once does Mother Courage see more deeply; she comprehends that the maintenance of her life is also its destruction, and she gives vent to the terrible recognition in an outcry: "Curse the war!" But that defense of the war quoted above follows like a retraction directly after this condemnation: Mother Courage can only exist if she "represses" the contradiction which goes to the root of the matter, if she gathers together all her strengths, even her intellectual and moral ones, for her "business." With bankruptcy and the destruction of her existence constantly before her eyes, she is determined to bring herself and her children through the war by means of her trade. Take part and keep aloof: this is the contradictory slogan of Mother Courage, born out of the senselessness of the situation. That her almost legendary courage to which she owes her name has nothing to do with idealistic, moral drives or even with a particularly daring personality, is drastically shown by the answer she gives the sergeant: "I'm called Courage because I was afraid of ruin, sergeant, and drove through the bombardment of Riga with fifty loaves of bread in my wagon. They were going moldy, it was high time, I had no choice."

The realistic hardness of Mother Courage, sharply drawn by Brecht, her active heroism which expresses itself in tireless haggling and reckoning, exhibits its tragic contradiction most emphatically where the "humane" comes into the picture. There it becomes clear that "courage," the last, "hard" virtue of the energetic sutler woman, is at bottom nothing more than the form in which she hides from herself the consciousness of the fruitlessness of *all* virtues. The highly dramatic scene in which Mother Courage loses her honest son Swiss Cheese presents the human conflict intensified as a business conflict. Despite the terrible, knife-edge suspense of the situation, Mother Courage begins to haggle in the moment when she hears that the box with the pay is lost. It is positively terrifying news; it means that Mother Courage cannot buy back the wagon which is to be leased to the camp prostitute Yvette. At first glance the scene has a brutal and inhuman effect. Swiss Cheese dies literally from the margin of difference about which they are haggling. Still, Mother Courage does not haggle for the sake of haggling. Brecht has constructed the situation as a true dilemma. Mother Courage is "desperate," as the stage direction notes. She reacts entirely as the "merchant-mother," that is, not as a sentimental abstraction, but as a sociologically concrete being when, stifling her first humane impulse, she considers the consequences: the fate of the helpless, mute Kattrin, a life without the wagon, a life without the possibility of living. It is not as though she had thought in the beginning that the life of her son would be risked in the terrible transaction; when the corruptibility of the constabulary turns out to be incorruptible, Mother Courage is ready to pay the whole sum. It is a single moment of reflection which deprives her of her son, just exactly that precautionary, prudent "virtue," that "courage," which is the only thing which up to now has kept her and her children alive through this inhuman war.

"Little people need courage. Why? They are lost." The collapse of all "virtues" runs like a dark ground bass through the scenes of the play. Mother Courage's excellent children are taken from her one after the other. Eilif, her daring son who is bent on a soldier's life, she loses to the recruiter when her attention is distracted by a small transaction (once again Brecht displays the fatal mixture of human and mercantile realities). In a moment of deceptive peace Eilif is executed for a deed for which he would have been rewarded earlier; a bloody sacrifice to the double morality of this world. Eilif's great moment is the scene in which he is distinguished by the commander and performs the saber dance. In the song of "The Fishwife and the Soldier" Brecht has written thrillingly of the short life of the warrior stretched between fame and death. Mother

Courage's daring son sings of his own end which comes so quickly. He has passed away like "smoke"; his deeds have nourished no one.

The mute Kattrin is also swallowed up by the war, also in a moment when her mother has gone away because of business. Kattrin's dumbness, symbol of the oppressed, tormented creature, brings a loud accusation against the inhuman condition of the world. The girl, who is obsessed by an animal-like drive for love and motherhood, who suffers from compassion, must never be played as an idiot. Kattrin is completely normal. It is the world that is abnormal, which has terribly deformed her. Because of her "friendliness" Kattrin—what a symbol!—must be constantly watched. She has only her mother's shameless art of living to thank that she exists at all in the middle of war and business and has even become twenty-five years old. Kattrin is only human and absolutely "incompetent"; consequently she exists in constant mortal danger. When Kattrin in one of the most dramatic scenes of the play climbs up on the peasants' roof and, sacrificing her life for strangers' children, awakens the sleeping town of Halle with a drum, it is not an act of "courage," not an action which qualifies one for business and maintaining one's life, but the exact opposite of all this: spontaneous, unplanned, so to speak biological humanity which transpires beyond all clichés of heroism like a birth: with groans and contortions, according to the stage direction. Tormented by a double anxiety, for her life and for the wagon, Kattrin, giving out "noises of distress," drums herself to death weeping: an innocent sacrifice of her friendliness. The human being does not go unpunished for violating the conditions of the Great Capitulation.

Brecht contrasted the action of the good Kattrin with the prayer of the peasants. While Kattrin, driven by her sympathetic nature, sacrifices herself, the peasants clear-headedly consider the fatal results for them of any action and escape into prayer, saving their own skins. "There's nothing we can do." A rational will to self-preservation and the wish that some kind of help might come from somewhere alternate in the prayer pathetically and mechanically. When suddenly help "comes," the pious resignation turns abruptly into a fearfully wild, instinctively egocentric attack upon the little mute girl. Brecht, as a true Marxist, has brought the instantly ready habit of prayer of these "poor" people into logical connection with the vital, courageous conformity which Mother Courage embraces in order to remain in undisturbed enjoyment of her business. Hard-boiled courage in the face of reality and ideological flight out of reality correspond to one another; both are forms of the Great Capitulation.

## Brecht's Epic Theater

The play does not condemn those who capitulate and avoids praising ideologically the suicidal, even if successful, action of the mute Kattrin.

No guide lines for political practice are offered as in Brecht's didactic plays. *Mother Courage* is also not an antiwar drama in the sense of the propaganda theater. Even if certain levels of the play can be comprehended with the concepts of dialectical materialism, the whole stubbornly resists classification into a political or philosophical "movement." The play has a deeply pessimistic impact. On the other hand it exhibits powerful humor and brings before the public in the midst of the depravity of the historical world examples of strong humanity. *Mother Courage,* despite its artistic arrangement and its undeniable basic attitude of philosophical materialism, is a play with many-leveled, "open" realism. Instead of providing the preconceived results of thought masquerading as literature, it only begins to set thought, along with its ideologies, in motion.

The superficial observer may miss a certain lofty air, the stirring spiritual note which one often connects with the concept of poetry. In point of fact Brecht depicts life without the mask of decency which it can afford in times of so-called peace, when the threatened and threatening character of human conditions has been repressed into the subconscious—which is why *Mother Courage* has often been misunderstood as an example of the popular, coarse, historicizing genre of literature and rejected as "culinary" [Brecht's own word for the easily digestible, merely enjoyable character of bourgeois theater. Tr.]. Brecht, who fights against the "culinary" attitude with angry contempt in his writings, meant his play to annoy "bourgeois" comfort. He offers no theses or recipes for avoiding catastrophes. But he warns men by presenting the catastrophe itself. Perhaps he is not even warning any more; no work of Brecht so obviously has the tone of lamentation.

The popular tradition which Brecht picks up and the well-known great names and historical settings enable him to work out the crying contradiction between monumental history forming its legends, expressed in the colorless monotony of the "Chronicle," and human reality, expressed in the fate of Mother Courage and her children by contrasting one with the other. In the style of the Baroque novel, but without its ingenuousness, each scene of the play is preceded by short, harmless-sounding "table of contents," which are at the same time confirmed and contradicted in a grim and surprising manner by the events as they are presented. The prefixed sentences thus do not only have the function of removing suspense and shifting the attention of the audience from the "what" of the event to the "how," but also the infinitely more important function of creating for the public a critical attitude toward historiography and its indifference to all individual human details. Formulas like the sober, summary sentence at the beginning of the sad ninth scene, "The great religious war has now lasted sixteen years," or like the sentence before the fifth scene, with its comic point, "Tilly's victory at Leipzig costs Mother Courage four shirts," discriminate against the "monumental" history of the historiographers in favor of the real, "little" history of "poor people" who experience the whole burden of reality. Brecht's epically "alienating" method, which appeals to the capacity of the audience to make critical comparisons, turns against the estrangement caused by a "history" dissociated from human beings, which presents fate as their enemy.

With an uncommonly sharp eye Brecht has constructed the fable and the characters of the play from the sociological aspect. In every sentence and in every gesture Mother Courage reflects her "business," which serves in the play as a fixed formula for the social and economic existence of men abandoned to the irresistible current of the perverted historical world. As a consequence the drama is not interested in the psychological development of character either. Mother Courage does not importunately exhibit her suffering to the observer, so that the complex historical reality with which Brecht is concerned is hidden. Intentionally, in part as an afterthought, Brecht has equipped Mother Courage with "disagreeable," "inhuman" characteristics which are supposed to sabotage the empathy-mechanism of the public which has been trained to expect the "humane." The good will the observer brings to Mother Courage is shaken again and again by shocks setting in motion reflections about the background of her actions.

Brecht's epic method achieves still another effect, at least equally decisive for this play. The classical play is constructed so that the action, piling up suspense from scene to scene and compressing time, flies like an arrow to the target waiting in the future. The result is that the audience paradoxically does not notice how time goes by. Epic theater radically breaks through this dramatic structure. It retrieves time in its reality, dragging itself wearily through the years, and presents it in this, its "natural," state. The above-mentioned chronicle-like texts inform the audience about the time interval between the individual scenes. The total action of *Mother Courage,* he learns, has a time span of twelve years as a background. This expanse of time is felt as doubly oppressive because no meaningful individual or social development justifies and overcomes the mighty stretch of time. Rather, one sees a crippling recurrence of the same thing, the hideous picture of a war constantly expanding and wantonly revolving within itself, from time to time threatening to sink to a deeper level, opening up the possibility of complete chaos. The elegantly bored attitude of the "Chronicle," which covers most of the time expanse, is destroyed simply by confronting it with its brutal reality.

There is no "great dramatic arc" in Mother Courage. If in the classical drama all the parts are dovetailed into a dynamic, progressive whole, in Brecht's play there is an artfully static structure which carefully balances individual scenes against each other. Scenes full of tense action are followed by more harmonious ones in which reflective elements predominate. Songs project out of the normal stream of action into a trans-individual, transdramatic dimension and correspond to each other through the play, creating an "indirect" linguistic medium which is both lyrical and meditative, refined and popular. By this means the meaning of the play is frequently broken and often intentionally veiled.

Even in *Mother Courage* there is dramatic tension in the traditional sense, except that it is limited to the action within the individual scenes. Brecht's mastery in forming a dramatic event can be clearly recognized in the third section of the third scene. Swiss Cheese has been captured and is to die. Mother Courage enters "excited." It is a matter of life and death. The first element of retardation appears in the haggling conversation about the wagon. Yvette, pompously "discussing" the matter with her recently hooked colonel, wants to buy; Mother Courage wants to lease it. When they have come to agreement, a further hindrance emerges. The novice businesswoman Yvette, instead of hurrying to save Swiss Cheese, falls greedily upon "her" wagon. Mother Courage has difficulty pushing her away. There is a tortuous wait. Yvette returns "panting." Her news, that Swiss Cheese has thrown the box into the river, creates a third retarding element as the high point of the "rising" action: the desperate cogitation of the merchant-mother. The suspense is concentrated almost to the point of physical pain. Yvette is sent away again, this time to bargain about the bribe. For those waiting, the minutes stretch to an eternity. Finally Yvette returns and reports the failure of her mission and the impatience of the constabulary. A third time she is sent away. Into the silence of those waiting comes the drum roll of the court martial. Mother Courage receives the reproaches of the prostitute, who has just been scolded for her own greed, in stony silence. But the tension is tightened up anew at one last point: Mother Courage must deny her dead son in order to save herself and her other children. The remarkable aspect of this incredibly compact scene is that every section is filled with social reality even to the intonation of the characters. No false pathos, no "noble" misery beclouds the pellucid atmosphere of the tragic action.

There are those who connect the concept of epic theater with the idea of a literary regression, namely from the concentrated manner of presentation back to the rich abundance of naturalistic detail. The opposite is the case, even with respect to technical aspects. *Mother Courage* shows very clearly that the popularly drastic, popularly intimate style of Brecht endeavors to re-create not so much reality as the "idea" of natural speech along with its typically alogical structure. The whole drama is alienated in a popular tone. The peculiarly moving melody of the songs, which has a distant effect even when, as in the "Camp Follower's Song," the age-old theme of love betrayed is intoned, grows organically out of the atmosphere of the play. "In you there's a young Caesar. You should see the king," says the commander to Eilif. Eilif: "I did, from a distance.

There's a glow about him. I'd like to make him my model." Commander:
"I bet your father was a soldier." Eilif: "A very great one. My mother
has warned me about it. In a little song." Upon this apparently realistic
dialogue which in fact has a stylized popular manner and operates with
elegant abbreviations, follows Eilif's song of "The Fishwife and the
Soldier." The prologue of the play, the conversation between the recruiter and the sergeant, makes the artful, non-naturalistic character of
the linguistic medium which Brecht has created especially noticeable.
The two slave traders in uniform speak, despite the coarse turns of
phrase with which their dialogue is spiced, a topsy-turvy, inverted
language of eerie comedy. With the countenances of gentlemen and the
vocabulary of standard morality the two are quite seriously indignant at
the immorality of a population which is not willing to accommodate
itself to military service and tribute. By a vivid dissociation of form and
content Brecht has brought to consciousness the absurd character of war
and its ideological, mendacious vocabulary. It is an example of elementary
dramatic style, typical for epic theater, which mixes excitement and
shock effects to the constant surprise of the audience.

Nevertheless Brecht's diction always remains close to the ground. His
play is a single triumph over the tendency to a bookish and scholarly
style with which German literature is always threatened. The over-
simplifying statement, to be sure, that Brecht took his words out of the
mouth of the people does not do justice to the complexity of this manner
of writing, drawn from the spirit of popular tradition, yet indirect and
full of veiled meaning. The language of *Mother Courage* provokes from
the member of the audience another, more direct mode of expression
which he must find himself.

# On Brecht's
# *The Caucasian Chalk Circle*

## by Ronald Gray

To turn from *Mother Courage* to *The Caucasian Chalk Circle,* not written till 1944-45, is to enter a completely different atmosphere, in which, nevertheless, many affinities can still be found. It is as well to say at the outset that the Communistic message which it seems to convey is only loosely connected with the main plot. This is the story of a young Georgian girl, Grusha, who saves the infant child of a tyrannical governor during an insurrection, who brings up the boy until the day when his real mother disputes possession of him before the "good, bad judge" Azdak, and who finally, through the unorthodox wisdom of the judge, is allowed to retain the child because she alone has shown a true motherly nature. It scarcely follows from this that (as the epilogue suggests) the Soviet authorities are entitled to deprive industrious dairy-farming peasants of their land in order to hand it over to others who will make use of it for viniculture. And the prologue, in which this contemporary problem is outlined (the play itself being performed as a means of persuading the reluctant dairy farmers to yield), is remarkable for the prim diction of the Soviet officials, the conventional picture it gives of shrewd, but goodhearted peasants, and the "socialist realism" of its style and presentation.

All this is in contrast to the non-naturalistic, manysided, lyrical, humorous, Rabelaisian, socially conscious elements of the "play within the play." The girl Grusha is not in the least conventionally drawn, though she, too, is shrewd and goodhearted. We do not sit back in uncomfortable or smug contentment telling ourselves that this is what sturdy peasants are really like, as we are invited to do in the prologue. She shows considerable courage in crossing a rickety bridge over a mountain chasm while being pursued by insurrectionist soldiers; she combines this with artfulness, a ready wit, blunt honesty, stubborn insistence, and

an unshakable moral probity. When she is married for convenience' sake
to a dying man who will be at least a nominal father for the child she
has saved, and when the man, a skrimshanker, rises from his "deathbed"
on hearing that the war is over, she continues to pay him a wifely respect,
shows no resentment or self-pity. When, later, her lover Simon to whom
she is betrothed returns from the war, she allows him to suspect her of
infidelity rather than betray the child to its enemies. Courage, perse-
verance, motherliness, dutifulness, self-sacrifice she shows time and again.
Yet because of her equanimity and lack of self-regard, these qualities have
no false ring. And this is due also in part to the deliberately non-
naturalistic language she speaks. Brecht makes no attempt to reproduce
peasant speech faithfully: Grusha's is sprinkled with proverbs and dialect
forms, but it also includes direct translations of English idiom; when
she sings a lullaby to the child it is at once a song that vividly recalls
ancient German folk art and at the same time has a modern ring. Subtly
and continuously through the language Brecht persuades us not quite
to believe in Grusha, to accept her as a creation of art, and to look
beyond her to a reality which in part we re-create ourselves. The
formality of his presentation reaches its climax in the scene, concluding
the first part of Grusha's adventures, where Simon returns and speaks
with her across a river that separates them. The lovers address each
other at first in an exchange of proverbs which is both humorous and
characteristic of their peasant origin. It is also, however, quite impersonal,
a drawing on common tradition, and it is only by reflexion that the
deep personal relationship between them is felt. In the climactic moment
of the scene, in fact, neither speaks, and it is left to the narrator to
reveal what each "thought, but did not say." Thus they confront each
other in formal attitudes which are never realistically portrayed but are
at the same time deeply moving, and it is by a similar estrangement
that Brecht succeeds in making the outstanding human qualities of
Grusha credible and acceptable.

The scenes of Grusha's escape, adventures, marriage and rejection by
Simon, forming about half the play, make a loosely strung narrative in
the fashion of "epic" theater. While there is a certain thread connecting
them, however—they do not stand "each for themselves," as Brecht suggested earlier that "epic" scenes should do—the interest is sustained
not so much by the thin plot as by the detailed interactions of the
characters and by the beauty of the portrayal. Since *Baal*, Brecht had
scarcely made any use in his plays of the natural scene. In *The Caucasian
Chalk Circle*, as in *Puntila* and *The Good Woman* and in his later
poetry, the world of nature returns. The scene by the river itself, indicated on the stage merely by two ground-rows of reeds, evokes by its
bareness, coupled with the lyrical song of the narrator preceding it, an
awareness of loveliness. The icicles above Grusha's hut, as she waits in
isolation for the winter to pass, become moving tokens of spring as they

melt, and the musical notes of a xylophone offstage, recording the falling drops of water, add excitement by their rising intensity. There is time for contemplation and for exhilaration in these austerely presented moments; the spectator is not whirled along as he was by the action of earlier plays, and not encouraged to indulge in ecstatic Nature worship, but rather to recognize with pleasure the delight that is to be had from Nature, off the stage. There is both detachment and attachment.

The settings also, in this part of the play, evoke an astringent delight. The descending white back cloth has already been mentioned. There is also the scene of Grusha's wedding, contrived to give a Breughelesque harmony of brown, oatmeal, sepia, and an occasional splash of red: peasant colors in a peasant setting, crowded, earthy, vulgarly frank, but shaped into a frame of unity that is comic, sympathetic, and has a lopsided symmetry of its own. There is the strange effect of the empty stage after the insurrection has passed by, with the voice of the narrator emerging from one side to comment on the silence and thereby, oddly enough, to intensify it. Meanwhile, from time to time, the prose speech breaks into verse such as that in which Grusha affirms her love at Simon's first departure:

> Simon Chachava, I will wait for you.
> Go in good heart to the battle, soldier,
> The bloody battle, the bitter battle
> From which not all come back:
> When you come back, I will be there.
> I will wait for you under the green elm
> I will wait for you under the bare elm
> I will wait till the last man comes back
> And longer . . .

It comes as a shock to go on from this moving language and these scenes to the following series which forgets Grusha entirely in order to introduce the story of the judge Azdak. From Azdak's first speech, the spectator is hit by a forceful language which English can barely reproduce: "Schnaub nicht, du bist kein Gaul. Und es hilft dir nicht bei der Polizei, wenn du läufst, wie ein Rotz im April. Steh, sag ich. . . . Setz dich nieder und futtre, da ist ein Stück Käse. Lang nichts gefressen? Warum bist du gerannt, du Arschloch?" The crudity of this, the rough vigor, the cynicism and humor and the underlying sympathy introduce the character of Azdak himself, which stands in strange contrast to Grusha's. Azdak is a thief, a timeserver, a coward, who by a lucky accident is raised during the insurrection to a position of authority. As a judge he is corrupt, licentious, contemptuous of law and order, a lickspittle. His life is spent, unlike Grusha's, not in rebellious opposition to society's moral standards, but in careful adaptation to them, going along with the tide, and keeping an eye on the main chance. But such an account does less than justice to this unpredictable rogue. In the first scene, finding that the poor man he thought he was sheltering is in fact the Grand Duke, fleeing from the insurrection, he still does not hand him over to the police, although whether from sheer contempt for the police, as he says, or contempt for the Duke, or from an inscrutable sympathy such as Ernst Busch implies when he plays him, is never clear. Promptly, he rushes into town to denounce himself, believing that the soldiery will welcome the news of his treachery—some strange conscientiousness is at work in him. Yet on discovering them to be indifferent to the rights and wrongs of the insurrection, he willingly allows them to clothe him in judicial robes, and goes off on his rampaging processions through the countryside, delivering sentences that completely reverse accepted standards of justice. He accepts bribes, but (though he keeps the money) only as an indication of the wealth of the litigants, which stands in his eyes in inverse proportion to their rights. He makes an award in favor of a poor woman who has been helped by a bandit, on the grounds that only a miracle could explain how a leg of pork came to fly through a poor woman's window: those who accuse the bandit of stealing the pork and throwing it through the window are condemned for godlessness and disbelief in miracles. When a buxom young woman accuses a farmhand of rape, he considers her luxurious gait and the shape of her buttocks and finds her guilty of assault and battery with a dangerous weapon, after which he goes off with her "to examine the scene of the crime." And when order is re-established he falls over himself with dutiful promises that Grusha, whom he has not yet met, shall be beheaded as soon as she is found.

Azdak is a standing affront, and at the same time a standing reminder of the questionable values on which society is based. He has one principle, that the rights of the poor are disregarded and that this situation must be reversed. Apart from that, he proceeds *ad hoc*. If a buxom girl is likely to commit rape he offers her the opportunity. On the other hand, if he foresees danger in maintaining his one principle, he gives way immediately: "I'm not doing any one the favor of showing human greatness." Yet all this is not mere self-gratification or concern for his own skin. There is nothing that can properly be called a self in Azdak, nothing consistent or foreseeable in his actions: he acts on impulse. He sets no store by his actions, any more than Grusha does by hers, and it is this that helps to make him the most fascinating character in the play, insulting and generous, preposterous and humble, ignorant and wise, blasphemous and pious. In his Villonesque song to the poor woman he addresses her as though she were the Virgin Mary and begs mercy for such damned creatures as himself—a strange translation from religious into human terms which still has an atmosphere of genuine devoutness. In the scene where he is buffeted in his false robes by the

soldiery, the production of the Berliner Ensemble is deliberately styled
to recall another buffeting. And in the comment of the narrator there
is a further suggestion of a wider scope: "And so he broke the laws, as
he broke bread, that it might feed them." The suggestion need not be
taken too far. Yet there is in Azdak, the scandal, the gnome, the cynical
good-liver, something immensely disturbing and provocative as well as
attractive. He denies all the virtues, mocks at repentance and charity,
ridicules courage, and, strangely enough, he gets our sympathy in the
process. For he is plainly being himself to the top of his bent, lusting
and helping the poor, crawling in abject fear and at the same time in-
viting the soldiers to recognize their own doglike obedience, answering
every prompting with instinctive recklessness. If we give him our sympathy, as we cannot help doing, in a way, so long as he dominates the
stage, he sets all Grusha's virtuousness at naught. This is Baal, returned
to the scene in a new guise, and all Baal's fascination pours out of him.

   In the final scene of all, the two sides are confronted with one another, the disruptive, ambiguous underminer and the calm, shrewd,
motherly girl who would rather die than forego her humanity. Azdak
is called to try the case in which the real mother of Grusha's "child," the
wife of the former governor of the province, claims possession of her
son. By a fortunate turn of events, the same Grand Duke whose life
Azdak saved earlier on has now returned to power, and thus Azdak's
servile promise to the governor's wife no longer has any hold over him,
if indeed he ever meant to keep it. Azdak proceeds, however, as usual,
accepting bribes from the wealthier party, while abusing Simon and
Grusha who have nothing to offer him, and it is this which brings on the
first serious opposition he has had to encounter. Grusha declares that she
has no respect for a judge such as he is, "no more than I have for a
thief and a murderer that does what he likes." Her moral protest is a
straightforward indictment of his libertinism (which is no mere show),
and none the worse for that; in fact she has all, or nearly all, our sympathy. Yet the end will have already been guessed. After the "trial of the
chalk circle" in which each woman is to pull at the child from different
sides, and Grusha fails to pull for fear of hurting the boy, Azdak
ceremonially declares that Grusha is the true mother since she alone has
shown true motherly feelings. This is not, however, a sentimental ending
awarding victory to justice against the run of the odds. Rather, it is the
fusion of two conceptions of justice. Azdak's instinctive prompting on
this occasion (he is, after all, in safety now, with the governor's wife in
political disgrace) is to award Grusha the custody of the child. But this
instinctive prompting is a part of his elemental originality, his closeness
to the roots of his nature, and his complete detachment from them. His
decision has gathered the weight and incontrovertibility of a natural
phenomenon, and despite his mockery of the virtues here is one virtue
in Grusha that he respects without thought of argument.

Thus the two sides come together. Like Nietzsche, Azdak demands opposition such as he gets from Grusha, and thrives on it. Like Nature itself, he is ambiguous and amoral and requires the rebelliousness of humanity to bring out his qualities to the full. Then, however, when he meets with opposition, he reveals an unexpected generosity (as Nietzsche never did). He is like Baal, it is true. But Baal was never opposed, lived his life in pure self-fulfillment, and died only to the tune of contempt from others. Azdak is Baal, and all that lies behind Baal, brought into relationship with human beings, and this relationship and conflict serve to make *The Caucasian Chalk Circle* far greater in scope than its predecessor. The virtue of Grusha is both convincingly stated and brought into question; the amoralism of Azdak is made to look both repugnant and curiously attractive; and yet in the final moments a fusion of Grusha's human demands and Azdak's inhuman unpredictability brings about a sense of at least temporary fulfillment. As the narrator has it, the period of Azdak's life as a judge could be looked back upon as "a brief Golden Age almost of justice." It was not *the* Golden Age, and it was not a time of complete justice. Both Azdak and Grusha have been too "estranged" for us to be able to accept them as models or heroes. But while steering clear of absolutes Brecht creates here an ending which is satisfying on a purely human plane. Despite the riotous exaggeration of a great part of the play, from which he never recants for an instant, the conclusion is moderately and accurately stated.

# Brecht: The Music

## by John Willett

Brecht was no trained musician, but far more than most writers he had musical ideas at the back of his mind, and his work is full of musical implications. This began with his early settings of the "Legende des Toten Soldaten" and other poems to his own tunes, where "actual delivery" became bound up with questions of intelligibility and of verbal punch. For the first few plays he assembled his own music in the same rather rudimentary fashion: for *Baal*, for *Edward II* and *Trommeln in der Nacht* [*Drums in the Night*]. Then for *Mann ist Mann* [*A Man's a Man*] and even for *The Threepenny Opera* he sketched rough drafts of the songs that Edmund Meisel and Weill actually composed; and from then on he found that he could collaborate with certain composers so closely and effectively as to realize many of his own musical aims. More than most playwrights, more even than the majority of poets, he has become known by the musical settings of his works. *The Threepenny Opera* lives mainly by its songs, *Happy End* by nothing else; *Mahagonny* and *Lucullus* are highly original operas; while the whole group of didactic pieces or *Lehrstücke* has a special part in the musical life of the time. Kurt Weill, Paul Hindemith, Hanns Eisler, Paul Dessau, Rudolf Wagner-Regeny: all the composers with whom Brecht worked are figures of some importance, and the particular movement with which they became linked—the socially orientated music promoted by the publishers Schott and Universal-Edition, and tried out at the Donaueschingen and Baden-Baden festivals—is among the most interesting and most neglected aspects of recent musical history. Like Jean Cocteau, Brecht had a strong influence on the form, orchestration and general approach adopted by his collaborators, but this was exercised by practice rather than by any public whip-cracking or polemics. It was just that poetically, as well as dramatically, he seemed to think in near-musical terms.

The musical movement in question developed out of that with which Cocteau was associated, for it started by reflecting many of Stravinsky's and Satie's ideas, while Darius Milhaud played a personal part in it from quite early on. Its objects were a new lightness and clarity after the heavy and uneconomic works of Mahler and Strauss; its methods a return to classical models and, much more closely bound up with this than we now realize, an exploitation of the trenchant, lively and still uncorrupted language of jazz. Stravinsky had set the ball rolling with the chamber opera *Renard* of 1915: a work of "predominantly dry timbre and bouncing resonance" which was intended "to be played by clowns, dancers or acrobats, preferably on a trestle stage with the orchestra placed behind." With Ansermet, Ramuz, and the painter René Auberjonois he then planned to found a traveling (wartime) theater on the same scale: a scheme whose sole realization was in *L'Histoire du soldat*, written for narrators, dancer, and seven musicians, and produced on a trestle stage (with podium either side), in Lausanne on 28 September 1918. This work showed the first influence of the jazz pieces which Ansermet had brought back from America the previous year: an influence openly admitted in Stravinsky's *Ragtime* of 1918 for eleven instruments, and in the *Piano-Rag-Music* of 1919.

In 1918 Cocteau, some nine years senior to Brecht, wrote his essay *Le Coq et l'harlequin* advocating a clear and popularly based musical style. A year before, his ballet *Parade* to Satie's music had been given by Diaghileff in Paris (it was repeated more successfully in 1920). Here was music "like an inspired village band," with a "Rag-time du Paquebot" and slogans shouted through megaphones; here were novel characters: the Chinaman, the Little American Girl, the Acrobats. In 1919, again with Cocteau, Darius Milhaud wrote his *Boeuf sur le toit* for an orchestra of twenty-five, which was given three performances that winter with the Fratellini and other clowns. This work was set, writes Milhaud, "in a bar in America during prohibition. With some very typical characters: a Boxer, a Negro Dwarf, an Elegant Woman, a Red-head dressed as a boy, a Bookmaker, a Gentleman in Tails. . . ." Its alternative title was in English: "The Nothing Doing Bar."

These are the obvious ancestors of Kurt Weill's *Mahagonny*; and the younger French composers continued exploring along these lines. Cocteau's *Mariés de la Tour Eiffel*, with more megaphones and a rowdy score by his friends "Les Six," was given on 19 June 1921; a Milhaud shimmy called *Caramel Mou* was performed by a Negro dancer that May; *La Création du monde*, his Negro ballet with book by Cendrars and settings by Léger, was produced by de Maré's Swedish Ballet in 1923. ("I followed the example of Harlem and had an orchestra of seventeen soloists, and freely used the language of jazz, which I combined with a classical feeling.") Jean Wiéner, that interesting composer and pianist who has long operated in the gap between "serious" music and jazz, sponsored a series of concerts in 1922 which included *Pierrot Lunaire* and *Mavra*, Stravinsky's other chamber opera; Milhaud met Cole Porter and recommended him to de Maré for a ballet; 1924 saw the first (American) performance of Gershwin's *Rhapsody in Blue*. Ravel himself, with whom Cole Porter took lessons, wrote his *Enfant et les sortilèges* "dans l'esprit de l'opérette américaine": a kind of sung ballet which was produced by Balanchine in March 1925 and represented a continuation of that process of extreme *dépouillement,* or stripping-bare, which began with his violin and cello sonata of 1920.

All this means that the relations between lowbrow music and the new anti-Wagnerian aims of the younger serious composers were for a time very close: that the actual scale of performance was being cut down, harmonies clarified, melody emphasized, orchestration tightened up. An element of classical balance was being reintroduced. And for some reason this trend expressed itself not in the orthodox opera but in short and rather frivolous stage works, where the means were economical and the words themselves—as in the rhythmic recitation devised by Milhaud for Claudel's *L'Ours et la lune* of 1918—treated in a clear and novel way: a process that led in 1923 to *Façade*.

In 1921 a group of German musicians, most of them born between 1890 and 1900, and including Hindemith and Heinrich Burkard, launched a small annual chamber music festival under the patronage of the Prince of Fürstenberg at Donaueschingen. This became in effect Stravinsky's platform in Germany, and from 1925 on he came to the festival each year. "Germany," he wrote in his *Chroniques*, "was plainly becoming the center of the musical movement." Milhaud's friendships with Hindemith and Kurt Weill had their origins here; Weill's own reputation was made with a Quartet at the second festival in 1922; Hindemith wrote a whole series of small-scale more or less neoclassical works. Other German musicians associated with this group carried the French experiments a good deal further, both inside and outside the actual festivals, and managed to bring them to a rather wider public. Ernst Křenek wrote his jazz operas *Sprung über den Schatten* (1924) and *Jonny Spielt Auf* (1927), with its Negro hero; Wilhelm Grosz (known to us as the composer of "It was on the Isle of Capri that I met her") wrote a *Jazzband* for violin (1925) and the ballet *Baby in the Bar* (1927), and set Ringelnatz's light verse to some very original music. A jazz class was instituted at the Frankfurt Hochsches Konservatorium under Matyas Seiber, who published a *Jazz Percussion Tutor*. In 1923 Hermann Scherchen introduced *L'Histoire du soldat* at Frankfurt with Carl Ebert as narrator, later taking it on tour with a cut-down version of Cocteau and Milhaud's short opera *Le pauvre matelot* (1926). It was performed at the Berlin State Opera in 1925, and in 1928 was produced there by Brecht's friend Jakob Geis, as part of the première of the Cocteau-Stravinsky *Oedipus Rex*. The Germans not only took the French ideas up; they took them seriously; and they took them to the public. And all this for more than "purely" musical reasons.

In 1927 the Donaueschingen festival shifted to Baden-Baden and began to reflect the same social and aesthetic ideas as were current in the theater at the time. "Thanks to Hindemith's severe and judicious selection," wrote Milhaud later, "the programmes had an undeniable aesthetic pattern." The pattern was that of *Gebrauchsmusik* and *Gemeinschafts-musik*, or applied music and amateur music, two terms expressing the broad social-aesthetic question: What ought music actually to do? "What didn't they try out there?" writes Heinrich Strobel in his study of Hindemith. "Film music, mechanical music, potted opera, radio music, music for young people, for amateurs. . . ." That first year they performed a batch of four chamber operas: Hindemith's own "film sketch" *Hin und Zurück*, whose action and music alike go suddenly into reverse in the middle of the work; Ernst Toch's *Prinzessin auf der Erbse*; and Milhaud's specially written nine-minute opera *L'Enlèvement de l'Europe* to a text by Claudel's friend Henri Hoppenot (later the Free French representative in Washington). The fourth work was the *Songspiel Mahagonny* by Weill and Brecht.

*Gebrauchsmusik*, or functional music, really originated with Satie's *musique d'ameublement*—musical furniture, to be listened to with half an ear—and Milhaud's *Machines agricoles* of 1919, settings of more or less random texts from farmers' and seedsmen's catalogues. Here is the new mechanized spirit that inspired Stravinsky's works for pianola, or Hindemith's various pieces for mechanical instruments (including the Bauhaus *Triadic Ballet*) of 1926 and 1927; and it had its own aesthetic appeal.

> Affiche, crime en couleurs. Piano mécanique,
> Nick Carter; c'est du joli!

—wrote Cocteau in his *Cocardes*, to convey the garish charm of the old silent cinema. The film indeed offered the one really new *Gebrauch*, or function for music, and at the same time it challenged the modern composer's technical and mechanical ingenuity. Antheil's *Ballet mécanique* (for eight pianos and percussion) was fitted to a film of 1924 by Dudley Murphy and Fernand Léger; L'Herbier's film *L'Inhumaine* of 1923 (made with the help of Léger, Cavalcanti, Autant-Lara and the jazz-modern architect Mallet-Stevens) included scenes of the rioting at Antheil's first Paris recital and was set to music by Milhaud; in 1927 Hindemith wrote a piece for mechanical organ to accompany a Felix cartoon. Film music figured at the Baden-Baden festival of 1928 (another Felix cartoon arranged by Ernst Toch, and a synchronization by Hindemith of a mechanical piano to fit Richter's *Spuk der Gegenstände*) and 1929 (a recording of this on soundtrack, plus another Richter film set by

Walter Gronostay, and Cavalcanti's *La p'tite Lili* to music by Milhaud).
Brecht was of course right when he suggested that the invention of sound
recording must knock such highbrow experiments on the head, but for
a moment the composers were encouraged to neglect the old orchestral
and operatic apparatus for an apparently new world: a world which,
like Piscator's theater audiences, got particular pleasure from seeing the
wheels go round.

*Gemeinschaftsmusik*, communal music, sprang, according to Dr. Strobel's account, from Hindemith's meeting with the singers of various
youth organizations at the Donaueschingen festival. He began writing
music for amateurs: first the instrumental *Schulwerk* (all in the first position) and *Spielmusik*, then the choruses (Op. 43, No. 2) and the *Sing
und Spielmusiken* of 1927 and 1928. Milhaud followed suit with the
cantata *Pour louer le Seigneur* and various pieces now included in his
*La Musique en famille et à l'école*, while at Baden-Baden in 1929 there
were amateur pieces by Wagner-Regeny and Walter Leigh, and in the
1930's Hindemith's *Plöner Musiktag* and Carl Orff's well-known *Schulwerk* carried the tradition on. These were the origins of the school opera
and the *Lehrstück*, or didactic piece, where the performers were meant to
learn as they went, and to learn not only the notes but the technique
and pleasure of working as a collective, too. Both the 1929 Baden-Baden
festival and the 1930 *Neue Musik* festival in Berlin were primarily devoted to such works. The object was as much social as musical, and the
writers of the texts were driven in the direction of a corresponding
simplicity of diction and clarity of sense.


Kurt Weill had already used texts by Kipling and Villon for his
pantomime *Zaubermacht* of 1923, and the poems in Brecht's *Hauspostille*
[*Domestic Breviary*] so impressed him that he proposed a collaboration
whose first result was the primitive *Mahagonny* of 1927. "Till then,"
wrote Brecht later,

> Weill had written relatively complicated music of a mainly psychological
> sort, and when he agreed to set a series of more or less banal *song* texts he
> was making a courageous break with a prejudice which the solid bulk of
> serious composers stubbornly hold.

This meant rejecting the sacred dogma according to which "folk" music
is respectable and popular music not. Despite the complaints of his
teacher Busoni that he was setting out to be "the poor man's Verdi,"
Weill saw that

> jazz has played a considerable part in the rhythmical, harmonic and formal
> liberation at which we have now attained, and above all in our music's
> steadily increasing simplicity and intelligibility,

while Brecht likewise held that it "signified a broad flow of popular musical elements into modern music, whatever our commercialized world may have made of it since."

Sharply orchestrated, and free from all mushiness, jazz not only fitted Brecht's conception of a down-to-earth vernacular language but also helped to establish his dramatic points.

> So-called "cheap" music, particularly that of the cabaret and the operetta, has for some time been a kind of *gestisch* music [i.e. one which expresses attitudes]. Serious music however still clings to a kind of lyricism and tries to express the individual.

Here, at a new low, economical level, the problem of the opera could be tackled much more effectively than in the top-heavy *Zeitoper*: the modernist operas of Křenek and Max Brand (*Maschinist Hopkins*, 1928) and Hindemith himself.

> Composers who aim to put new blood in the opera are inevitably (like Hindemith and Stravinsky) brought up against the whole operatic apparatus. Great apparati like the opera, the stage, the Press, etc., impose their views as it were incognito.

Spurred by reading the libretto of the *Beggar's Opera* during the winter of 1927-28, Brecht saw the chance to undermine this apparatus as Gay and Pepusch had done two centuries earlier: by writing a "ballad opera" in the new popular terms.

In *The Threepenny Opera*, which he and Weill wrote in a considerable hurry in the summer of 1928, the singers were primarily actors and the songs interruptions; the music was never allowed to swamp the continually lucid text. The melodies were nostalgic, the counterpoint neat and the harmonies often disconcertingly prickly, but it was scored for a band of eight musicians only, and the singers came from the world of the theater and the cabaret, not from the grand operatic stage. "I couldn't read a note," writes Weill's widow Lotte Lenja, of her appearance in the first *Mahagonny*, "—exactly why I was chosen." Such methods imposed new rules, which were outlined by Brecht in *The Threepenny Opera* notes:

> Nothing is more revolting than when the actor pretends not to notice that he has left the level of plain speech and started to sing. The three levels—plain speech, heightened speech, and singing—must always remain distinct. . . . As for the melody, he must not follow it blindly: there is a kind of speaking-against-the-music which can have strong effects; the results of a stubborn, incorruptible sobriety which is independent of music and rhythm.

Music here becomes a kind of punctuation, an underlining of the words, a well-aimed comment giving the gist of the action or the text. And this remains its prime function in all Brecht's plays.

*Happy End*, with its very successful songs, was composed on the same pattern, but the completed *Aufstieg und Fall der Stadt Mahagonny* represents a swing toward the orthodox opera, for although it has the same lightness and punch and the same nostalgic jazz tunes the music runs almost continuously throughout the work. The orchestra in the original version was some forty strong, including strings (which Brecht always disliked), plus a stage orchestra of twenty-one; the writing was less disjointed, and the bass often less percussive and monotonous than in the two musical plays. The real innovation, never followed up by Brecht, lay in the alternation of rhythmical and free dialogue, some-times over the orchestra, sometimes unaccompanied, and in the ingenious combination of solos and chorus. The words emerged as clear as ever, but the general effect, even after the work had been rescored for some-thing more like a dance band, was further from unadulterated theater than Brecht cared to go.

In the notes which he and Suhrkamp wrote on this work about 1930 he admitted that it was what he called a "culinary opera," whose differ-ent elements are cooked into a common mush, even though it is also a *Spass;* a joke, which a guilty conscience has stopped its authors from making too easy to swallow.

> The opera *Mahagonny* pays conscious tribute to the idiocy of the operatic form. The idiocy of opera lies in the fact that rational elements are em-ployed, solid reality is aimed at, but at the same time it is all washed out by the music.

So he returned to the principles of *The Threepenny Opera*: clear division of songs from dialogue; no illustrative or "psychological" element in the music; an orchestra of not more than thirty; and the singer as a "reporter" whose private feelings must remain a private affair. He now classed *Mahagonny* with the new opera of Hindemith and Křenek: an attempt to modernize the content and mechanize the form of the opera without querying the "apparatus" or the social function which it performed. He himself set out "more and more to emphasize the didactic at the expense of the culinary element."

The close connection of these works with the experiments being con-ducted at Baden-Baden was recognized by the serious critics and stressed by Weill himself:

> The *Threepenny Opera* takes its place in a movement which today embraces nearly all the young musicians. The sacrificing of "art for art's sake," the

playing down of the artist's individuality, the idea of film music, the link with the musical youth movement, and arising from these the simplification of musical means of expression—they are all stages along the same road.

Two new steps in this direction were taken at the 1929 Baden-Baden festival, which was devoted to the didactic cantata and to works specially written for radio. For this Walter Goehr composed a setting for Feuchtwanger's pseudo-American poems *Pep*; Hanns Eisler wrote his cantata *Tempo der Zeit*; while Brecht provided the text for two pieces: *Lindberghflug* (for radio) with music by Hindemith and Weill, and the *Badener Lehrstück* [*Baden Cantata of Acquiescence*] to a score by Hindemith alone. The second work started with the final chorus of the first.

Unfortunately the collaboration with Hindemith was not entirely successful. "Every word can be understood," wrote Heinrich Strobel of Kurt Weill's part of *Lindberghflug*.

> Hindemith's music is much more atmospheric: it uses precisely the same means of characterization as his stage works have made familiar.

At the same time Brecht pushed the conception of the *Lehrstück* a good way further than Hindemith wished to go, writing that

> The *Lehrstück*, product of certain musical, dramatic and political theories, all of which envisage the collective practice of art, is designed to clarify the ideas of the authors and of all those taking part, not to provide anybody with an emotional experience.

Hindemith wanted his work to be played by any instrumentalists available, and left them free to omit whole sections if they wished; Brecht was concerned with the instructive aspects of the text as a whole. The question at issue was whether *Gemeinschaftsmusik* was to teach the writer's ideas, or to restrict itself to teaching music, plus the simple social pleasure of performing together. It was with this purely musical didacticism that Brecht so disagreed: "The cellist in the orchestra, father of a numerous family, now began to play not from philosophical conviction but for pleasure. The culinary principle was saved."

The performance of the *Lehrstück*, with Hindemith conducting an audience that included Gide and Gerhardt Hauptmann, and the words of the choruses projected on a screen, caused a major scandal at Baden-Baden, thanks largely to the gratuitous and, on paper, laboriously unfunny scene for the three clowns. (This, according to Dr. Strobel, was the reason why the festival had to shift the following year to Berlin.) Brecht then added further sections to his text, which he had not regarded as complete, but Hindemith refused to set them to music, with the result that each refused to let the work be performed except in his own version, and it became impossible to perform it publicly at all. The irresistible poet had met the immovable musician, and they had arrived at a stalemate: a great pity, because Hindemith's score was judged to be one of his finest achievements:

> Without in any way sacrificing his individual point of view Hindemith has simplified his style to the point of universal intelligibility. His music has an unsentimental dignity: powerful and serious. . . .

It was also, says Dr. Strobel, "the only occasion on which Hindemith collaborated with a writer of real importance."

At the festival in 1930 further *Lehrstücke* (like *Das Wasser* by Döblin and Ernst Toch) were followed by the first "school opera," written on very similar principles. "The practical value of a school opera," wrote Weill, "consists precisely in the learning of it." He and Brecht had turned, as we saw, to the noh drama, and found there the material for the school opera *Der Jasager* [*He Who Says Yes*]. *Lindberghflug*, henceforward given with Weill's music only, was rechristened "a radio *Lehrstück* for boys and girls." Other school operas followed: Hindemith's *Wir bauen eine Stadt* (1931), Milhaud's *A propos de bottes* (1932); but *Der Jasager* was one of the most successful of them all, and was widely performed in German schools before 1933. It was arranged, according to Weill,

> in such a way that all the parts (chorus, orchestra and soloists) can be performed by school-children. . . . The score is laid out to suit the resources of a school orchestra: a basic orchestra of strings (less violas) and two pianos, with *ad lib* three woodwind (flute, clarinet, saxophone), percussion and plucked instruments.

He emphasized the instructional value of the text, and also the possible emergence of a new musical market. This he saw not only in the schools but also in "the working-class movement."

Yet when at the end of the year Brecht came into contact with this movement it was through another composer; and although there was no break between him and Weill the really productive period of their collaboration ends at this stage. It was in a sense logical, for it was a turning point in Brecht's work, and Weill's music was becoming too light and nostalgic; apt even, with its very genuine charm, to "wash out" the new-found roughness of Brecht's verse. They worked together on the 1931 productions of *Mahagonny* and *Mann ist Mann*, for which Weill wrote fresh incidental music; they planned a number of works, including an opera called *Der Moabiter Pferdehandel*; and later in America they discussed the music for *The Good Woman of Setzuan* and an operatic version of *Schweik*. But all that has so far come down to us of these plans is some isolated songs, and their one major work after 1930 remains the ballet *Die Sieben Todsünden* [*The Seven Deadly Sins*] of 1934, which the late Constant Lambert regarded not only as Weill's best stage work but as "the most important work in ballet form since *Les Noces* and *Parade*." Whatever the truth of this judgment it was a quite conscious regression on Brecht's part. He never cared to print the songs which he wrote for it, and it seems a plain attempt to earn money in exile by recapturing the spirit of his greatest success.

Hanns Eisler, five months younger than Brecht, and a pupil of Schönberg and Webern, had come from Vienna to Berlin in 1925. He was an austerer composer than Weill; his sister Ruth Fischer and his brother Gerhard Eisler were both prominent Communist party officials; and he had already become well-known as a composer of Communist songs. As such he was prepared to do what Hindemith evidently would not, and give a certain supremacy to the text. Thus although *Die Massnahme*, the *Lehrstück* which he and Brecht wrote for the 1930 festival, was in one sense a logical continuation of the two pieces of 1929 and a natural companion to the *Jasager* (whose essential theme it repeated in Communist dress), the whole work had a strong political flavor, and Eisler's songs were revolutionary in their impact. Hindemith and the other directors of the *Neue Musik* objected to this. *Die Massnahme* was not performed at the festival; and Brecht's connection with the bulk of the new movement now ceased.

He and Eisler turned instead to the Socialist-Communist workers' choral societies, one of which (the *Gemischte Chor Berlin*) had originally been conducted by Hermann Scherchen, just as Anton Webern in Vienna had conducted the *Arbeiter-Sinfonie*. The didactic aim now became narrowed to these left-wing singers:

> As there are half-a-million working-class singers in Germany, the effect on the singer is at least as important as that on the hearer.

So Brecht thought. But when three of the Berlin societies agreed to perform *Die Massnahme* at the end of 1930 the unfortunate effect was to split this whole movement; and in the end it was only the converted to whom Brecht was left preaching. In these circumstances the Baden-Baden principle of actual participation no longer seemed so important. Two years later *Die Mutter*, the last of the Berlin didactic works, was played mainly by professional actors, with the chorus relegated to a very minor role. And from then on Eisler's position in the partnership was a good deal less prominent than Weill's had been: at least, so far as the major works were concerned, though Brecht also supplied the words for individual choruses of a more or less rousing kind, such as Eisler had already been composing for some years.

Eisler was exactly the right composer for Brecht's mature poetic style. He had none of the faintly cheap nostalgia that haunts much of the work of Weill: he is an even more skilled (and in many ways highbrow) composer, who used his gifts like Brecht himself to make the meaning simple and clear. Like Brecht he used ecclesiastical (the Lutheran chorale) and popular models (folksong, popular ballads, and jazz), and made of them something in no way imitative or spiced-up but recognizably his own. "What is essential in modern music?" he asks in an article of 1949.

> It is not the increased resources in discordances or in new colours, but the dissolution of the conventional musical language as handed down to us. A piece which is full of discords can be perfectly conventional in its approach, and one which uses relatively simpler material may, if the means are applied in an individual way, seem completely advanced and new.

This is true of most of his settings of Brecht's words: their originality consists in the chamber music orchestration and lively counterpoint, in those changing rhythms that match Brecht's irregular lines, in the dry flavor and the persistent yet slightly unexpected melodies, at once logical and fresh. Eisler's music for *Die Mutter*, wrote Brecht,

> can by no means be called simple. Quâ music it is relatively complicated, and I cannot think of any that is more serious. In a remarkable manner it makes possible a certain simplification of the toughest political problems, whose solution is a life and death matter for the working class.

It underlined the words and interrupted the story, exactly as Brecht had demanded in *The Threepenny Opera* notes.

During 1931 Brecht and Eisler collaborated on a third work: the semidocumentary film *Kuhle Wampe*, which culminates in the singing (by Ernst Busch) of the well-known Solidarity Song. They next worked together on the songs for *Die Rundköpfe und die Spitzköpfe* [*The Roundheads and the Peakheads*], which was staged during Brecht's exile in Denmark; then in 1937 Eisler emigrated to the U.S.A., where Kurt Weill had already gone. Among the various theatrical and film figures whom Brecht listed for membership of his proposed "Society for Theatrical Science," or Diderot Society, that year, Eisler is the only composer mentioned; and it is plain that Brecht relied on his opinions where much more than the music was concerned. They worked together again in Hollywood in 1942 on Fritz Lang's film *Hangmen Also Die*, then on Brecht's own play *Simone Machard*, while for the Hollywood production

of *Galileo* in 1947 Eisler wrote a long *Moritat*-like ballad and a series
of short songs for boys' voices to go between the scenes.

These boys' or women's choruses, sometimes unaccompanied, recur in
the incidental music which he wrote after 1949 for some of the productions of the *Berliner Ensemble*; but Brecht and he never again seem to
have collaborated on any work of major interest, and most of these
pieces are very slight. There are also a great number of individual songs
by Eisler, and these range from the more private and esoteric settings of
Brecht's exiled poems to the disappointing banalities of the children's
poems and other "positive" political songs written after Brecht's return
home. The East German Academy's plan for publishing Eisler's collected
songs and cantatas embraces something like one hundred and fifty songs
to texts by Brecht.

But if it was Brecht who gave Eisler much of his sense of words and
of the stage, his own ideas of music (as outlined in his essay "Über die
Verwendung der Musik für eine epische Bühne" of 1935) were very
largely Eisler's work. Thus they are not always easy to reconcile with
the musical settings of his third major collaborator Paul Dessau, or even
with the amusing Weill-like songs which Rudolf Wagner-Regeny wrote
for *Trumpets and Drums*. Both these composers had made their mark in
the same school as the others: Dessau with some "thin, pathetic" film
music at Baden-Baden in 1929, and two school operas in 1932: Wagner-
Regeny with three short operas (one of them called *Moritat*) staged at
Essen in 1929 in sets by Neher, and three full-scale "culinary" operas to
Neher's librettos, of which *Der Günstling* became well known during
the Nazi period. But it was only in America that Dessau came to work
with Brecht, and Brecht never gave his name as a *Mitarbeiter*. Evidently
he did not play the same part as Weill and Eisler at the planning stage;
and it is perhaps for this reason that his scores for the big late plays—
*Mother Courage* (1946), *The Good Woman of Setzuan* (1947-48), *Puntila*
and the semioperatic *The Caucasian Chalk Circle* all tend to be brittle
rather than clear. They may respect Brecht's ideas of instrumentation:
they may have been worked out in close consultation with him: they
may be a fair illustration of the plays. But time and again they blur the
text, and the music seems exotic where it ought to be precise.

Dessau's settings of Brecht's words represent a reversion to the gingered-
up folk or pseudofolk style of the early Stravinsky. Thus the *Mother
Courage* songs, he writes,

> based on the folk-song, extend it by enriching it with rhythmical and
> harmonic multiplicity

—that is to say, by abruptly changing rhythms, ragged discords, and the
insertion of tin tacks in the piano hammers. This is certainly not in-
effective: the bitter, sometimes violent orchestration gives the play a

distinctive flavor, and the self-conscious "modernism" of the method is less specious than it seems at first. But the general effect is to underline Brecht's own mannerisms—an affected orientalism or a deliberate tattered squalor. The music is basically atmospheric; and except in the *Mother Courage* songs it fails to bring out, or even to let through, the sense. Both *The Caucasian Chalk Circle* and, still more, the opera *Die Verurteilung des Lukullus* [*The Condemnation of Lucullus*] represent a return to the despised "culinary" approach. *Lucullus'* score is in many ways brilliantly exciting, but the critic is right who complained that the music "is bogged down in illustrative externalities," and the opera remains within the orthodox framework because the composer is heading in a quite different direction from Brecht's austerely didactic verse. No doubt Brecht could have checked this if he had wished, and perhaps one can read a certain disillusionment with didactic methods into his new tolerance of the "idiotic" operatic form. But for all his surface innovations Dessau is not an opponent of the "apparatus," and when Brecht in the 1940's returned to the orthodox theater this collaboration helped him to adopt a more orthodox attitude to the opera as well.

In England today we seem once more to be getting interested in the origins of this whole musical movement. We are reviving the small-scale works of Stravinsky, like *Mavra* and *Renard* and *L'Histoire du soldat*; we see some connection between these and the economical, almost chamber form of opera being evolved at Aldeburgh by Benjamin Britten; but we forget what came between. The German social-musical developments of the Twenties have remained in the shadow since 1933; to imply that music has any social aspect at all is now rank Bolshevism; and the part played by Brecht and his collaborators is wholly ignored. Yet surely there was a quite continuous process, to which such works as the Honegger Concertino or the Falla Harpsichord Concerto or Auric's score for *A nous la liberté* all contributed, as well as neglected pieces like Křenek's Little Suite for Piano (Op. 13a) or Wilhelm Grosz's Ringelnatz songs (Op. 31) or Kästner's and Edmund Nick's charming satirical cantata of 1931, *Leben in dieser Zeit*.

It all represents a certain deflation of the pompous, difficult, uneconomic approach to music. And once we no longer look only at Stravinsky and Britten, the two extremities, we see that this is bound up with a new, largely social urge towards intelligibility, and a corresponding need for composers and writers to have something definite to say. Nowhere is this so clear as in *Die Mutter*, but the movement continues through Gershwin's and Kaufmann's *Of Thee I Sing* and later, American, works by Weill such as *One Touch of Venus* or the "school opera" *Down in the Valley*, to bring fresh sense and artistry also to the popular musical show. "Its effect on the stage," said the citation by Columbia University, who in 1932 gave *Of Thee I Sing* the first Pulitzer Prize to be gained by a lowbrow work,

> promises to be very considerable, because musical plays are always popular, and by injecting genuine satire and point into them, a very large public is reached.

Compared with *The Threepenny Opera,* or even with Antheil's *Transatlantic,* which it in some ways resembles, the Gershwin work was pure Gilbert and Sullivan. None the less, this suggestion proved true. In America at least (where Stravinsky, Bartok and Milhaud all wrote works during the 1940's for musical-comedy kings or dance band leaders) the lowbrow media have remained open to the highbrow artist, with the results that we saw in *Oklahoma!* and Leonard Bernstein's ballet *Fancy Free* and many other good and successful works. And Marc Blitzstein rightly dedicated his *The Cradle Will Rock* (one of the landmarks in this particular story) to Brecht. For the combination of accessibility, artistry, and solid content is fundamental to Brecht's ideas.

# Brecht's Language
# and Its Sources

## by Martin Esslin

Brecht was a poet, first and foremost. However much interest his writings may have aroused as expressions of the problems and anxieties of the age, as political pamphlets, manifestoes of stage reform, or social documents, their chief distinction lies in their being "memorable speech." This is their primary significance. It underlies, and from it derives, any other significance they may possess.

Brecht's plays may be discussed and imitated as examples of a new kind of dramatic construction or stage technique. Nevertheless their main importance lies in their poetic quality. The new dramatic convention they represent lives above all through the grace of their language and the poetic vision of the world it conveys. Without the stamp of greatness impressed upon them by their poetry, these plays could never have been exercised such an influence. They would not even have been noticed. And so it is with Brecht's ideas in other fields. They become important only as the ideas of a major poet.

But this also makes any discussion of Brecht particularly difficult outside his own linguistic sphere. While writers like Sartre or Thomas Mann lose relatively little by translation and their ideas come across in any language, Brecht's ideas, in their own way as significant as theirs, are so intimately bound up with the manner in which they are expressed that any account of Brecht's work which has to ignore this quality becomes unreal. Hence the champions of Brecht in the English-speaking world often appear to be overstating their case. Brecht's poetry does not translate well. Its power, to a large extent, lies in its directness and simplicity, in the bold use of hackneyed words in unhackneyed contexts. Inevitably in translation simplicity often turns into mere simplemindedness or banality and the common word subtly used into the merely commonplace.

"Brecht's Language and Its Sources." From *Brecht: The Man and His Work* (London: Eyre & Spottiswoode, 1959; New York: Doubleday & Company, Inc., 1960). Copyright © 1959, 1960 by Martin Esslin. Reprinted by permission of Eyre & Spottiswoode and Doubleday & Company, Inc.

It is clearly futile to try to *describe* the beauties of a poet's style at second hand. Yet an attempt must be made here to convey, without deeper analysis of Brecht's use of words, syntax, and imagery, some of the features that account for its impact, and to trace the varied sources and influences that lie behind it.

Literary German, and above all stage German, is essentially an artificial dead language. While standard English, standard French, and standard American are spoken, if not by the whole population at least by important sections of it, standard German exists only on paper and on the stage. In ordinary life even the most educated Germans have a clearly defined regional accent and vocabulary. It is thus far more difficult in German to write dramatic dialogue that sounds like real speech and that is free from the local overtones and limitations of mere dialect. Some of the greatest achievements of German dramatic literature are in fact dialect plays and confined to a limited area: the Viennese folk theater of Raimund and Nestroy, or the Darmstadt comedies of Niebergall. When naturalism reached the German stage, its first successful exponent, Gerhart Hauptmann, wrote his early plays in Silesian and later in Berlin dialect. He turned to standard "poetic" German only when he took up a vague and bloodless romanticism.

In poetry, even more than in the drama, the language used tends to diverge from real speech and to assume a highly formalized hieratic tone, which some poets like Stefan George and Rilke have used with consummate skill and great effect, but which tends to degenerate into empty and abstract phrasemaking in the hand of lesser men.

Brecht, however, achieved the rare feat of creating in his poetry and plays a language all his own, which suggested the rhythms and gave the feeling of real speech without being tied to any particular regional dialect. It is still not a language spoken by anyone in reality—with the exception perhaps of Brecht himself. But while it is a synthesis, it is such a vital and original synthesis, so deeply rooted in a number of different traditions, that it creates the illusion of real speech.

This was the quality that overwhelmed the audience even in Brecht's first chaotic plays. As one critic said at that time:

> If it weren't for Brecht's diction! Again and again it simply forces you to listen. His characters may talk the silliest stuff for quarters of an hour on end. In parts what they say is completely devoid of sense. But the point is: *how* they say it! No other writer has caught the speech of the masses of the people as Brecht has. In comparison Toller's leading-article-German is ridiculous; even Hauptmann sounds like reams of paper beside him. . . . For Brecht language is no longer a secondary, indirect matter, no longer merely a question of intellectual expression, but something elementary, a function of the body. . . . This language rises up from depths in which the

conscious self only flickers as a far-off, little taper. It is no coincidence that in Brecht's plays there are so many drunkards, and that almost all his characters are good drinkers: *in vino veritas*. This language never lies, there is not the least bit of padding in it. All rational inhibitions are here dissolved. . . . The choice of words itself is *banal*, but the way they are put together almost amounts to genius.[1]

This intensely personal idiom, chaotic and uncontrolled in his early years, disciplined into severe and monumental simplicity later on, is the product of the fusion of many diverse and disparate elements.

Ernest Borneman has most perceptively isolated the four main sources of Brecht's language:

1—the daily speech of southern Germany; 2—an antimetaphorical poetry of colors, textures, and other concrete images; 3—bureaucratic jargon; 4—Anglicisms and exotic expressions.[2]

These elements, which are already clearly present in Brecht's earliest published writings, are the basis of his personal idiom; the regional Bavarian accent is always to be detected, but never lapses into mere local color. It is stylized and fused with archaic elements from an earlier, baroque layer of the German language. The use of phrases and constructions from the jargon of the civil service is in itself a somewhat baroque device. The stilted locutions of the bureaucrats are to a large extent historical relics, and Brecht used their dusty flavor and demented pedantry not only as parody but somehow turned it into poetic imagery through which the desiccated, fossilized clichés suddenly sprang into new and unexpected life.

Brecht's language also has a firm basis in the chief source of modern standard German. Once, when asked by a magazine to name the strongest literary influence in his life, Brecht replied in a single sentence: "You will laugh: the Bible!"[3] And in fact the vigorous, outspoken language of Luther's Bible pervades the writings of the atheist and blasphemer Brecht. He made masterly use of Biblical constructions: the juxtaposition of contrasted half-sentences, parallelism, repetition, and inversion.

Equally marked throughout Brecht's life was the influence of the street ballad, the *Moritat* (morality), as it was sung by balladmongers at country fairs—lurid accounts of murders and executions couched in the strident language of lachrymose sentiment and naïve horror. Brecht turned to this "vulgar" style in protest against the gentility and respectability of the bourgeois society he abhorred. Disgusted by the insipid classical

---

[1] Harry Kahn, "Bert Brecht," *Die Weltbühne*, Berlin, 1.17. 1928.
[2] E. Borneman, "Ein Epitaph für Bertolt Brecht," *Sinn und Form*, Second Special Brecht Issue, 1957, p. 142; also in *Kenyon Review*, Spring 1959.
[3] *Die Dame*, Berlin, 10.1.1928.

poetry taught at school, he reveled in the powerful emotions and garish
colors of the entertainments of the common people, the songs of kitchen
maids, and the pleasures offered by the sideshows of fair grounds and
beer gardens.

In protesting against the canons and conventions of German poetry,
the stately idealism of Goethe or Schiller which he had been taught at
school, Brecht returned to the last relics of an older tradition which
these reformers of the German language and purgers of its "coarseness"
and "irregularity" had tried to eradicate. Goethe and Schiller had been
the crowning glory of the literary movement of the eighteenth century,
whose aim it had been to base the greatness of the united German nation
they sought to create upon the sure foundation of a German national
literature as respectable and regular, as elegant and polite as the literatures of France and England. To achieve this aim the exuberance of the
baroque, the earthiness of the folk tradition had to be banished from
polite society. The victory of the reformers seemed complete. Yet among
the comics of the beer gardens, in the peepshows and fair-ground
"panoramas" the old German baroque drama, the earlier traditions of
Hans Sachs, the Austrian and Bavarian forms of the Italian *commedia
dell' arte,* and even some relics of the mystery plays of the Middle Ages
were still alive when Brecht was young.

The Austrian and Bavarian folk theater, which reached its peak in the
Viennese popular drama of the late eighteenth and early nineteenth centuries, is a branch of the same tradition that also survives in English
pantomime. The only example of the genre which has achieved international fame is Schikaneder's *Magic Flute,* carried to immortality by
Mozart's music. If one imagines *The Magic Flute* with the music much
reduced in weight, it can serve as a good example of its type. The main
plot is a fantastic fairy tale with a strong moral lesson, but parallel to
it there always runs a coarsely comic plot that parodies and debunks the
highfalutin antics of the noble lovers and matches their ethereal sentiments with earthy common sense. While the "high" plot is intended as
historical drama, the "low" plot lapses into constant anachronisms. The
spoken dialogue is interrupted by musical numbers—"couplets" with recurring refrains that resemble the comic character songs of the Victorian
music hall.

This is a genuinely common, "plebeian" kind of theater. As the
romantic plot is no longer taken seriously, the higher world of upper-
class sentiments is presented from the ruthless viewpoint of the common
people. The heroes are seen through the eyes of their valets and chamber-
maids. This produces a characteristic duality of language: the high-flown
bombast of the "noble" characters stands against the homely, vigorous
common sense of the people.

The sketches that Brecht's greatly admired friend Karl Valentin performed in the beer gardens of Munich were direct descendants of this

tradition. He was the last in a long line of great clowns and Hans Wursts stretching back to the eighteenth century.

Brecht's theater with its use of fairy tale elements, musical numbers, and broadly comical characters is a continuation of this old and once despised tradition and has re-established it as a vehicle for the expression of ideas. His language drew much of its vigor and force from the earthy speech of clowns who never failed to call a spade a spade.

The affinities between this comicoheroic drama and Shakespeare are clear enough, and the early Brecht was deeply indebted to the Elizabethans, both directly, and indirectly through their greatest follower in German literature, Georg Büchner, the author of *Woyzeck* and *Danton's Death*. Brecht regarded Büchner as the greatest German dramatist and modeled his early plays on him. In *Baal* and *Drums in the Night* we find the same feverish, rhythmic prose, tender and coarse in turn, direct and daring in its images:

> And love is like letting one's naked arm swim in the water of a pond, with weeds between one's fingers; like the torment of which the drunken tree begins to sing as it creaks when the wild wind rides it; like drowning in the wine you gulp down on a hot day, and her body pours into you like very cool wine and penetrates every fold of your skin; soft like plants in the winds are the joints; and the force of the impact to which you yield is like flying against a storm and her body tumbles over you like cool gravel. . . .[4]

This ecstatic prose of Brecht's first play also shows the influence of another great rebel among German dramatists, Frank Wedekind (1864-1918), another follower of Büchner, who spent his life struggling for the sexual liberation of mankind like D. H. Lawrence after him, acted in his own plays, and sang his ballads in the Munich cabarets.

Brecht saw himself as one of this band of outsiders. He was fascinated by all the *poètes maudits* of world literature: François Villon, whose ballads he used in *The Threepenny Opera,* Baudelaire, Verlaine, and Rimbaud. The plot of *Baal* contains echoes of the relationship between Rimbaud and Verlaine, and so does another early play, *In the Jungle of Cities* [*In the Swamp*], in which Brecht quotes extensively from *Une saison en enfer* in K. L. Ammer's translation. Many of the poems in Brecht's first published collection, the *Domestic Breviary,* are modeled on Rimbaud's language.

Surprising as it may seem at first sight, Brecht was at least as strongly influenced by a poet of an entirely different stamp: Rudyard Kipling. The same impulse that drove him from the drab respectability of provincial society to the vagabonds among the poets, street entertainers,

4 *Baal. Erste Stücke 1,* p. 18.

and fair ground comics also made Brecht dream of the wide, wide world
he found in the *Barrack-Room Ballads*. There, too, he met a vigorous
plebeian language—spiced with deliciously exotic names of places and
things that breathed an air of boundless freedom and adventure.

Kipling was the main source of the exotic, mythical Anglo-Saxon
world which forms the background to a great deal of Brecht's earlier
writing. Other elements in it come from Swift and Gay, Upton Sinclair,
Jack London, the Chicago stories of the Danish novelist J. V. Jensen
(*The Wheel*), Dickens, innumerable crime stories, and gangster films.
This world, in which English and American elements are inextricably
mixed up, is as unlike real England or America as it could possibly be.
It is a world inhabited by huge, hard-drinking lumberjacks from the
Yukon *en route* for Benares, laden with gold and ready to spend it; a
world where Chicago merges into Soho and John Gay's rogues and highwaymen are blood brothers to bootleggers and gangsters. This is the
world of *The Threepenny Opera*: eighteenth century London inhabited
by highwaymen, whores, and Victorian bankers, ruled by the police chief
Brown, who is addressed as "Sheriff" and has served with Macheath in
the Indian Army, where they freely made mincemeat out of any brown
or yellow race they met between "the Cape and Cooch Behar." Chicago,
on the other hand, is the home of the demonic merchant Shlink in
*In the Swamp*, who happens to be a Malay from Yokohama and is
lynched for having lived with a white girl. In Chicago, too, we find, in
*St. Joan of the Stockyards*, the mighty canned-meat king Pierpont Mauler,
in whose factories careless workers disappear into the mincing machines
to reappear in the form of meatloaf; Pierpont Mauler, who ruins whole
industries by his ruthlessness on the Stock Exchange and has his starving
locked-out workers beaten up by the police. Everything in this mythical
Anglo-Saxon empire, which extends from Alaska to the South Seas, is
bigger than life-size, savage, adventurous, and free. Brecht was so fascinated by it that he even wrote a number of "songs" in his own peculiar
English, which he thought could alone express its flavor:

> There is no whisky in this **town**
> There is no bar to sit us down
> Oh!
> Where is the telephone?
> Is here no telephone?
> Oh, Sir, God damn me:
> No!
> Let's go to Benares
> Where the sun is shining
> Let's go to Benares!
> Johnny, let us go.[5]

---

[5] "Benares Song," *Hauspostille*, Berlin, 1927, p. 42.

Brecht's ostensible loathing of the capitalist ruthlessness of this dream-
land can never quite conceal the magnetic attraction its size, freedom
and adventurousness had for him. The drunken pirates of the "Ballade
von den Seeräubern" ("Ballad of the Pirates"), who murder and rape
their way across a boundless azure sea, the Kiplingesque soldiers of
*Man Equals Man [A Man's a Man]*, who ransack the treasures of ancient
pagodas if they want to pay for a pint of beer and storm the mountain
fastnesses of Tibet, are the symbols of Brecht's passionate protest against
the respectability of small town bourgeois life in a landlocked country.
His love for these images springs from precisely the same roots as his
antibourgeois, anticapitalist politics. Even at a later stage of his development, in so openly political a poem as the one in which at the time of
the great depression he somewhat prematurely mourned the "Forgotten
Glories of the Giant City of New York," we can detect an undertone of
awe and nostalgia:

> Harmonious sounds at evening time of the waters of Miami!
> Irresistible gaiety of generations driving fast along unending highways!
> Powerful sorrows of singing women, hopefully bewailing
> Broad-chested men, but still surrounded by
> Broad-chested men! 6

Such was the curious mixture of influences that shaped Brecht's early
poetry and the tense, extravagant prose of his first plays. While the
Expressionist fashion of the period also left some superficial traces in his
style, his basic attitude remained fundamentally different from that of
the Expressionists. They were entirely preoccupied with their own ego
and projected their own personal emotions onto a cosmic plane, while
Brecht's poetry, even in its wildest effusions of riotous imagery, remains
strangely impersonal. Like the ballads of the street singers, whose strident
tones he tried to reproduce, most of his poems are reports on the acci-
dents and crimes of other people, or dramatic monologues whose first
person singular or plural is clearly that of historical or imagined characters. The only really personal poems in Brecht's first published volume
of poetry, *Domestic Breviary,* are relegated to an appendix, headed "Of
poor B.B." (an echo of *"pauvre François Villon"*), and even here the
lyrical self-portrait of the author is put forward in the exhibitionist tone
of a music hall performer presenting a character sketch, masking the
private emotion by the posturing of a public performance.

The publication of the *Domestic Breviary* marks the transition to an
even more impersonal approach than that represented by many of the
early poems collected in that book. By the time Brecht published these
poems (1926) his attitude had become austere and didactic. He had made

---

6 "Verschollener Ruhm der Riesenstadt New York," *Hundert Gedichte,* East Berlin,
1951, p. 130.

himself one of the main exponents of *Gebrauchslyrik*, the view that poetry should not be an outlet of private emotions but should be judged solely by its social usefulness. Hence the arrangement of the *Domestic Breviary* on the model of a religious breviary as a kind of blasphemous prayer book, in which each poem is designed for use in a certain situation. The collection is prefaced by a detailed "Direction for Use of the Lessons contained in this Book," which starts with the injunction:

> This domestic breviary is designed for the use of readers. It must not be gobbled up in a senseless manner.[7]

Detailed indications follow as to the situations in which the poems should be used:

> Chapter 2 ("Ballad on Many Ships") is to be read in hours of danger. . . . Chapter 6 ("Ballad of the Pirates") is mainly designed for the light nights of June; but the second part of this ballad, as far as it deals with the sinking of the ship, can still be sung in October, etc.[8]

This is parody, but behind the jest there was a serious and growing conviction. As the frenzy of the Expressionist era died down and the fooleries of Dadaism lost their novelty, many of the younger poets and artists in Germany tried to get away from the fruitless preoccupation with their own selves to the real problems of the age. The plush curtains and ornamental bric-a-brac of the previous, now discredited generation had been torn down and cast aside. The new beauty of the machine, its economy of outline resulting from perfect adaptation to the function for which it had been created, now became the ideal before the artist. This was the creed of a movement labeled *Neue Sachlichkeit*. If social usefulness, however, was to be the new criterion of beauty, literature and the stage also would have to be didactic and to serve the community by teaching it how to live.

And so Brecht's language cast off all ornament and became functional and austere. The *Lehrstücke* and "school operas" are meant to be "teaching aids" rather than art, and their language is severely factual. In *The Flight of the Lindberghs*, for example, the chorus, which embodies the collective personality of the hero, introduces itself:

> My name is Charles Lindbergh
> I am twenty-five years old
> My grandfather was Swedish
> I am American.
> I have picked my aircraft myself

[7] *Hauspostille*, Berlin, 1927, p. ix.
[8] *Ibid.*, p. xi.

> Its name is "Spirit of St. Louis"
> The Ryan Aircraft works in San Diego
> Have built it in sixty days. . . .[9]

The poetry of facts and figures is extracted from the most unpromising material:

> I carry with me:
> 2 electric torches
> 1 coil of rope
> 1 roll of string
> 1 hunting knife
> 4 red flares, sealed in rubber tubes
> 1 waterproof box of matches, etc., etc.[10]

It is a measure of Brecht's stature as a poet that he did succeed in achieving the effect of functional elegance he aimed at and that some of the later *Lehrstücke* have a monolithic, stark beauty of their own. The sudden rejection of the anarchic exuberance of his early style reflects Brecht's yearning for discipline and order, which led him to Marxism, and it is significant that one of the models for his new didactic style was provided by a civilization that followed a pattern of equally strict military discipline: the Japan of the samurai. The school operas *He Who Says Yes* and *He Who Says No* are based on a Japanese no play, *Taniko,* in Arthur Waley's translation, and Brecht's most important didactic play, *The Measures Taken,* also derives from this Japanese model.

Arthur Waley's translations of Chinese poetry made a deep impression on Brecht in his next, more mellowed and relaxed stage of development. The Confucian urbanity and courtesy, the quietly ironical tone and free rhythm of these translations became a decisive influence in his progress toward mature simplicity. The gentle politeness of the Chinese, the undogmatic authority of their classical teachers, represented for him the ultimate socialist ideal of friendliness as the basis of human relations. Brecht made German versions of a number of Waley's Chinese poems, and some of his most successful later verse is clearly modeled on them. In one of these poems, which relates a dream vision of a visit to the once exiled poets in the land of the dead, Brecht sees himself in the company of the shades of Po Chü-i and Tu-fu, together with those of Villon, Dante, Heine, Voltaire, Shakespeare (exiled to Stratford by James I!), Euripides, and Ovid.

Brecht, who knew his own facility in writing verse, deliberately at-

[9] *Der Flug der Lindberghs, Versuche 1,* p. 3.
[10] *Ibid.*

tempted to get away from smooth, easy rhythms. "I needed a heightened language, but I was repelled by the oily smoothness of the usual iambic pentameter," [11] he writes in his essay *On Unrhymed Verse with Irregular Rhythms,* in which he describes his efforts to find a style that could dispense with rhymes and regular rhythms and yet remain poetry, a poetry expressing the disharmonies of society.

> As a consequence, apart from ballads and rhymed (political) songs for the masses, I wrote more and more poems without rhyme in irregular rhythms. It must be remembered that my main work was done for the stage; I always thought of the spoken word. And I had worked out a special technique for the speaking of prose or verse. I called it *gestisch,*

i.e., a language in which the words already contain the gesture that must accompany them. Characteristically Brecht illustrates what he means by quoting the Bible. To say "Pluck out the eye that offends thee" is far less effective than "If thine eye offend thee, pluck it out." Here the language itself implies and compels the corresponding action. Brecht argues that it is this element of implied gesture which can make un-rhymed, irregular verse still keep the quality of poetry. He describes how he discovered the power of such irregular rhythms in the slogans shouted in unison by demonstrating masses of unemployed workers and in the headlines called out by news vendors on the street corners of Berlin.

Apart from political marching songs, for which he used a rhymed stereotype of German "folk song," and some of the songs in his plays, most of Brecht's later poetry is in this unrhymed, irregular verse, the rhythmic subtleties of which he compared to those of the syncopations of jazz or tap dancing. This highly personal style is equally effective in the robust anti-Nazi *German Satires* he wrote for broadcasting from the "German Freedom Station" before the war and the elegiac poetry of his exile as well as in the very short, epigrammatic poems resembling Japanese Haiku he composed with masterly economy of words in the last years of his life.

But it is in the great plays he wrote between 1937 and 1947 that the overflowing richness of his early language and the didactic severity of the phase that followed are blended in a masterly idiom unequaled by any other German dramatist of this century. The Biblical allusions, the Bavarian local accent, the exotic names, the archaisms, and the garish rhythms of the street ballad are still there, but controlled and put into their place by the conciseness and economy acquired in the austere at-mosphere of the didactic plays and mellowed and relaxed by the influence of the Chinese example. Each play has its own individual tone: *Mother Courage* the earthy flavor of seventeenth century German and the picaresque novels of Grimmelshausen, *Puntila* a racy folk language,

[11] Über reimlose Lyrik mit unregelmässigen Rhythmen," *Versuche 12,* p. 143.

*Galileo* the richness of baroque scientific and religious disputation, *The Good Woman of Setzuan* a Confucian urbanity, *The Caucasian Chalk Circle* a different blend of Oriental colors, and *Schweik in the Second World War* a brilliant pastiche of the language of Hašek's novel.

The various and openly acknowledged influences which shaped Brecht's work throughout his life have inevitably led to his being accused of plagiarism and lack of originality. In fact, his originality consisted of his uncanny ability to absorb and assimilate the most diverse and seemingly incompatible elements. Under the influence of the Romantics an even greater value is attached in Germany than elsewhere to the quality of uniqueness, the originality, which is said to be the essence of genius. Brecht thought little of this cult of originality. In one of his Keuner stories he makes his alter ego quote the example of the Chinese philosopher Chuang Tzu, who wrote a book of a hundred thousand words, nine-tenths of which consisted of extracts from other books.

> Such books can no longer be written in our country, because we have not enough intelligence. That is why we manufacture ideas only in our own workshops. Anyone who is unable to put enough of them together feels that he is lazy. That is why there are no ideas worth taking up, and no phrases worth quoting. . . . They build their huts without help and with nothing but the miserable amount of material a single person can carry. They know no larger buildings than those one man can build by himself! [12]

Brecht loved to adapt and to modify the work of others. He needed the challenge of another mind to get the best from his own talent. He based many of his plays on existing originals—Marlowe's *Edward II*, Gay's *Beggar's Opera*, Hašek's *Schweik*, old Japanese or Chinese legends. Again and again he drew on motifs from Shakespeare. His satire against racialism, *The Roundheads and the Peakheads*, contains elements from the plot of *Measure for Measure*; in *Arturo Ui*, in which the rise of Hitler is parodied through that of a Chicago gangster, the character of the villainous hero is modeled on Richard III, so that the murder of Roehm echoes the downfall of Buckingham and the Hitler character woos the widow of one of his victims. But while the Shakespearean models are used with reverence and admiration, the German classics are always ruthlessly parodied. Brecht even went so far as to parody the Bible: Macheath, for example, is betrayed by a kiss on a Thursday evening.

Besides reverent adaptation or cruel parody, Brecht had a third way of assimilating the work of others: the counterplay, written as a reply to, or refutation of, an existing work. His first play, *Baal*, was written

---

[12] "Herr Keuner und die Originalität," *Versuche 5*, p. 456.

to show how Johst's *Der Einsame* could be bettered. *The Days of the Commune* was a reply to Nordahl Grieg, and at the time of his death Brecht planned a counterplay to Beckett's *Waiting for Godot*.

It would be tedious to pursue the countless literary parallels, concealed quotations, and examples of pastiche and parody in Brecht's work. This will provide employment for generations of students to come. Brecht shares his predilection for literary allusion with writers like T. S. Eliot, Ezra Pound, and James Joyce. It marks him as an intellectual, in spite of his sincere attempts and avowed intention to write for the common people. The use of parody, moreover, particularly the iconoclastic mockery of the German classics, the Bible, and religious hymns and anthems, reveals Brecht's ambivalent attitude toward these models. Parody gave Brecht an opportunity to fulfill an unconscious desire to emulate and follow these examples. Under the cover of ridicule he could indulge the "high-minded," even religious impulses which his rational, cynical self would not allow him to acknowledge. In his later phase, when he had found a positive framework of belief and had attained recognition as a classic of his own time, the tendency to parody great literary examples disappeared, while his love for open adaptation and imitation continued unabated.

Brecht's readiness to sink his own personality in the work of his predecessors and contemporaries, to use the whole storehouse of past literature as so much material for his own handiwork, was in accordance with his views about the nature of poetry itself and the poet's function in society. Here, too, he rejected the mystical, romantic view of the poet as the vessel of divinely inspired intuitions, called upon to fulfill and express his unique personality. To him the poet was a craftsman serving the community and relying on his reason and acquired skill, a man among men, not a being set apart by virtue of some special quality or power. That is why Brecht was ready to accept the advice of numerous collaborators, whom he conscientiously named when his works were published. As he did not consider the work of art divinely inspired, he never hesitated to alter, and often debase, his own work, according to the circumstances of the moment.

After the banning of the operatic version of *The Trial of Lucullus* Brecht told a Swiss journalist that he regarded the indignation of his Western admirers about the interference of the authorities with an artist's work as sheer hypocrisy. After all, the authorities had paid for his opera, so they could demand alterations from the craftsman they employed. "When princes commissioned works of art, they, too, interfered a great deal with the artists." [13]

Within his own sphere of craftsmanship, however, Brecht never suf-

[13] Gody Suter, "Brecht," *Tagesanzeiger*, Zurich, 9.1.1956.

fered from undue humility. Lion Feuchtwanger tells how he used to counter criticisms of his often very unorthodox use of grammar by saying: *"Ego, poeta Germanus, supra Grammaticos sto."* [14] And when during his stay in the United States someone drew his attention to a literal translation of an English idiom, pointing out that such a phrase did not exist in German, Brecht replied: "All right. So it exists from now on!" [15]

But this arrogance remained confined to the sphere in which he regarded himself as a craftsman, an expert. It never led him to regard the poet as a higher being. For, as he said in a poem dedicated to the Danish writer Andersen-Nexoe, the time will come when the works of the most exquisite poets will be looked at with different eyes:

> . . . not for their elevated thoughts
> Will their books be searched through; but
> Some casual sentence, which allows conclusions
> As to some feature of those who were weavers of coats,
> Will be read with interest. . . .[16]

# Chronology of Important Dates

*Dates and places in parentheses*
*indicate first production.*

| | |
|---|---|
| 1898 (February 10) | Brecht born in Augsburg, Germany. |
| 1908 | *Realgymnasium,* Augsburg. First literary contributions to *Augsburger Neueste Nachrichten* (1914). |
| 1917 | Munich University (premedical courses, and Professor Kutscher's seminar on the history of the theater). |
| 1918 | Orderly at Augsburg Military Hospital; work on *Baal* (first produced Leipzig 1923). |
| 1920 | Munich; free-lance writer. |
| 1922 | *Drum in the Night [Trommeln in der Nacht]* (Munich) Kleist prize. |
| 1923 | *In the Swamp [Im Dickicht der Städte]* *(Munich);* collaboration with Otto Falckenberg (Munich *Kammerspiele*). |
| 1924 | Berlin; Assistant *Dramaturg* at the *Deutsches Theater* (until 1926). |
| 1926 | *A Man's a Man [Mann ist Mann]* (Darmstadt); Marxist studies at Berlin *Workers' School.* |

[14] Lion Feuchtwanger, "Bertolt Brecht," *Sinn und Form,* Second Special Brecht Issue, 1957, p. 106.
[15] H. Winge, "Brecht en privé," *Europe,* January/February, 1957, p. 46.
[16] "Die Literatur wird durchforscht werden," *Hundert Gedichte,* East Berlin, 1951, p. 173.

| 1927 | Domestic Breviary published. |
|---|---|
| 1929 | The Baden Cantata of Acquiescence [Das Badener Lehrstück vom Einverständnis] (Baden-Baden). |
| 1930 | The Rise and Fall of the City of Mahagonny [Aufstieg und Fall der Stadt Mahagonny] (Leipzig): The Measures Taken [Die Massnahme] (Berlin). Saint Joan of the Stockyards [Die Heilige Johanna der Schlachthöfe] completed. Work on The Mother. |
| 1933 | Exile: Prague, Vienna, Zurich; Denmark (1938), Sweden (1939), Finland (1940). |
| 1935 | Trip to Moscow. |
| 1936 | The Roundheads and the Peakheads [Die Rundköpfe und die Spitzköpfe] (Copenhagen). |
| 1938 | The Private Life of the Master Race [Furcht und Elend des Dritten Reiches] (Paris). |
| 1941 | Brecht arrives in the United States. Occasional jobs for Hollywood. Mother Courage [Mutter Courage und ihre Kinder] (Zurich). |
| 1943 | The Good Woman of Setzuan [Der gute Mensch von Sezuan] (Zurich). |
| 1944/5 | Work on The Caucasian Chalk Circle [Der Kaukasische Kreidekreis]. First performed, in English, at Carleton College, Northfield, Minnesota (1948). |
| 1947 | Galileo (2nd version; Hollywood). Brecht testifies before the House Committee on Un-American Activities. Return to Europe. |
| 1948 | Herr Puntila and his Servant Matti [Herr Puntila und sein Knecht Matti] (Zurich). Brecht returns to [East] Berlin. Little Organon for the Theater. |
| 1949 | The Berliner Ensemble established (Director: Helene Weigel). Brecht becomes "a member of the artistic advisory board." |
| 1951 | East German National Prize. |
| 1954 | Stalin Peace Prize. Brecht's production of Mother Courage receives the first prize at the International Theater Festival (Paris). |
| 1956 (August 14) | Brecht dies in East Berlin and is buried near Hegel (Dorotheenfriedhof). |

# Selected Bibliography

## BOOKS

Bertolt Brechts Dreigroschenbuch. Edited by Siegfried Unseld. Frankfurt: Suhrkamp Verlag, 1960. Useful materials concerning The Threepenny Opera; includes a record, "Brecht sings." The Brecht fan's Christmas present.

Esslin, Martin. *Brecht: The Man and his Work.* New York: Doubleday & Company, Inc., 1960. Particularly illuminating on Brecht's politics, and his literary sources.

Gray, Ronald. *Bertolt Brecht.* New York: Grove Press, Inc., 1961. Useful introduction.

Grimm, Reinhold. *Bertolt Brecht: Die Struktur seines Werkes.* Nuremberg: Carl Verlag, 1959. The Rhetoric of "Alienation."

———. *Bertolt Brecht.* Stuttgart: Metzlersche Verlagsbuchhandlung, 1961. Indispensable bibliographical and research material.

Hink, Walter. *Die Dramaturgie des späten Brecht.* Göttingen: Vandenhoeck und Ruprecht, 1959. Competent analysis of dramatic techniques.

Kesting, Marianne. *Bertolt Brecht: Dargestellt in Selbstzeugnissen und Bilddokumenten.* Hamburg: Rowohlt, 1959. Bertolt Brecht's life, compiled from his own writings; instructive illustrations.

Klotz, Volker. *Bertolt Brecht: Versuch über das Werk.* Darmstadt: Gentner, 1957. Lucid analysis of style and poetics.

Mayer, Hans. *Bertolt Brecht und die Tradition.* Pfullingen: Neske, 1961. Intelligent, sensitive Marxist appraisal.

Schumacher, Ernst. *Die dramatischen Versuche Bertolt Brechts 1918-1933.* East Berlin: Rütten und Loening, 1955. Important for knowledge about the young Brecht; from an orthodox Communist point of view.

Willett, John. *The Theatre of Bertolt Brecht.* New York: New Directions, 1959. Useful information about Brecht the producer.


ESSAYS

Benjamin, Walter. "Was ist episches Theater?" *Akzente,* I (1954), 163-170. Reprint of an important early essay on Brecht's theory.

Bentley, Eric. "Introduction" to *Seven Plays by Bertolt Brecht* (New York: Grove Press, Inc., 1961), pp. ix-li. Essential statements by the pioneer of American Brecht criticism.

Bornemann, Ernest. "Credo quia Absurdum: An Epitaph for Bertolt Brecht," *Kenyon Review,* XXI (1959), 169-180. Rich in details on Brecht's poetry and dramatic achievements.

Frisch, Max. "Recollections of Brecht," *The Tulane Drama Review,* VI (1961), 33-36. The noted Swiss playwright reports on Brecht's return from his American exile.

Hays, H. R. "The Poetry of Bertolt Brecht," *Poetry,* LXVII (1945), 148-155. Brecht's anti-individualism.

Hecht, Werner. "The Development of Brecht's Theory of Epic Theater: 1918-1933," *The Tulane Drama Review,* VI (1961), 40-97. Important compilation of relevant material; the Marxist a priori tends to blur the critic's perception.

Lüthy, Herbert. "Of Poor Brecht," *Encounter,* XXXIV (1956), 33-53. A skeptical view of the Communist Brecht, brilliantly presented.

Sartre, Jean-Paul. "Brecht et les classiques," *World Theater,* VII (1958), 11-14. Tenuous links between Brecht and French tragedy.

Tynan, Kenneth. "The Theater Abroad: Germany," *The New Yorker,* September 12, 1959.

Wekwerth, Manfred. "Auffinden einer Kategorie," *Sinn und Form* (Second Special Brecht Issue [East Berlin: Rütten und Loening, 1957]), pp. 260-268. Old Brecht musing on the "dialectical" and the "naive." Of fundamental importance.

### RECORDS

*Lotte Lenya sings Berlin Theater songs by Kurt Weill* (Columbia LP ML 5056)
*Aufstieg und Fall der Stadt Mahagonny*. With Lotte Lenya. (Columbia LP 3L-243)
*Die Dreigroschenoper*. With Lotte Lenya. (Columbia LP O2L-257)
*The Threepenny Opera*. New York Production. (MGM 3121)

# Notes on the Editor and Contributors

PETER DEMETZ, editor of this volume, teaches German and Comparative Literature at Yale University. He is the author of *René Rilkes Prager Jahre* (1953) and *Marx, Engels und die Dichter* (1959).

SERGEY TRETIAKOV (1892-1938?), Soviet novelist and playwright, once belonged to the "Futurists" and the *Left Front* Group. He died in the Stalinist purges of the late Thirties.

HANNAH ARENDT, critic and political philosopher, has made her home in New York. Her books, including *The Origins of Totalitarianism* (1951) and *Between Past and Present* (1961) have been translated into many languages.

Professor ERIC BENTLEY (Columbia) first met Brecht in the early Forties. Since that time he has interpreted and translated many of Brecht's plays and critical writings for American audiences.

ERNST SCHUMACHER, a disciple of the East German critic Hans Mayer, explicates the work of the young Brecht from an orthodox Communist point of view.

OSCAR BÜDEL is a member of the Department of Romance Languages at the University of Washington, Seattle.

The Moscow critic I. FRADKIN was particularly active when Brecht's *Berliner Ensemble* visited the Soviet Union.

HANS EGON HOLTHUSEN, German poet and critic, is director of the Goethe House in New York. His collections of essays include *Die Welt ohne Transzendenz* (1949), *Der unbehauste Mensch* (1951), and *Das Schöne und das Wahre* (1958).

GÜNTER ROHRMOSER and FRANZ NORBERT MENNEMEIR belong to the younger generation of German scholars concentrating on recent literature.

WALTER H. SOKEL, Associate Professor of German at Columbia University, is the author of *The Writer in Extremis: Expressionism in Twentieth Century German Literature* (1959).

Before turning to Brecht, the British scholar RONALD GRAY published important studies of Goethe and of Kafka's *The Castle*.

The young British critic JOHN WILLETT has done extensive research on Brecht and his contemporaries.

MARTIN ESSLIN writes and produces literary scripts for BBC and frequently contributes to European periodicals. His book on Brecht was widely discussed in Europe and in the United States.